Days for Decision

by Anthony Eden

★

FOREIGN AFFAIRS

FREEDOM AND ORDER

PLACES IN THE SUN
(*John Murray*)

DAYS FOR DECISION

by

The Rt. Hon.
ANTHONY EDEN
M.C., M.P.

HOUGHTON MIFFLIN COMPANY BOSTON
THE RIVERSIDE PRESS CAMBRIDGE
1950
KRAUS REPRINT CO.
New York
1969

Foreword

Throughout our long history each generation has sought to choose its way and has influenced thereby the course of its successors. The present choice must be decisive for ourselves and for our children.

Politics are essentially concerned with conflicting human claims: freedom and order, the individual and the state, tradition and change, personal security and adventure, ideals and reality, independence and interdependence. The art of statesmanship is to reconcile these claims and to build a way of life that gives them fair expression. These pages show how I, as a member of the Conservative Party, have attempted to set out my thoughts on these vital issues.

Those who cherish our conception of a free parliamentary democracy have to meet two threats. The first is incidental to the growth of scientific discovery and to our inability to make political progress which measures up to it. The second is the growth of a harsh materialistic creed which, under the name of Communism, would impose a new serfdom upon a war-wearied and baffled humanity in an atomic age.

Our own ability to meet this challenge must depend upon the vision of our leadership and the steadfast unity of our nation and the Commonwealth.

The General Election of 1945 gave the Socialist Party a triumphant parliamentary majority. The margin among the electorate was narrower, but had no practical influence on events. The Socialists had their mandate and have been putting it into effect ever since.

As one re-reads these pages one is struck, in the domestic sphere, by this Parliament's alternating themes of Socialist nationalization measures and financial and economic crises.

Foreword

Memory being mercifully short, the tale of these last is already fading in recollection.

First, the fuel crisis, with its loss of £200,000,000 in exports at a time when our national opportunity was at its greatest; the fuel crisis which everybody foresaw, except the expostulating and uncomprehending Minister of Fuel and Power. Then the dollar crisis, and this time it is the Chancellor of the Exchequer of the day, Dr. Dalton, who is hopelessly bewildered. Convertibility presents no peril, he is sure. By the end of 1946 only £150,000,000 had been drawn from the Loan of £937,500,000. Six months later only £250,000,000 were left of the American Loan and only £125,000,000 of the Canadian £300,000,000 credit.

Finally, we have the gold crisis when Sir Stafford Cripps takes his turn in the queue of lamentable misjudgment. After a long period of alternating warning and comfort, he suddenly announces in July this year drastic reductions in our dollar imports at the rate of £100,000,000 *a year* to help close the widening gap in our balance of payments. This action is accompanied by a speech of extraordinary optimism which exaggerates the contribution the cuts can make to stem the drain on sterling area gold, and belittles the consequences to British industry of the loss of these dollar imports. It is all to be so smooth and painless, too easy by half. Repeated Opposition questions and warnings are unanswered or unheeded, with bland or blind assurance. Even some Government supporters express concern at this display of optimism.

In any event, there is to be no question of devaluation, the Chancellor repeatedly instructs us, and most of us applaud. Personally, I specifically endorsed his attitude upon this issue, for I felt, and still feel, that unilateral devaluation in present conditions and as a first step was too dangerous a gamble with the nation's life. In any event, its effect must be, I thought, to raise the cost of living appreciably, nor was I confident that we could sell the additional goods in dollar markets soon enough for the result to be an early gain even to our balance of payments across the Atlantic. This July debate, memorable at least for all who took part in it, was

Foreword

wound up by the Foreign Secretary in a desultory ramble that answered none of the points raised but assured us that all would be well in the bright hereafter of the Washington talks.

And so we adjourned at the end of July with relief and with misgivings. Unhappily, within a very few weeks our worst fears were realized. The Chancellor's half-hearted measures entirely failed to restore confidence in sterling. No significant reductions in expenditure were announced or effected; no further attempt was made to put our house in order. Our gold reserve drained away still faster. So that when the Chancellor returned from his cure in Switzerland the cupboard was bare. The Government decided on devaluation in an attempt to protect their remaining gold reserves. Finally, in a moment of ingenuous frankness the Chancellor confessed to a Press Conference on September 19th: 'At the end of the war we all thought it was going to be easier than it turned out to be in the economic sphere, and we have been trying to deal with it by a series of temporary expedients which have led to a series of crises as each expedient has been exhausted. Now we recognize that this is not enough.'

The patient reader of these pages will find just this warning and this charge repeated over and over again in Parliament and in the country. Until the date of this confession it was met every time with complacent confidence or obstinate denial. How can a Government which, on its own confession, has so completely misjudged our financial and economic problems make any further claim upon the confidence of the electors?

But it is not these past blunders, formidable and costly as they have been, which should be the main background of the next General Election. Even graver issues are at stake. The country has to pronounce upon nationalization. It has to decide how far existing schemes have been successful and whether it desires their extension to yet wider fields of industry and commerce. The future of the iron and steel industry is in the forefront of this controversy. It will be for the country to determine whether nationalization can be judged so far successful that further

Foreword

experiments can be safely indulged, or whether a halt must be called to our evolution as a Socialist state. This issue transcends all others in importance, and is capital to those of us who believe that there is no future at all for this country as a Socialist state with its rigid and costly centralized control of our national life.

It is our unshakable Conservative conviction that

'our strength and our prosperity have been built on countless different activities, producing, selling, banking, insurance, sending goods of all kinds to every corner of the world. All these things were done under the system of free enterprise'.

It is undeniable that the success of our export drive to date has been overwhelmingly the achievement of free enterprise. Coal is the only direct contributor from a nationalized industry, and its overseas sales are still far below the pre-war level. Sheffield has increased its production of crude steel by 40 per cent compared with 1938. How fortunate should we be if the coal-mining industry could show a comparable record. As it is, we have the nationalized railways constrained to work on coal of poorer quality and having to meet an annual coal bill which is about £24,000,000 more than the pre-war figure of about £12,500,000. Small wonder, then, that a year ago a Government supporter, the Hon. Member for Walton, should have felt impelled to this confession:

'I am disappointed at the fact that what I have advocated on public platforms for the last twenty-five years, that as we nationalized an industry the people in that industry would work harder because they were working for the state than if they were working for a private employer, has not altogether worked out. I am very disappointed that we have not had the results one would expect.'

Here, then, is the triple task which confronts the Conservative Party: to restore confidence in the pound; to halt and, where possible, reverse the threat of nationalization to industry; to reduce government expenditure and the burden of taxation upon industry and our national life. These three objectives are intertwined. All must be realized or none can be achieved. Upon success in this task our future depends.

Acknowledgments

I am very much indebted to Brigadier A. R. W. Low, C.B.E., D.S.O., M.P., who has arranged these speeches and provided valuable notes on the background against which they were made, and also to the many friends who have helped me in the reading and checking of proofs.

The reports of the speeches delivered in the House of Commons and reprinted here have been taken from the Official Report of Parliamentary Debates. I should like to express my thanks to the Controller, His Majesty's Stationery Office, for permission to reproduce them.

Acknowledgment is also due to the *Yorkshire Post, Daily Telegraph*, International News Service, and International Co-operation Press Service for permission to reprint here certain of my articles.

Contents

xiii

Contents

PART ONE

DOMESTIC AFFAIRS

INTRODUCTION

The Conservative Party's programme at the 1945 General Election had been set out in concise and comprehensive terms in Mr. Churchill's Declaration of Policy. Soon after the Socialist victory at the polls it became clear that many Conservatives were not satisfied that either their policy or their programme had been understood by the electorate. Many asked for an early restatement of policy; some for a statement of programme.

In the four following years, Mr. Eden set out to explain to the people of Britain, first the principles of Conservatism, and secondly the general line of policy which a Conservative Government would pursue. As it became possible to anticipate the circumstances which would prevail at the time of and after the next General Election, he developed the general lines of policy into specific proposals. But throughout the period Mr. Eden showed that the Conservatives had practical solutions to offer to existing problems.

Chapter 1

The Aims of the Conservative Party

A. OUR PRINCIPLES

In 1946 Mr. Eden used the occasions of his public speeches to restate in general terms the principles that would guide the Conservative Party in the conduct of Parliamentary opposition and in the development of their policy. In the best known of these speeches, delivered at the Party Conference at Blackpool, he defined the Conservative objective as 'a nationwide property-owning democracy'. He ended that speech with these words:

'We base ourselves upon the individual, upon the need to develop the individual personality; we recognize that the individual can develop only through membership of a living united community. But unity is not mere uniformity; it can be created only out of diversity, only from harmonizing the desires, the aspirations and the efforts of the human beings who make a nation.

'Socialism says to a man: "You are a unit in the State. Work hard for the State, as the State thinks best, and the State will provide you with what it thinks you should have."

'We say: "You are an individual. Choose your own way in life and seek to develop to the full your own talents. If you do this, and if you are prepared to accept the obligations that are essential to life in an ordered community, then we regard it as the duty of government to see that out of the fruits of your labour you can build a life of your own for yourself and your family, and at the same time feel the satisfaction of sharing in the common purpose of a free society" ' (see *Freedom and Order*, Chapter 49).

The following speech was made at the annual general meeting of his own constituency Conservative Association (Warwick, Stratford upon Avon and Leamington) in mid-1946. Five days

B   3

before there had been a debate in the House of Commons on the statement by Mr. Wilmot, then Minister of Supply, that the Government had decided on a large measure of public ownership of the iron and steel industry. This statement had been delayed for several months whilst the Socialist Cabinet considered the plan for iron and steel, proposed by the British Iron and Steel Federation on the invitation of Mr. Churchill's Government in May 1945, and submitted to the Socialist Government in December 1945. The debate had not disclosed any practical reason for the course which the Government had decided to take, nor made it clear which firms would be nationalized and which left free. It was not until nearly two and a half years later that the Iron and Steel Bill was published.

Let me now speak to you of our present duty as members of the Conservative and Unionist Party. First of all, we have an important function to discharge as His Majesty's Opposition. It is our duty to scrutinize most closely the proposals put forward by the Government. We must search out their weaknesses; we must expose their dangers and their follies. We must not hesitate to make plain their shortcomings to the electorate so that the people may know precisely what is being done in their name. We must offer stubborn opposition to the Government whenever they bring forward proposals which we do not consider to be in the best interests of our people. At the same time we must, of course, be prepared to indicate what alternatives we think the Government should adopt. Our criticisms, our opposition will be based upon the fundamental principles of our political faith.

Let me re-state those principles. We believe in the British tradition. We take pride in the history of our race and Empire. We believe there is a vast deal of good in this structure of the British way of life that has been built up over so many centuries by patience and far-seeing effort. We believe in using all that is good in our existing institutions, in our law, in our way of life,

The Aims of the Conservative Party

in our economy, as the only sound and sure basis for future progress.

We recognize that there is much, indeed, to be put right. Our social and economic structure needs to be continually amended and improved if it is to be kept up to date. But it must, we believe, be based upon firm foundations, which take account of our national character, if it is to be strong and enduring. The growth of modern industrial society, the steady spread of Marxist materialism, lead inevitably to the development of a society where the emphasis is increasingly upon quantity.

The final development of this process must be the reduction of our society to a single, drab, dull monotone. We are fundamentally opposed to such a conception. We believe in emphasizing quality. We believe that the strength and the greatness of this country depend on the quality of our institutions, the quality of our industrial processes and, above all, upon the quality of our individual citizens. It is our intention to develop such qualities to the full, and this, to my mind, can be done only in a society where there is a maximum of freedom for the development of the individual, and where effort and quality are accorded their due reward.

It must be our constant concern to see that the amenities of life are available for all. But I do firmly believe that we will not develop our strength and the prosperity of the country unless we recognize that varying qualities should be accorded varying rewards. We must encourage greatness amongst our people. Beware the man who penalizes success. For a successful country depends upon successful citizens.

Now as to the method to be employed for the application of these principles. We must, as a party, at all times base our approach to the problems of government and statecraft upon realism, upon practical requirements. We must not be tempted by the doctrinaire approach of our Socialist opponents to fall ourselves into the pit of doctrinaire anti-Socialism. All prejudices are equally fatal to good government.

Domestic Affairs

We must be prepared to regard each problem as it arises, be it in the social or the industrial sphere, on its own merits. In particular, we must bring to the problems of industrial organization minds that are free from bias. For it is as wrong to oppose nationalization on grounds of prejudice as it is to support nationalization from blind subservience to a theory.

We must always determine our actions by the true needs of the whole nation, not by the requirements of doctrine or by sectional interests of any single class of the community. There could be no better example of the contrast between our approach to industrial problems and that of the Government than the recent debate on the iron and steel industry. The treatment which the Government propose to mete out to this industry can only be described as an ill-considered and costly gesture of political prejudice.

Here you have an industry of vast size and complexity and of fundamental importance to our national life. It is an industry which in the dark days of the 1920s and early 1930s suffered severely from world conditions. In 1932 the National Government of the day granted to the industry the protection of tariffs on imported iron and steel products.

But at the same time it insisted that the industry should set about reorganizing itself under the general supervision of a Government-appointed body, the Import Duties Advisory Committee. This reorganization was carried out, the industry spending in the years 1934 to 1939 no less than £50,000,000 on the provision of new capital equipment. At the same time the industry was closely organized by the formation and development of the British Iron and Steel Federation.

Throughout the war the industry answered all calls made upon it. Since the conclusion of the war it has built up its production and its exports to a level well above that of the pre-war years. Yet, despite its extensive reorganization and its remarkable record of recent times, the Government have decided to nationalize the industry, or at any rate a large proportion of it.

We do not deny that in any industry of this fundamental

6

The Aims of the Conservative Party

importance, an industry which has developed such a high degree of integration, there must be a measure of public supervision. There must be control in the public interest to ensure that the consumer is not exploited, for example, by excessive prices.

Such control already existed before the war in the shape of the Import Duties Advisory Committee, which supervised the price structure of the industry. The industry itself was wholly prepared to accept the continuation of such control. But the Government, although they admittedly have full powers over price, structure, location, capital equipment, imports and exports, decided that they must 'nationalize the industry'. At the best the result can only be confusion. At the worst it may entail a national disaster.

No one yet knows what section of the industry is to be nationalized and what is to be left free. No one can say what will be the result of competition over a wide area between the Government and private enterprise producing the same products. At a moment when every effort should have been devoted to assisting the industry to maintain its very creditable production and export drive, the Government have decided to jeopardize the future life of the industry.

If ever there was a clear example of doctrine run riot, it is this. The public interest demands that the iron and steel industry should be treated on the basis of practical requirements. This industry is a perfect example of how the true interests of the nation would best be served by a realistic approach combining the benefit of State direction and control at the highest level with full freedom of management and operation throughout the main body of the industry.

As this twentieth century develops it becomes ever more apparent that the problem of the relation of the individual to the State is the most urgent and vexatious problem of politics. It is not a problem to which one can give a single answer. It is as foolish to say that the State should have no authority over individual lives as it is to say that the individual has no right to freedom from the State.

7

Domestic Affairs

The truth is that we can only develop our own lives, our individual characters within the context of an ordered society; yet ordered society inevitably involves some restriction upon individual liberty. The great danger is that in the development of our society we may lose sight of its fundamental purpose, which is the true liberty of the individual, and we may submerge that liberty in the State machine which, paradoxically enough, has been created solely to ensure it.

This is precisely where Socialism is leading us. There can be no doubt that the responsibilities of government are growing. There can be no doubt that the benefits that good government can bring, particularly in the economic sphere, to our people are increasing. We welcome this. It is our desire to see the full capacity of modern government organization harnessed to the service of the individual citizen.

We will, therefore, not oppose but encourage all developments in the activities of the State which are clearly conducive to this end. But at the same time we are convinced that the development of a Socialist form of society in which all political and economic power is concentrated in the State, where everyone depends upon the State for his livelihood, for his job, his food, his clothing, can but mean the disappearance of liberty as we know it today, and produce finally something akin to the slave State.

Let us not, in seeking to improve the material conditions of our people, as seek we must with all our power, forget that material requirements are only one part of the picture. If, in pursuing this objective of improved material conditions, we cast aside the great moral requirements of individual liberty and responsibility, then we shall, on balance, be bringing not good but harm to our people.

The truth is surely that material and spiritual requirements are together the concern of government. We must have regard for the whole man. We recognize that man cannot develop as a moral being unless his material life is properly ordered. But at the same time we recognize that the excessive ordering and regulation of his material life may in the end destroy his moral and intellectual freedom.

We must, I am sure, concentrate on finding, not a compromise, but a just balance between material and spiritual requirements. I have been speaking in very broad outlines. I have been speaking of what appear to me to be the principles of the Conservative and Unionist Party. Principles are broad and general and must be so. Yet, unless our principles are clearly established in our minds, we cannot hope to develop programmes that are consistent, coherent and effective.

I believe that if you look at the history of our Party you will find these great principles running through it. The maintenance of the British tradition, the confident faith in the future of the British Commonwealth and Empire, the development of the full quality of our institutions and of our citizens, the essential need of realism in our approach to all the political problems, and finally a deep conviction of the sanctity of individual liberty within a society where the whole machinery of the State is designed to foster the material wellbeing and the spiritual development of the individual citizen.

These, I believe, are the principles of our Party, and I think that if we will keep them as a guide they will show us our way through the maze and tangle of problems, difficulties and dangers that face our hard-tried people in these most troubled times.

B. THE INDUSTRIAL CHARTER

In the course of 1946 Mr. Eden had several times outlined the fundamentals of Conservative industrial policy. 'Life', he had said in October 1946, 'must be taken as a whole. You cannot draw a clear line of distinction between man's working life and his leisure. If he is to have the status of a free individual he must have it in his work just as much as in his leisure.'

And in the same month, at Liverpool:

'The keynote of any industrial policy for the country must be output. Upon the increasing volume of production depends the

9

achievement of our great social and economic plans. Upon the reduction of effort required for a given volume of production depends the possibility of reducing hours of work. Upon the achievement, above all, of a level of production cost that will match up to world competitive conditions depends our chance of maintaining a stable, let alone an expanding, economy in the future. I believe that this task of increasing production and lowering production costs can best be achieved by co-operation on the part of government, capital and labour. Free enterprise working in competitive conditions for profit provides the best means of raising levels of efficiency and lowering costs throughout the overwhelming majority of our industries. I am not afraid of the word profit, for, so long as profits be related to services rendered, I see nothing to object to in the profit motive any more than in the wages motive. Though neither is wholly adequate by itself as an incentive to work, each is of the utmost importance. While we can best rely upon free enterprise to provide the driving force necessary in our various industries, the dispersal of decision and flexibility of operation, it is to the organizing power of government that we must look to help to achieve the necessary balance in our economic structure: a balance between demand and supply, between requirements and resources, between industry and industry.'

As the result of a resolution passed at the Blackpool Conference in October 1946, a Committee under the chairmanship of the Rt. Hon. R. A. Butler, M.P., drew up a report known as the Industrial Charter in which was set out an outline of—

first, the immediate steps which should be taken to deal with the 'present crisis';
second, the relationship which should be established between Government and industry;
third, a Charter of Rights and duties to give the workers in industry opportunity and status.

The Charter was published in mid-May 1947. On May 17th Mr. Eden addressed a large meeting of over 20,000 people at a fête at Cardiff Castle. In the course of his speech he welcomed the Industrial Charter and said:

The Aims of the Conservative Party

I ask you to examine with me the statement of Conservative industrial policy prepared by Mr. Butler's Committee and issued at the beginning of this week. I think you will agree that we are deeply indebted to the authors of this report for the work which they have done.

Nor have we, I think, any cause to complain of the way in which the proposals have been received by the nation at large. At least, if we are to judge by our sales, we are reaching the people much more effectively than did the Government White Paper. It is true that some of our critics maintain that, though our plans are good, we are not sincere in propounding them. Well, if they can think of no better argument against us than that, it is indeed a sign of their bankruptcy in criticism.

Again some of our Liberal friends have maintained that, while our projects are worthy of support, they are essentially Liberal. Well, I would reply that they are not necessarily any the worse for that, particularly if you spell liberal with a small 'l'. This Charter is a statement of industrial policy, but it is not, of course, a detailed Party programme. It is a sincere and sober attempt to place the issue fairly before the country and to propound remedies for our present and growing ills. Its purpose is to bring government, capital and labour together in a common partnership in pursuit of a common objective, the expansion of production. It seeks to show the respective functions and responsibilities of each of the three partners and to demonstrate how in a practical and realistic manner these separate functions can be welded together.

We hold out to the people a prospect of true freedom and fuller achievement. But we have no intention of trying to buy the support of the electors by a series of grandiose promises which we know cannot be honoured. Our policy is based solely upon what we conceive to be the real needs of the nation at the present time. We do not shrink from recommending Government action when we consider

11

Domestic Affairs

it to be necessary. But, on the other hand, we have throughout as our major objective to encourage individual enterprise and to free private industry and commerce on the widest possible scale. We believe in planning, but in planning for freedom. We believe not in equality of misery imposed from the centre, but in equality of opportunity achieved by common effort. We believe that the benefits both of Government leadership and of individual initiative can be secured. We have an unshaken faith in Britain's industrial future, but we are not prepared to pretend that the way will be easy, or that we can win economic stability and prosperity except through hard work.

And now a word about planning. If by planning you mean the detailed control of the whole of our economic life, the imposition of a central bureaucratic machine upon all our trade and industry, then planning must mean disaster. Do not forget that this is the Socialist objective. The aim of the Socialist Party is avowedly the establishment of the Socialist Commonwealth of Great Britain. What they claim to be their moderation at the moment does not reveal their true intentions. It merely indicates a well-founded doubt as to the readiness of the country to swallow the whole Socialist dose at one gulp.

But if by planning you mean wise national housekeeping, the balancing of resources and requirements, the settling of the broad strategy of our economic effort, then I say that this is precisely what the country does require, but that this is fundamentally the Conservative and not the Socialist conception of what planning means.

Ever since this Government took office they have shown by their actions that they constantly confuse planning with interference. I do not believe that any Socialist Government can by the very nature of its economic doctrine and political background solve our national problems. The Socialist Party has risen to power largely on the cry that the workers need only get rid of the capitalists in order to be able to work far less and obtain far more in exchange. There is no doubt that many people have been led to

12

The Aims of the Conservative Party

believe that the return of the Socialist Government to power would mean a rapid and substantial improvement in their own standards of living that need not be accompanied by any extra effort on their part.

Mr. Strachey, for example, in his now famous book, *Why You Should Be a Socialist,* said that what Socialism really means is giving nine-tenths of us the chance to get at least ten times as much clothing, houses, gardens, motor cars, supplies of food and furniture as we ever get today. Yet in the same book Mr. Strachey maintained that 'Hard work will not make the workers any richer, but it will make their employers much richer'. Therefore Mr. Strachey clearly does not think that more production by the workers is needed to produce this greater wealth. He even warns them against what he calls the old 'Produce More' cry, and says: 'I suppose we shall get it again after this war too.'

Well, we have got it, and from the Socialists. How can a party, which for years has been preaching the kind of gospel in Mr. Strachey's book, today turn to the country and expect to be believed when they say 'we work or want'?

Chapter 2

Britain's Economic Struggle

INTRODUCTION

During the first session of the post-war Parliament the Socialist Government nationalized the Bank of England and the coal industry. They threatened the iron and steel industry with nationalization before the end of the Parliament. They passed into law the National Insurance Act and the National Health Act, both based on plans made and agreed by the Conservative Party during the war-time Coalition Government.

At the beginning of 1946 a food crisis developed without any warning having been given to the country. Cuts in rations followed and bread rationing was imposed in June by Mr. John Strachey, who had succeeded Sir Ben Smith as Food Minister.

During 1946 the total acreage of tillage in Britain declined and the 1946 harvest was considerably smaller than that of the previous year. In 1945 the Government had begun with a policy of livestock expansion, but reversed this policy six months later, and during 1946 constant reductions and alterations in the feeding-stuff rations caused the premature slaughter of many valuable animals. Attempts were made to encourage livestock production early in 1947 by a small increase in the feeding-stuff ration.

Meanwhile the Government were using every known method of exhortation to encourage industry to increase production. Mr. Attlee, the Prime Minister, asked the country for a united national drive in his broadcast of 3rd March 1946; he called for a revival of the Dunkirk spirit. Mr. Eden had been emphasizing the need for increased production in his speeches. Some Socialist Ministers, however, continued to attack private enterprise on which an industrial revival must largely depend.

There were demands for the general acceptance of a forty-hour

Britain's Economic Struggle

week, which the Government refused, and for a five-day week in the coal mines, which was granted by the National Coal Board in 1947. Unofficial strikes in a number of places occurred, but the main anxiety concerned coal. Despite warnings from the Opposition, Mr. Shinwell, then the Minister of Fuel, remained unconvinced even in October 1946 that there would be a coal crisis. He had, however, appealed for a 10 per cent voluntary reduction in the consumption of coal, gas and electricity. Those in charge of electricity undertakings insisted that some form of rationing of electricity was inevitable during the winter. It was known that electrical generating capacity was inadequate and that electrical generators were being exported. Moreover, the 1946 Budget, by removing purchase tax from electric heaters, had encouraged their use, and had increased the load on the power stations. A fuel crisis did in fact develop, with all the consequences forecast by the Conservatives.

The U.S. Loan, negotiated in December 1945, came into operation on 15th July 1946. It was then anticipated by the Government that it would last for at least three years.

The second session of this Parliament began in November. The Government's programme included the nationalization of electricity, of transport and of cables and wireless. It had previously been announced that the Liverpool Cotton Exchange would not be reopened, and the Cotton (Centralized Buying) Bill was now proposed. The London rubber market was, however, reopened in November. The Government had made serious mistakes in bulk buying of rubber and of cotton; at one time spinners were paying twopence per lb. more for cotton than those who bought in a free world market, and rubber was twopence per lb. dearer than in the U.S.A.

During the debate on the Address in reply to the King's Speech on November 14th Mr. Eden spoke of the need for the Government to encourage and to increase the productivity of industry. He referred to the shortage of essential commodities and of manpower, to the fact that although 50 per cent more people were working for exports now than in 1938 the volume of exports was only 17 per cent above 1938, and to the past teaching of Socialist Ministers which had discouraged hard work. Nine days earlier Mr. Marquand, the Secretary for Overseas Trade, had said: 'I think that what we might have to anticipate in the near future may be something like the slump we experienced in 1921.' Mr. Eden pointed out that in 1921:

Domestic Affairs

'What was available to the consuming industries and to the public was not required by them. Now, the exact opposite is the position. Today the whole emphasis is on the shortage of materials. If there is a slump in future it will be because there is not enough production of these essential commodities.'

A. SPRING, 1947

1947 began with exceptionally severe weather. This coincided with a most serious shortage of coal stocks, foreseen by the Opposition, but against which the Government had neglected to insure. The Ministry of Fuel and Power had been busy with coal nationalization, which came into effect on 1st January 1947. The fuel crisis began on February 10th, and for varying periods the greater part of industry was shut down, whilst for several months individuals suffered hardships from severe restrictions of fuel and light. This industrial dislocation had a serious but temporary effect upon the increase of exports.

On February 21st the Government issued their 'Economic Survey for 1947' as a White Paper. Mr. Eden said of it: 'The diagnosis of the Government is admirable, the remedy is wholly absent.' The survey outlined a number of immediate objectives, including coal production, exports and expansion of industrial manpower. The coal target for the year was 200,000,000 tons, which, allowing for open-cast coal, was 15,000,000 tons less than that produced in 1941 with less machinery. It was reckoned by many that the needs of industry required a total of 215,000,000 to 220,000,000 tons and that coal could not therefore be exported. The general export target was set at 40 per cent above the 1938 volume. In the first quarter the volume achieved was only ½ per cent above the 1938 average and 10 per cent below that achieved in the last quarter of 1946.

Mr. Eden had much to say about the handling of the fuel question, both by itself and as part of general economic planning. On March 20th he spoke in the series of Parliamentary Political Broadcasts:

Britain's Economic Struggle

No one will deny the seriousness of the economic crisis that now confronts us. It is not merely the weather that has caused this. The weather has made things worse, but the origin of our troubles goes much deeper than that. The immediate cause of the breakdown has been shortage of coal and shortage of electric generators. The fuel and power crisis, coming just at the time when industry was regaining rhythm in post-war production, has been a cruel blow to our prospects. Its effects will long be felt.

But these immediate problems must be set against the wider background. Before the war our overseas investments, themselves the result of the thrift and enterprise of our ancestors, played an important part in our national economy. Today these have been largely spent on the war. We are heavily pledged overseas, particularly by the existence of the so-called sterling balances, those vast debts which are one of our principal rewards for saving the world. Our export task is truly gigantic.

To meet all these commitments we have a labour force which is ill distributed, and industrial equipment which is suffering from the strain of six years of war. Finally, in our internal finances, we have a dangerous situation. Too much money is chasing too few goods, while Government expenditure greatly exceeds revenue.

All this is most serious. But these difficulties can be overcome, provided that we set about them in the right way. Within the limits of the time I have, it is my duty to show you where I think the Government have made mistakes and to suggest what we think should now be done. This is not indeed an occasion for faction, but it is most emphatically an occasion for fair and constructive criticism.

The British people, after all the strain of war, are now called upon to put forth further efforts in order to win the peace. In these circumstances they are entitled to the best of leadership, and they are entitled to make sure that they are getting it. It is not enough that we should be satisfied that the Government means well. We must also be satisfied that they have the ability to administer the country in these difficult times and the determination and power of leadership to bring the country through the dangers that lie before us.

We must have economic planning of a kind and of a quality that will ensure the fullest possible use of all the resources we possess, both at home and abroad. I have for some time been saying, both in the House of Commons and in the country, that in their concern to interfere with the working and control of individual industries the Government have been losing sight of their first task, which is broad strategic planning. The aim of planning should be to guide and stimulate the efforts of industries and individuals, not to restrict and distort them.

Let me give you an example of what I mean. The dislocation of industry from which we have suffered this winter, the discomfort which the public has had to endure, have been caused by a shortage of 5,000,000 tons of coal, or about ten days' output. That is relatively a very small margin indeed. Moreover, the danger of a breakdown must have been evident last spring; for it is in the spring that the coal budget for the next twelve months is prepared. Surely it would have been wiser to take precautions then against such a calamity, even if this meant buying 5,000,000 tons of coal abroad, or cutting down our exports, which amounted to 9,000,000 tons last year in bunkers and otherwise. This would have been better than allowing ourselves to stumble unprepared into such wholesale dislocation. Even now the coal production target for this year is too low for the needs of the nation. It is below what was achieved in 1941 by the same number of men with less machinery.

Stranger still, the Government have, by speeches and by reductions in the purchase tax, encouraged us to buy electric fires and gadgets at a time when they must have known that our generating plant was inadequate to carry a further load. Nor,

Britain's Economic Struggle

apparently, was the manufacture of generators for the home market given any adequate priority at all. It is also disturbing to note that throughout 1946 we were exporting mining equipment and electric generators. Again, there is a substantial figure for the export of agricultural machinery, badly wanted on our own farms. That is what I mean by a failure to plan.

Now I turn to the question of our export trade. Here again nobody denies the importance of exports if we are to obtain the necessary equipment and raw materials for our industries and the necessary food for our families. In present circumstances the concern of government should be with the pattern of our import and export programmes. And here all is far from well.

It is disturbing to note how small a portion of our exports are at present going to the so-called hard-currency countries, principally the American continent, for these are the countries who have the things we really want. According to the Government's White Paper, only 14 per cent of our exports are going to hard-currency countries, while we are taking as much as 42 per cent of our imports from them. It becomes all the more urgent to sell goods to the hard-currency areas because the sellers' market, which is at present available all over the world, is not going to last for ever. When this market begins to dry up, and by the summer I am afraid we shall begin to see the first signs of it, we shall be faced with stern competition. Then our increased costs, which a continuance of present conditions will make inevitable, are going to add to the difficulties of our manufacturers in winning their way to world markets.

Again, I cannot feel happy about the use which we are making of the American Loan. I had always understood that by far the greater part of this loan would be used to re-equip our industry, to provide us with essential raw materials, and perhaps some foodstuffs. But actually in the last half of 1946 we spent only 5 per cent of our dollars on all kinds of machinery as against 7 per cent on films and still more on tobacco. Surely these figures do not make sense.

Domestic Affairs

Now let us look at money and taxes. The rate of Government expenditure is still today about three times above the peak pre-war budget. You see the consequences of this in a crippling level of taxation, which acts as a definite brake on effort and incentive in all walks of our national life. I think it is of the utmost importance that there should be tax reliefs of a kind that will encourage effort and output. I have in mind, for example, further reliefs on earned income. Effort must be rewarded. There should also be a revision of the methods of the operation of P.A.Y.E. and the transference, if possible, of a further proportion of the weight of taxation from direct to indirect taxation. But none of these reliefs can safely be given as things are today, unless there is a substantial decrease in the rate of Government expenditure.

Perhaps the most striking of all the failings of the present Government is their apparent indifference to public opinion and their inability to make their policies intelligible to the ordinary men and women, who are most closely affected by them. Small wonder that many people are bewildered by what has happened in the past few weeks, so very different from what they have been led to expect. As a nation we possess all the qualities of character needed for our tremendous task. Our democratic institutions are fashioned for change and progress. We are addicted to the best kind of discipline, which has been described as organized un-selfishness. It is surely the duty of those who govern to make their policies not only clearly understood but true to British character and in accord with tried and valued British institutions.

Let us consider how our free institutions, that are a vital feature of our democratic system, are in danger of being weakened by excessive interference and regimentation. The influence of Parliament is affected if ill-digested bills are forced through by methods such as the guillotine, which will prevent large chunks of them ever being discussed at all. Hasty and careless legislation impairs the authority of Parliament, and so imperils the sovereignty of the people which reposes in Parliament.

The British Civil Service is a source of national pride for its

Britain's Economic Struggle

efficiency and its integrity. An honest, impartial and efficient Civil Service is an essential of democracy as we understand it. But, as the Government rushes legislation through at breakneck speed, our Civil Service is being overloaded with work, and its efficiency is in grave danger of being reduced.

Local government is the centre of democratic activity in the provinces. The municipal service, which has so often been the training ground of our national representatives, is being discouraged and belittled by over-centralization of administration in London.

If our industrial system is to tackle the great task before it there is need for Government aid and general direction, but not for so many over-centralized and confusing controls.

Incentives to hard work there must be. In totalitarian States the threat of force operates. It is well that we should never forget this forbidding fact. We need to create an incentive based on pride in achievement and a sense of service to the community, plus reward for effort and a true partnership between capital and labour. There are many ways in which such a partnership can be formed, differing in detail to suit the varying conditions in industry. The Conservative Party has for some time been studying this vital problem and will shortly present its proposals. I believe we will offer the rank-and-file worker a position in industry that will cause him to feel that he is more than a mere cog in the wheel. The question I ask my listeners to ponder is whether the workers, brought under a vast system of State monopolies, will be able to achieve a higher sense of personal responsibility and greater pride of achievement than they can attain under a system of enlightened free enterprise.

I have tried to make an objective analysis of our problems and to propound some remedies for our ills. But it is an essential condition of the success of any policy that there should be true leadership.

The Prime Minister appeals for support of the Government on national grounds, but unfortunately the Government persist in pursuing policies which divide the nation. The state of the nation

today is very different from that at the time of the General
Election. There has been a marked deterioration in our affairs.
We hear of the Dunkirk spirit, but the essence of that spirit was
that we all set aside partisan programmes and joined in a
national effort.

Mr. Attlee said he did not intend to score party points. But what
he repeatedly called his plan, which appeared to be merely to
nationalize transport, electricity, and perhaps other industries
also, is the most controversial of party politics. You cannot unite
the nation on that basis, for even on the figures of the last General
Election about half the nation was against the Government on
these issues. Nor, whatever their merits, do they offer any cure for
our immediate ills. They merely cramp and confuse industrialists
and clutter up the desks of civil servants who should be attending
to more urgent tasks. Though our hands must be free for the
future, nobody is going to ask this Government to go back now on
what is already law. But I say to the Government: stop galloping
down nationalization avenue and pay attention to the things that
matter most now: food and fuel, houses and clothes, the balance
of trade and the balance of the Budget, and the fate of home
agriculture. Make no mistake about it. Home agriculture is going
to be a vital issue in 1947. All who work on the land will need
every assistance we can give them. These are the things a Government should be troubling its head about, and not whether
electricity should become a State monopoly in 1948 or not. The
Government must put first things first.

For my part I am more than ever convinced that giant State
monopolies offer no cure for our national ills. On the contrary,
the success and stability of a civilized State depend upon the
widest possible extension among all its citizens of the private
ownership of property. That is our faith, and I know that it is
poles asunder from Socialism.

But there is an immediate task, and on this I conclude.

The Government is faced with issues as complex and as urgent
as have ever confronted our State in time of peace. Let them face

these difficulties in a national spirit. Let them give a true national lead and we can win through.

The British people will always respond to a lead. If they are told the truth, and if they are given the lead they require, they will never fail you. If what has to be done is unpleasant and unpopular, they will not flinch if they know it to be necessary. Let them be given a national lead. Let them be told in clear language what is required of them. Let them be given a term and a purpose.

Today the nation is like a runner who starts, as he thinks, to run his half a mile. He strains every nerve, he almost drops from exhaustion, he reaches the winning-post, but, alas, the tape is not there. Nor can anyone tell him where it will be.

Instead of an endless vista of growing restrictions and dismal forebodings, let our people be given a clear and definite task, which, though harsh, holds out at its conclusion the prospect of a freer and fuller life for ourselves and for our children.

For close on three hundred years the British people have solved their own political differences peacefully by democratic methods and parliamentary processes. Now has come our greatest testing time. It is not only that we have a democratic duty to ourselves to solve our political problems by debate and vote, but we must set an example to Europe of the virtues and virility of free discussion and the other liberties we cherish, and show that they lead, under God's guidance, to a healthy way of life and high achievement.

I ask you to examine these matters without political prejudice and with characteristic common sense, and I am confident that your democratic answer will be against State regimentation, and in favour of a system of free enterprise adapted by modern thought and brought more closely into line with popular aspiration. I call that the democratic answer because democracy stands for the pursuit of individual happiness, and I believe that without the free development of the human personality and the joy of personal achievement there can be no true happiness for the individual or lasting prosperity for the nation.

Domestic Affairs

B. THE STORM BREAKS

In April Dr. Dalton budgeted for a surplus of £270,000,000, which Conservatives showed was fictitious owing to the large capital payments expected. He imposed a heavy tax on tobacco in an attempt to reduce its consumption. He admitted that there was 'a tendency towards inflation', but estimated a total expenditure of over £3,000,000,000 and continued with his cheap money policy. Direct taxation remained at its oppressive level.

By the end of July exports had reached 125 per cent of the 1938 volume, but imports had risen both in volume and in price. The increase in import prices during the year up to May had been 19 per cent against an increase in export prices of 15 per cent. The seller's market was disappearing and the export market was becoming more difficult. The high adverse balance of trade, running at an annual rate of £700,000,000 in July, resulted in heavy drawings on the American Loan. By the end of 1946 only £150,000,000 had been drawn from the Loan of £937,500,000. Six months later only £250,000,000 were left of the American Loan and only £125,000,000 of the Canadian £300,000,000 credit.

Despite these portents, a number of optimistic statements were made by Ministers during the summer about rations and our general recovery. But on June 30th Dr. Dalton announced a programme of import cuts estimated to save £25,000,000. On July 8th Mr. Eden described this as 'tinkering with the problem'. The Government seemed to be relying on the prospect of further U.S. help held out by Mr. Marshall's offer a month earlier on which no firm steps had yet been taken. Mr. Eden's comment was: 'We cannot become the permanent pensioners of the United States. We have a role of our own to play as the heart and centre of a great Empire.'

On July 15th sterling again became convertible in accordance with a stipulation in the American Loan. Despite many warnings, Dr. Dalton had maintained that convertibility would not be a serious burden. In the event we had to draw from the American Loan £175,000,000 in July and £60,500,000 in the first nineteen days of August. Convertibility, which had been ruinously expensive in dollars, was suspended on August 20th.

The full force of the economic storm broke upon the country at the end of July. The House of Commons remained in session

Britain's Economic Struggle

until August 13th. On the 6th and 7th they discussed the Government's proposals to meet the crisis. These consisted of revised targets for the basic industries and export plans, an increase of 20 per cent on agricultural output by 1951-2, a form of direction of labour and full emergency powers to be given by a Supplies and Services Bill to be rushed through Parliament, cuts in the Defence forces and cuts in imports amounting to an annual saving of £175,000,000. This resulted in reduced rations, the abolition of the basic petrol ration, a ban on foreign travel and a reduction in the housing programme. Mr. Attlee, in introducing the proposals, said that we could not and would not base our plans on the assumption that there would be further American help.

Mr. Eden spoke last for the Opposition. The following is the main part of his speech:

I have listened, as the House has listened, with growing concern to the course of this Debate during the last two days. We have all our party views and party faith in whichever part of the House we sit, but over and above that there is a concern for the future of our country. I had sincerely hoped, and I say this to the right hon. and learned Gentleman (Sir S. Cripps) who is to follow me, that as the outcome of this Debate we would have been presented with a comprehensive and coherent plan to lead our country out of the present quagmire on to the firmer ground of solvency and self-respect. That is what I had hoped for. With real reluctance I am bound to say that I cannot consider that the Government have produced any such plan at all. I am indeed disappointed at their proposals, and several of their own supporters have expressed themselves as disappointed during the last two hours. They seem to me to be just a hasty improvisation, ill-considered and incomplete. In many spheres we are called upon to consider not policy but hopes.

The Prime Minister yesterday made a good deal of play with the undoubted fact that any Government in power at this time

25

would have grave difficulties to face. We do not deny that, but what we do say, and what the right hon. Gentleman's speech did much to confirm, is that in facing these difficulties the performance of the present Government has been wholly inadequate.

They have stumbled undecided, unprepared and without a plan into a crisis which they had not foreseen. As far as we can judge from this afternoon they appear to hope to stumble out again in the same way. The Prime Minister's statement was not a coherent or a clear-cut plan to overcome an imminent danger. It seemed to me to be a hastily contrived collection of expedients, not designed, because there was no design in them at all, but produced in the hope that they would do something to meet a situation which clearly the Government do not even yet seem fully to understand. Let me remind you, Sir, that there is a remarkable contrast between what the Prime Minister had to say yesterday and what the Lord President of the Council and the Chancellor of the Exchequer had to tell us in the Import Programme Debate as recently as July 8th. I have looked up the Lord President's words. He said this:

'The only remedy, pending the restoration of European agriculture and industry, lies in devising some means whereby billions of dollars' worth of North and South American production can be transferred across the Atlantic without the necessity for immediate payment in the form of an equal and opposite flow of European goods.'—[OFFICIAL REPORT, 8th July 1947; Vol. 439, c. 2076.]

That is the Lord President on July 8th. Yesterday we had the Prime Minister:

'It may be that the chain of events started by Secretary Marshall's speech will lead to further American help towards the recovery of the Old World, and that we shall share in this help. But we cannot and will not base our plans on that assumption.'—[OFFICIAL REPORT, 6th August 1947; Vol. 441, c. 1501.]

In other words, the only assumption on which the Lord President on July 8th bases his plan is repudiated by the Prime Minister less than a month later—[HON. MEMBERS: 'No.']—Well, it is true.

Britain's Economic Struggle

Let hon. Members themselves confirm the quotation. On July 8th the Chancellor of the Exchequer himself argued against an immediate cut in our import programme. He said that it was not the right thing to do at this moment. Yet, yesterday the Prime Minister announced, and today the right hon. Gentleman endorsed, these extensive cuts in our food supplies. If they are right today, why were they not right on July 8th, or why were they not right at an earlier date still? The right hon. Gentlemen cannot be surprised, and the Government cannot be surprised. With such conflicting voices from the Treasury Bench—and there is the Attorney-General, the prize conflicter—how can the House or the country have any confidence in the Government's ability to understand the situation or to plan the way out? The Prime Minister said how many were the difficulties which the Government had to face. Of course, we admit that.

The Prime Minister went on to say that in all the circumstances the Government were not unwise to hold a balance. That is precisely what the Government have not done. They have held no balance. On the contrary, week by week, Ministers have made a number of contradictory statements. What the learned Attorney-General says one week, the President of the Board of Trade contradicts the next. The trouble is that the Government mistake a see-saw for a balance. That is their policy. What has happened? Let us analyse this matter again. Before the war—and this confirms what the Chancellor said; I agree with him in this respect— we lived to a very considerable extent upon our overseas investments, the result of the thrift of our ancestors, or if hon. Gentlemen like it better——

Mr. Harrison (Nottingham, East): Hear, hear.

Mr. Eden: I thought they might like it better—of the wicked capitalist instincts of our forebears. On that we have lived for a considerable time. We also benefited before the war largely from invisible exports, that is to say from our shipping, our banking and our insurance business. To a considerable extent, these sources of income are now reduced, but, despite this impoverishment, we

27

Domestic Affairs

have behaved as if we are richer than before the war, and this applies particularly to capital expenditure, about which I want to say a word or two. In that respect, I say to the House that we have been trying to do too much, and this is a warning which I have been repeating to the Government for many months past.

Let me try to put the picture in military terms. Let us suppose that we are back in the darkest days of 1940, which parallel has been drawn many times in this Debate. Suppose the War Cabinet of that day, after the collapse of France, decided that they wanted to set on foot, let us say, one hundred divisions. When the time came to work out our resources, that War Cabinet would have found that there just simply was not the manpower available to give them that hundred divisions, and so they had to cut their coat accordingly, and decided, perhaps, that they could raise only fifty divisions and a certain number of air squadrons, while maintaining our indispensable naval forces. I say that there has been no similar calculation by the Government in respect of the period of reconstruction. Has there ever been, I ask the President of the Board of Trade, any budget of our expenditure on capital reconstruction? The truth is that, despite their avowed belief in planning, of which we have heard so much from the Government and their supporters, it is precisely in the broad strategic planning of national resources that the Government have shown their worst failure.

For a long time, my colleagues and I have been telling the Government and Ministers that they have been trying to do far more at one time than is possible with the nation's resources. Let us look at what they are trying to do. There is the fulfilment of our commitments overseas, on which, although there may be differences among back benchers, the Government and we are agreed. There are new factories in the development areas, new social services, new hospitals, new schools, all highly desirable in themselves; higher wages, shorter working hours, all these, too, infinitely desirable; the development of great schemes of town planning, of capital investment of all kinds, all to be welcomed in themselves; but what, surely, must have been apparent long since to all but hon. Gentlemen opposite is that to try to attain all these things together now, at one time, might mean failure to attain any single one of them. It is all a question of priority.

I am stating what I believe to be our national position. Of what use is it, for instance, to build new factories to use steel if the existing factories working for export have not enough steel for their own use? The right hon. Gentleman knows that there are examples of it. I hope he will tell us of what value it is. Is it not true, for instance, today, that the motor-car industry could increase its production for export if its full steel requirements were made available? That is so; it is not disputed. Then, where are we going in our planning, if that be so?

I turn to food. The right hon. Gentleman the Prime Minister told us that our food supplies from the hard-currency areas are to be cut by £12,000,000 a month. I do not know what are the factors that brought the Government to achieve that particular figure. Why £12,000,000, or even £10,000,000 or £15,000,000? I do not know. Perhaps they will tell us. I reckon that this cut means a reduction of at least 40 per cent in our present food supplies from the so-called hard-currency countries. This would, indeed, be a formidable reduction in our standard of life if the supplies cannot be replaced from anywhere else.

Let the House note this. The Prime Minister did not tell us yesterday that of the food supplies which we at present receive from these hard-currency areas, about 55 per cent are, I think, staple foodstuffs—grain, meat, dairy produce, and sugar. If I understand the Government aright, they propose to replace part of this loss from the soft-currency countries. I would ask the President of the Board of Trade to tell us how this is going to be done. I feel certain that the Government cannot have decided on a cut of this kind—so drastic—without having a clearer view of the consequence than was given by the Prime Minister yesterday. How much of this cut do the Government think they can replace

Domestic Affairs

from the soft-currency areas, and from which of those countries do they expect to obtain the necessary supplies? We really must know that.

During the past two years, presumably, the Government have been obtaining as much of our foodstuffs as they could from the soft-currency countries anyway; they would have been open to grave censure if they had not. How can it be that, all at once, they see the possibility of increasing our supplies from the soft-currency areas to anything approaching the very large figure of £12,000,000 a month? I hope that the right hon. and learned Gentleman will enlighten us about that. If they cannot increase their purchases by £12,000,000 a month, or near it, from the soft-currency countries, is it not clear that there will have to be drastic cuts in the rations? We really must be given the full facts of this situation to-night so that we can judge. I say, quite frankly, that we on this side, equally with hon. Members opposite, and the country as a whole, will not flinch if told the whole truth, but I think that we have still only been given a part of the picture. The Government must not be surprised if we complain that they have not, in past months, prepared the country for just the state of affairs which the Prime Minister described yesterday.

I must remind the right hon. and learned Gentleman that it is only a few weeks ago that we had the pleasure of listening to the Minister of Food (Mr. Strachey) in this House. He was enthusiastically cheered by his supporters. I do not blame them; but we were all derided for not joining in the cheers. The Minister was telling them that there was no need whatever for the housewives or the people of this country to feel that it would be difficult, or impossible, to obtain, partly from home and partly from abroad, the food they need. How in the world can that be reconciled with a 40 per cent cut in our food imports from the hard-currency areas which has been announced by the Government today? I would like to appoint the right hon. and learned Gentleman the President of the Board of Trade, for whom I have a great respect, to a new office, that for the co-ordination of ministerial speeches.

Britain's Economic Struggle

Now I come to the next topic about which we are far from satisfied—agriculture. Is it not true that, in fact, there has been a decline during the last two years in every section of the agricultural industry, except milk production? The cattle population has gone down; the sheep population fell by half a million even before the appalling weather conditions of the early spring of this year. The pig and poultry population declined by about one-fifth in numbers, and the total area under arable crops in this country at this time last summer was half a million acres less than when this Government took office, and, at the moment, it is declining still further.

I must say that, in our opinion, the Government's target of £100,000,000 of increased output by 1951–2 is inadequate, and I will tell the Government why I think that. In the first place, that target only gets us back, four years hence, to the value of our output two years ago, in 1945. That is not very glorious, in view of the present difficulties. At that time, the House will recall, our production was mainly cereal crops, while the hope is that by 1951 the increase will be mainly livestock. Therefore, we ought to expect it to be much more valuable. So I say that that target is not at all sufficient. The industry is woefully short of labour, and simply because of lack of accommodation. If labour is to be attracted or directed, accommodation must be provided. Apart from the question of new houses, would it not have been a help through this period if the Housing (Rural Workers) Acts had been continued? Would we not have been better off? Two years ago the Minister without Portfolio (Mr. Arthur Greenwood) promised us that some substitute for this Act was going to be produced. We are still waiting, but nothing has yet materialized.

The next point I wish to raise in connection with agriculture is that, as the right hon. Gentleman knows very well, great strides were made in the mechanization of the industry, and many of the machines which the industry now possesses, such as tractors and harvesters, are today idle for want of spare parts, and many more new machines are needed. What has been going on? In spite of

Domestic Affairs

this shortage at home, and of what the Chancellor calls our first dollar saver—and I agree with him—over £6,000,000 worth of agricultural machinery was exported last year, and over £3,500,000 worth has already gone abroad this year. Can this be justified?

Mr. Parkin (Stroud): Groundnuts.

Mr. Eden: Groundnuts! Is agricultural machinery going to be exported to harvest groundnuts, when there is not yet enough machinery available at home? Is the production of food at home a No. 1 priority, or is it not? If it is a No. 1 priority, then the steel required is trivial in comparison with the output of food that would result. I say to the President of the Board of Trade that there ought to be a revision of the steel allocation, so that the agricultural industry can receive its full requirements of new machinery and spare parts; and only after those requirements have been met should consideration be given to the manufacture of agricultural machinery for export. Our home needs must come first in that sphere.

With regard to livestock production, we have been retarded in that sphere by want of feeding-stuffs. The Prime Minister said that the Government had been doing their utmost to get feeding-stuffs. No doubt they have, but hon. Members will readily understand that it is not much good doing one's utmost if one comes last in the race. Certainly we have been infinitely less successful than anybody else. [HON. MEMBERS: 'No.'] If we have not been less successful, will hon. Members please explain to me how it is that countries like Holland, Denmark and other European countries are now in a position to export to us pig and poultry produce? Does not that mean that they have been able to get feeding-stuffs over and above the requirements of their own people? [*Interruption.*] I do not think I quite caught that remark. Did the hon. Gentleman say they are eating groundnuts? It seems to be the universal explanation of all the Government's troubles. I wish to deal seriously with the present position of feeding-stuffs, and I would like the right hon. and learned Gentleman to give me some information.

Britain's Economic Struggle

They are available to an increasing extent in the world today, and if we are going to cut our supplies of foreign meat to the extent that, apparently, we are to do, judging from the figures given us yesterday and earlier today, it is essential that we should have greatly increased imports of feeding-stuffs in order that we may, as far as we can, make good the cut that will otherwise have to be made in our rations.

I am told that the exportable surplus of Argentine maize this year is estimated at between 5,000,000 and 6,000,000 tons. All we know so far is that the Minister of Food hopes to obtain some 700,000 tons of this, but if, as the right hon. Gentleman says, we are to expand our livestock production, we need at least three times as much. I do not know how much more the Government can get. We want three times more than what we are said to be getting now. The feeding-stuffs position would be enormously eased for our farmers if they were allowed to retain from this year's harvest up to 20 per cent of their wheat and barley for stock and poultry rations. If the industry is going to be called on to play its part it must be provided with the means. So I ask the Government what they can do in that respect.

I turn now to the next subject, and it is a vexatious one—to what the Prime Minister had to tell us about the direction of labour. It seemed to me that the Prime Minister's references to this subject were far from clear. Let me say at once that I hate the direction of labour and all that it implies. Such a restriction is wholly foreign to our national conception of freedom of choice in time of peace. But if anything of the kind is intended let it be clearly defined. How far is this direction of labour to extend? What categories are to be affected? And what penalties are to be imposed and exacted? For instance, are women to be included? These are grim questions, but they are questions to which we must have an answer. I must repeat that the sacrifice of the principle implied in the limited direction of labour—even though it be limited—is as odious to me as the general direction of labour. I am not at all sure that in some respects it is not worse,

33

Domestic Affairs

because if we are all subject to the same restrictions there is a certain rough justice in the event, whereas the subjection of selected groups of workers to this direction seems to me to be dangerously open to abuse. But that is not all. Let us suppose for a moment that the House will be prepared, under the stress of present conditions, to accept that principle. Are we sure, even then, that to apply it in present conditions is going to solve our problems?

I thought yesterday that the Prime Minister's speech did not face reality, because it did not meet what is our fundamental problem. It is really no use for the Government to appeal to workers in all productive industries for a greater effort unless those workers can be assured of the necessary supplies of raw materials with which to make that effort. I ask the President of the Board of Trade, let him go outside and look at the nearest Government poster, and there he will find written up:

'We need 11,000,000 tons more coal. What for?'

In order that industry shall work at full production instead of at two-thirds production as it is doing at the present time, I say to the right hon. and learned Gentleman that nothing is more exasperating to workers in an industry than to be appealed to for greater efforts when they know they have not got the fuel and materials available with which to work.

Here I turn to what was said yesterday by the hon. Member for Bolton (Mr. Jack Jones). He said:

'Our steel industry wants to do more, but again more coal is necessary. I pointed out at one of our recent meetings that the works in which I have had the privilege to work for thirty-two years closed down for a fortnight, the first time they had closed down since the General Strike of 1926.'

I hope the Chancellor will not tell me again that there is no serious industrial crisis, as he told me a while back.

'They closed down three weeks ago because they had used up their allocations of coal and had to put the rest of their coal to stock, with the result that 16,000 tons of ingot steel were lost.'— [OFFICIAL REPORT, 6th August 1947; Vol. 441, c. 1550.]

Britain's Economic Struggle

That is the situation confronting the Government, and it is not the slightest use appealing for longer hours or greater effort unless supplies of material are dealt with above all. I ask the Government: Where are we on this issue of coal, which is fundamental to our efforts? Everybody admits disappointment with the output figures so far this year. I confess that, though I do not pretend to be an advocate of nationalization, I had hoped that when the mines were nationalized we might well see—because I knew it was a step dear to the hearts of the miners themselves—an upsurge of production due to their contentment at the new conditions.

Mr. Kirkwood (Dumbarton Burghs): There has been.

Mr. Eden: The hon. Member cannot call it an upsurge. We have only to compare the figures today—as I have done in this House more than once, unhappily—with the figures for 1941, when the miners were away fighting at the front in, for instance, the 50th Division, which won unrivalled glory. In 1941, with fewer miners and less machinery, we produced 206,000,000 tons of deep-mined coal. Would not we be feeling much more content if we could be producing that this year? . . .

Now let me turn to the Government. The Government have not presented us with a plan. They have presented us with a series of expedients which are to take the place of a plan, and there are many gaps in the Government's proposals. They speak of a reduction of the Services. As far as I can judge, the run-down of the total in the Services, by the Government's plan, has not really been very greatly accelerated. I am not awfully impressed by it. Indeed the reduction in total strength by March 31st next is in the order of about 7½ per cent. It ought to be possible to achieve that by the operation of the table, with which my right hon. Friend is very familiar, without any considerable loss of efficiency. But we do not know what is the size of the previously intended repatriation figures, and so what the Government have told us about reductions abroad is impossible to assess. We have never been told the original programme, so it is impossible to judge the significance of the revised programme. I take note of what the Prime Minister told us, that the Government propose to maintain their foreign policy, and to fulfil their defence commitments which result from their foreign policy.

I must point out that this reduction in the Armed Forces is in most marked contrast to what is happening in the Civil Service. Is there to be no reduction there, or are the swollen figures to continue? I am casting no reflection in any way on the industry of civil servants, and I join in the warmest tribute to the hard work they are doing; but the question is, cannot their tasks be reduced as the tasks of the military, naval and air forces are to be reduced? I cannot believe that this is beyond the wit of man to devise; yet, there is not the slightest indication that the Government intend anything of the kind.

I must say a word to the Prime Minister about his appeal in respect of the Dunkirk spirit. I think I understood what moved the Prime Minister to make that appeal, but I must ask hon. Members to be as patient as they can with the reply I have to make to it. It seems to me that the Prime Minister did not understand that his speech of yesterday—and the Chancellor of the Exchequer today did not seem to understand it—with all its insistence upon Socialism, destroys completely the Dunkirk parallel. It is quite true that after Dunkirk this nation made an unprecedented effort, but it made that effort as a united nation.

We did not attempt, although we were a majority in Parliament at that time, and had an overwhelming majority, to pass any party legislation. [HON. MEMBERS: 'Oh.'] If any hon. Member can point to a single party measure we introduced after 1940, I should be glad to know of it. [An HON. MEMBER: 'You kept things as they were.'] Our supreme crime apparently was to keep things as they were, but we also had another job, which was to keep Hitler out of this land, and we did both. [*Interruption.*] I am not claiming that I did it personally. The hon. Member need not be so impatient. I never suggested that I kept the Germans out of Britain. What I was pointing out was that the war Coalition

36

Britain's Economic Struggle

leadership made a certain contribution to the defeat of the enemy.

If the hon. Member will have a little patience, I think I can make myself clear. The Prime Minister yesterday appealed for a Dunkirk spirit. I am trying to point out that at the time of Dunkirk, when there was a majority of our party in the Government, we interpreted the Dunkirk spirit in the sense that we brought in no legislation which represented our party point of view. We could easily have done so, with our large majority. It is now impossible for the Government to appeal for a Dunkirk spirit and, at the same time, announce that they intend to bring in the most violent partisan legislation. I will give one example, the iron and steel industry. [Hon. Members: 'Ah.'] That is precisely the answer I expected. Members opposite know that all of us on this side—and even after the last election we had the majority of voters —know that to proceed with that policy at present is anathema. Whatever the Government Front Bench may wish, Members of the party opposite clearly wish to proceed with that policy, yet, at the same time, are calling for a Dunkirk spirit. The position is utterly unacceptable.

I will sum up my complaint against the Government's present policy. They have told us that Europe and Asia have taken a long time to settle down. That is true. But when did the Government first discover that? It must have been apparent, even to the least-informed observer, a year ago, so why could not some of these proposals have been brought before us then? My main charge against the Government is this: even at this stage of the Debate we have not been given a clear picture. We still have not been told what the continuing rate of exhaustion of our dollar resources, including our reserves, is likely to be. We have not been told what the cumulative effect of the Government's proposals is likely to be. Neither the House nor the country has been given any indication of how long this struggle and the privations are to last.

I say, as I have said before, that the people of this country will always respond to a clear and definite lead. Tell them clearly

37

Domestic Affairs

what is required of them; show them the size and nature of the task; tell them clearly what has to be endured, and for how long; set a term to their efforts and sacrifices. Then you will get from them the response for which you ask. Up to now they have been presented with nothing but muddle, confusion, conflicting Ministerial statements, and a dreary vista of continuing shortages. More than once we have said plainly that we would support the Government in any constructive effort they might make to meet our present difficulties. That undertaking stands. But we cannot regard this present hotchpotch of certain cuts and uncertain hopes as a serious remedy for our ills. We must, therefore, vote against the Adjournment tonight.

C. IMPROVEMENT—THE END OF 1948

When the trade figures were published for the first half of 1948, it was seen that there had been a great improvement, the most marked being on invisible account. Exports had exceeded the estimate in price and volume, but so had imports. The terms of trade were still moving against Britain.

This improvement continued into the autumn, but the international position demanded greater expenditure on defences by Britain and the European countries. It was estimated that by the middle of 1948 industrial production as a whole was running at about 20 per cent above pre-war. Output per man year had recovered the pre-war level in many industries.

But despite this improvement, the standard of consumption in Britain was not as high as in 1947, and Sir Stafford Cripps stated that in the next year there would be no material improvements in the standard of living.

The Board of Trade Journal in October gave an interesting estimate of the position that would have prevailed if there had been no aid from the U.S.A. The rations of butter, sugar, cheese and bacon would have been cut by one-third, and the ration of meat and eggs would have been lower. Only one-quarter of the existing tobacco supplies, less footwear and cotton goods would have been available for the home market. There would have been even less petrol, fewer films, newspapers and books. Short-

38

age of timber would have reduced house building to perhaps 50,000 per year. Owing to shortage of raw materials unemployment would have risen to 1,500,000 and would have become progressively worse thereafter.

Despite our efforts, it has been said we were—at the best— after four years of peace, back in the position we had been in after the first eighteen months.

The third session opened in October 1947. The Government programme included the nationalization of gas and a measure to reduce from two years to one the suspensory veto which the House of Lords could impose on legislation. Sir Stafford Cripps had been appointed Minister of Economic Affairs and had taken over the general co-ordination of Government economic policy from Mr. Herbert Morrison. A special budget was introduced by Dr. Dalton on November 12th, with the object of reducing purchasing power. Dr. Dalton resigned, following an incident in the Lobby, and was succeeded by Sir Stafford Cripps, who now combined the duties of Chancellor and Minister of Economic Affairs. One of his first actions was to cut capital expenditure which Mr. Eden had advocated earlier in the year so that we could match our plans with our resources. At the end of the year the adverse balance of payments was £675,000,000 and the total dollar deficit for the year was £1,023,000,000. Our total reserves had fallen to £512,000,000; in addition, there was still £75,000,000 of the American Loan outstanding, £70,000,000 of the Canadian credit and a gold loan of £80,000,000 from South Africa, which with other items brought the total to £758,000,000.

After a detailed investigation of the plan for Marshall Aid put forward by the sixteen European nations, it was proposed in January 1948 in Washington that £1,700,000,000 should be provided for aid of Europe for the first fifteen months, of which it was estimated Britain might expect £440,000,000. These figures were subsequently reduced to £1,325,000,000 and £331,000,000, but in February no final decision had been taken by Congress.

On 4th February 1948 the Government issued a White Paper on Personal Incomes, Costs and Prices, in which the danger of inflation, the effect of increased wages, salaries and profits on costs and therefore on the export trade and the effect on inflation of our attempts to achieve a balance of payments was clearly set out. The Government asked that there should be no increase of dividends or of wages except in certain specified conditions and promised a number of new price-control orders. Mr. Eden took part in a debate on this White Paper on February 12th. He welcomed all measures to check inflation, but gave the Government this warning:

'In the last resort, the only way in which we will get out of this position is by increased output. It is therefore essential that in the Government's very proper desire now to combat inflation they should not take any action which may kill incentive. It is incentive which maintains our output and which alone makes a rising export trade at competitive prices possible at all.'

He added that the drain on our reserves could only be partially met by Marshall Aid. He spoke of the need to take a long-term view as well as to seek a solution of the short-term problem and he reminded the House of the resources and strength of the British Commonwealth in whose greater unity lay our hope for the future.

An Anglo-Argentine Trade Agreement was announced on 16th February 1948, but £150,000,000 raised by the sale of the British-owned Argentine Railways would be largely used up by one year's purchase of food.

On March 9th the Government published the Economic Survey for 1948, which, because of its gloomy tidings, quickly earned the name of the 'Black Paper'. A production target of 14,000,000 tons was set for the steel industry, a figure which in the event was well surpassed. Yet there were known to be difficulties in allocation. The Government appeared to have no steel budget.

On April 3rd President Truman signed the Foreign Assistance Bill, which allowed Britain £331,000,000 for the first fifteen months of the European Recovery Programme.

On April 6th Sir Stafford Cripps introduced a budget showing a genuine surplus of £330,000,000 to reduce inflation. In setting out the nation's accounts, he adopted a new method of which the House of Commons showed its approval. Recent financial policy had shown that he had revised Dr. Dalton's dogmatic cheap money policy which had expanded credit by forcing down interest rates. Expenditure remained enormous at just under £3,000,000,000. Taxes on beer, wines, spirits and tobacco, totes and pools were increased; purchase tax was amended, but retained at a high rate. Certain reliefs were given on income tax and these had been pressed on the Government by Conservatives

40

Britain's Economic Struggle

for the past two years. A new tax, or levy, was imposed on capital and described as a special contribution 'once for all'. Several Socialists, including Dr. Dalton, asked for a true capital levy.

. . . . .

Mr. Eden reviewed the position as it was in the autumn of 1948, when he spoke at Reading on November 3rd. The following is an extract from his speech.

We can rightly draw a measure of encouragement from the improvement in our economic affairs that has taken place in the first half of this year. We can take pride in the achievements of our export industries, and the progress that has been made gives us ground for increasing confidence in our ability to save ourselves and our country from the economic dangers that hang over us. But it would be most unwise for us to be led away by this improvement into thinking that all our problems on the economic front have been solved.

After the mounting perils and disasters of 1947 it is with sincere relief that we see genuine progress being made. But that progress is but a small step along the arduous and uphill road to full recovery and full economic independence.

We are still to a large extent dependent upon the help we are receiving from our friends across the Atlantic. We must not allow ourselves to forget that without the £300,000,000 worth of dollars we are receiving this year under the Marshall Aid scheme there would be one and a half to two million unemployed, and we should all suffer further drastic reductions in our present standards of living.

This much Ministers themselves admit. Moreover, Marshall Aid will not last for ever. It is a respite, not a remedy.

The knowledge that the stream of dollar aid must cease, coupled with the promptings of our own national pride, demands

41

Domestic Affairs

that we set as our target the achievement of complete economic independence as soon as possible. We cannot in this country remain permanent pensioners of the United States.

This is going to call for further sustained efforts in increasing our exports in the face of growing difficulties. There are two particularly disturbing facts.

First, while our exports have been steadily increasing, it looks from the latest published figures that the increase in total production of goods in this country is slowing down. In fact, there has been no further increase in the last month or two. Already, as you well know, exports represent a very high proportion of the goods that we produce in this country.

If we are going to be called upon to export more and more, we can do it only in one of two ways, either by increasing our total production, or by reducing still further what is available for the home consumer. This last would be indeed a disturbing prospect. It emphasizes the importance of ensuring that the upward trend of production is resumed at the earliest possible moment.

The other disturbing fact is the danger to our export trade of rising prices. For a period after the end of the war the problem of selling goods practically did not exist. There was a seller's market all over the world. Anything we could make we could sell, such was the shortage of all kinds of goods after six years of war. But the heyday of the seller's market has already passed, and in one line of goods after another British exporters are finding themselves faced with severe price competition. In other words, now that competition is reviving we are finding that we will not be able to sell the goods we produce unless we can offer them at competitive prices. Two of the heaviest burdens laid upon industry are the weight of taxation, and the cost and quality of coal.

These, then, are important facts which I would ask you to bear in mind when you hear the rather optimistic accounts that Ministers are now giving of the progress that this country has made in improving its economic situation in recent months.

Britain's Economic Struggle

There is, thirdly, the problem of strengthening our national and Imperial defences, which cannot be effected without further strains and stresses on our manpower.

A word as regards our general economic position. The improvement that has been made in our exports is not the achievement of Socialism; it is the achievement of free enterprise. The industries that have made the major contribution to this great export drive, industries producing motor cars, machinery, metal manufactures, pottery, cutlery, biscuits, are all owned and operated by free enterprise. There is no nationalized industry among them. There is not even an industry which is threatened with nationalization among them.

I notice that the latest argument of some Government supporters is that some of these industries, like iron and steel, are doing so well because they are looking forward to being nationalized.

I cannot believe that even supporters of the Government take this argument seriously. In any event, the great improvement in our export drive has taken place under this free-enterprise system that I have described.

The only nationalized industry that makes a direct contribution to our export programme is the coal industry. Here we see coal exports still lagging very far behind the level maintained before the war under free enterprise. Meanwhile coal has increased by 6s. 6d. a ton since nationalization, and as to quality, well, I leave you to judge for yourselves. This does not help our manufacturing industries much.

So when Ministers talk about the achievements of recent months let us not forget that these are the achievements, not of Socialism, but of those free-enterprise industries that Socialists constantly deride.

A particularly encouraging feature of our trade returns has been the improvement in what are called invisible exports. In fact, in the first half of this year, although our export of goods increased greatly, the cost of our imports increased even more,

43

and so the deficit on our visible balance of trade was £69,000,000 *more* than the Government estimated. Fortunately for them, and for us, however, the balance of trade on what is called invisible account, that is the rest of our manifold commercial and trading activities, was £64,000,000 *better* than they had forecast.

Now what are the activities that go to make up these so-called invisible exports?

Well, there are many different trades and industries that contribute. There is our shipping to start with. That is now earning a profit for this country at a rate of £66,000,000 a year. Then there are the activities of the British oil companies operating overseas. These are becoming increasingly important. There are the commissions earned by our bankers and the income of insurance companies obtained from their activities in foreign countries. These together are making an important contribution to the solving of our difficulties.

But look at these industries for a moment.

Shipping is not nationalized, and indeed I do not think that anyone has seriously suggested that it should be. The oil companies are not nationalized. They are not merely private enterprise; they are indeed typical of the companies that have for years developed the world's resources in the raw materials of industries, often earning for themselves Socialist abuse as wicked exploiters. The banks and the insurance companies are the next. Here again are citadels of free enterprise, accustomed to hear the thunder of Socialist propaganda attacking them. Yet their contributions to solving the problems that confront us are very substantial.

The improvement in our invisible exports has two lessons for us today. First, it underlines once again the fact that we are the greatest commercial and trading nation in the world, and therefore singularly unsuited to Socialism. Secondly, it makes abundantly clear that further nationalization plans cannot hope to meet the challenge of the difficulties of the day.

Everybody knows how expensive nationalization has proved

to be. We have had enough. If the Government persists in yet more forcible feeding from the trough of State monopolies, it can only mean disaster for us all.

And then there is the outstanding example of Malaya. Here the great tin and rubber industries developed by free enterprise are the greatest dollar earners of the sterling area. Last year exports from Malaya to the United States totalled 284,000,000 dollars, which was more than the value of the total exports from this country to the United States, which was 240,000,000 dollars.

Socialism has had nothing to do with that.

The truth is that our strength and our prosperity have been built on countless different activities, producing, selling, banking, insurance, sending goods of all kinds to every corner of the world. All these things were done under the system of free enterprise. It was in this way that we built up the vast overseas investments that stood us in good stead before and during the recent war, and the reduction of which presses so sorely upon us today. It is these activities of private trade and commerce that are now trying to solve the problem of our balance of payments.

There is another aspect of our affairs that causes us concern. We are living, in part, on money given or lent by the United States. We are also living upon our own accumulated capital. For instance, all this year we have been eating the Argentine railways. This is a process that cannot be repeated.

Gradually we are parting with other capital assets in South America, the Brazilian railways and so forth. But they have served us well. They were made possible by a low level of taxation and by the ability of our ancestors to save.

Unhappily, as Lord Catto said the other day, 'Even a Scotsman cannot save and also pay existing taxation.' This is a very serious state of affairs. For we cannot hope to rebuild our strength, still less restore our overseas investments, which paid for a quarter of everything we imported before the war, while we are staggering under the present heavy load of Government expenditure.

Domestic Affairs

Our national expenditure is still more than three times its rate before the war. This is much too high.

Economies are always difficult to effect, but they must be effected, if we are going to be able to stand on our own feet when the help of the Marshall Plan is ended.

D. CRISIS AGAIN

The volume of exports in the last months of 1948 reached the Government's target of 150 per cent of the 1938 volume. Industrial production continued to rise until the end of the year. The provisional statement of balance of payments during the last half of 1948 showed that we were in overall balance with the rest of the world. But it also showed that we were still far from paying for our dollar imports with current dollar earnings; our total deficit with the Western hemisphere during 1948 was £340,000,000 and was expected to be £115,000,000 for the first half of 1949.

The Economic Survey for 1949 gave as paramount objectives for 1949: expansion of exports to Canada and U.S.A.; further expansion in industrial and agricultural production; reduction of costs and prices, particularly in exports.

In April Sir Stafford Cripps budgeted for a small real surplus on a total expenditure of £3,300,000,000. His important proposals were: an increase in death duties, in the tax on football and other pools; a decrease in taxes on beer; and the doubling of the initial allowances for industry. But the most important part of his budget speech lay not in his proposals but in his emphasis on hard facts and common sense concerning food subsidies, for which he laid down a maximum, and the payment for social services.

During the early months of 1949 exporters were experiencing increasing difficulties, particularly in the U.S.A. Monthly trade figures showed a widening gap between exports and imports. Special steps were taken by the Government and industry to encourage exports to Canada, and these began to bear fruit in April. But it became clear that the high prices of British goods would make the exporters' task more and more difficult, especially as prices in the U.S.A. began to drop substantially.

Wholesale prices had continued to rise throughout 1948, and despite the Government's policy the average rate of wages increased during 1948, so that at the end of the year it was 7 per cent above the level of June 1947. The railway trades unions were asking for substantial increases in wages during the beginning of 1949.

On April 13th the Socialist Party issued the draft of its General Election programme in a sixpenny pamphlet entitled, *Labour Believes in Britain*. This draft, which was to be considered by the Party at its Whitsuntide conference at Blackpool, contained a number of promises about price stabilization, housing and the development of the health scheme. But certain industrial proposals aroused the most interest. These included the nationalization of Industrial Assurance, sugar refining and manufacture, the cement industry, water supplies, and the wholesale meat trade. There were further proposals in the nature of a blank cheque for starting up new public enterprises, for the nationalization of existing enterprises in certain conditions and for allowing public enterprises to compete with private firms.

Sir Stafford Cripps emphasized many times during the first quarter of 1949 how dependent we were on Marshall Aid. The programme of imports for 1949–50, published in December, required about £235,000,000 in dollars from the European Recovery Programme. This would not be assured until Congress approved the second year's aid in late summer.

The Iron and Steel Bill reached the report stage in the House of Commons by April. The guillotine restricted discussion in the Committee and Report stages.

Early in June reports indicated that our gold and dollar reserves were being heavily drawn upon despite Marshall Aid. Sir Stafford Cripps reached agreement with the U.S.A. representative and the O.E.C.C. over the limited convertibility of sterling made available by the U.K. to other European countries under the European payments scheme and thus avoided one source of a possible further increase in the dollar drain.

Early in July the publication of the balance of payments figures for the first half-year revealed that the gold and dollar reserve of the sterling area had fallen from £471,000,000 to £406,000,000 in the past three months. The net gold and dollar deficit for the second quarter had been £44,000,000 more than the estimate, and £75,000,000 more than in the first quarter. On July 6th the Chancellor announced a postponement of all new dollar purchases for at least three months to the maximum possible extent.

Domestic Affairs

The House of Commons debated the economic situation on July 14th and 18th. In his opening speech the Chancellor gave some details of cuts in dollar expenditure. He assumed that Britain could not afford in the next year to import more than three-quarters of the 1948 level of dollar imports. This would save £100,000,000 in dollars. The cuts affected imports of sugar, tobacco, timber, paper pulp, steel, non-ferrous metals and other raw materials. He called these cuts an evil necessity and expressly denied that they were a remedy. The import programme would not be settled until September. His forecast that the cuts would not prevent industry from maintaining the present overall level of production was criticized by Opposition speakers. He expressly denied that sterling was to be devalued.

He had nothing new to say about long-term policy, but announced that conversations would take place between the U.S.A. and U.K. Governments in Washington early in September. Meanwhile talks were in progress in London with the Finance Ministers of the countries of the British Commonwealth.

Sir Stafford Cripps appeared in his speech to be trying to avoid making too much of the gravity of the nation's position. This was in contrast to an emotional speech made by the Minister of Fuel and Power a week earlier in which the Government was said to be in 'a moment of supreme crisis'.

During the week-end it was announced that Sir Stafford Cripps was unwell and would go to Switzerland for a few weeks' course of treatment. On Monday, July 18th, Mr. Eden opened the second day's Debate:

I am glad to be able to begin with at least one comment which I think will be non-controversial, and that is to express the gratitude which the whole House feels towards the six Finance Ministers of the Commonwealth for responding so immediately to the call for a meeting which was issued to them; it ·was characteristic of the spirit that our sister nations always show when we have to face together the urgent needs of the hour.

48

Britain's Economic Struggle

On the whole I think it was perhaps fortunate that this Debate was adjourned over the week-end so that we could have a chance, in the interval, to consider last Thursday's Debate and to weigh and confront the stern realities of our national problems. After re-reading that Debate carefully my own reflection remains unchanged: it is that the Minister of Fuel and Power, in his comment ten days ago, seems to have been much nearer the mark than the Chancellor of the Exchequer was last Thursday. The Minister of Fuel and Power at Porthcawl spoke of 'this moment of supreme crisis for the Government'. I agree with him, and I would add of supreme crisis for the nation, also.

On the other hand, the Chancellor gave me the impression—whether he intended to do so or not I cannot tell; and here I am in agreement with the hon. Member for Ipswich (Mr. Stokes), and not a secret agreement, either—that he was much too optimistic, that he was trying to play down the gravity of the situation. I do not want to play up the gravity of the situation; I want to state the situation exactly as I see it, and as fairly as I can. I think it is too serious to try to tilt the balance either way, although I do not wish to be gloomy.

To reduce our imports from the dollar area by a quarter of their total or by £100,000,000 sterling would at any time be an extremely serious step, but it is much more so when already, over a long period, we have been striving hard to reduce our dollar imports to the very minimum. Yet the whole tenor of the Chancellor's speech seemed to me to minimize the effect of these cuts. The right hon. and learned Gentleman seemed as if he were saying: 'You will lose a little here and a little there, but you will not really feel it because we shall make it up somewhere else.' I do not believe that to be a true assessment of the situation. Indeed, that mood seems rather contrary to the right hon. and learned Gentleman's own character. I often disagree with him on political issues, but I always thought he was a man who would not hesitate to put the picture, however starkly, before the nation. He has done so before, and has done a service in doing so.

Domestic Affairs

I believe it is better that we should be given the warning that the nation is going down the slippery slope if, indeed, it is going down the slippery slope. I just do not believe that we can cut £100,000,000 sterling from our dollar imports without the nation feeling it severely. Out of the proposed reduction of 400,000,000 dollars on last year's imports the cut in sugar and the restoration of sweet rationing will save, on the Government's own estimate, less than 20,000,000 dollars—a twentieth part of the whole. As for tobacco, the Chancellor said that we should spend substantially more dollars in the United States this year than we expended on payments for last year's crop. That is rather surprising in the circumstances.

It follows that practically the whole weight of the cuts will fall upon imports of raw materials for industry and American machinery. I do not think that that is disputed. The Chancellor said we should make up these losses by buying elsewhere, but without more evidence I cannot accept that as true, and I am astonished that the Chancellor should suggest it. If there are these alternative supplies available why have not we been using them all this time? Are we to believe that they have become available to us now, at the time when we are in need of them? It all sounds rather like a too fortunate circumstance to be acceptable. We have been buying machinery and raw materials from the dollar area because we could not buy them elsewhere. They will not suddenly become available from other countries because we badly need them today.

May I give one or two figures by way of illustration? In 1948 we obtained from the United States and Canada £34,000,000 worth of timber out of total imports amounting to £93,000,000 and £7,600,000 worth of papermaking materials out of a total import of £16,700,000; and £19,000,000 worth of cotton out of a total import of £106,000,000. This underestimates the importance in terms of volume because, in many cases, they were cheaper than the purchases from the sterling area. From America, Canada and Chile came about one-third of our copper, a quarter of our lead and half our zinc. Even if we exclude questions of special qualities and special material, how can these quantities be replaced from elsewhere? Certainly American price reductions will help, and no doubt that is what the right hon. and learned Gentleman had in mind. But I cannot see how they can eliminate the effect of the 25 per cent cut, and how it can still fail to be very serious.

I hope the Foreign Secretary will tell us how large a proportion of these cuts will fall on Canada and how much on the United States. I ask this deliberately because we must all feel the greatest reluctance to stop any purchases from Canada. No country in all our history has ever treated us more generously than Canada, or stood more loyally by us, and it must be hateful to have to take any action which must create difficulties for her economy and prosperity.

I know that when I was in Canada—and the President of the Board of Trade will bear this out—manifest good will was shown by Canadians towards this country. They desired to take our goods so far as possible, and it seems all the harder and harsher, therefore, that we should have to inflict cuts on Canada at this time, especially as we have to face the fact that there are some people there who do not feel that we have treated Canada as well as we might have done. I do not say we are right or wrong, but the right hon. and learned Gentleman knows that bilateral agreements are not very popular in Canada. I did what I could to defend them, as he no doubt knows, but there is that sentiment.

Mr. Stokes (Ipswich): Can the right hon. Gentleman justify Canada buying something in the order of 560,000,000 dollars worth less of goods than we are buying from her, and 305,000,000 dollars worth more goods from the United States than the United States is taking from her?

Mr. Eden: The hon. Gentleman knows very well that the whole Canadian position has been queered by the post-war situation. Canadian pre-war trade was entirely three-legged, but that has now gone. It is no easy thing for the Canadians with all their adaptations to trade with the United States to swing from American markets to this one. If I could give one illustration, the contents of the advertisements in the Canadian papers are almost exclusively American, and they have become used to certain lines of goods and to turning to the American market. I do not say that it cannot be changed, but it is going to be a large task to undertake and it is going to cost a great expenditure of dollars to bring it about.

There is another aspect of this problem about which I hope we may be given some explanation. It is true that the prices of raw materials we import from the dollar countries are lower than they are from the non-dollar world. It is certainly true of oils and fats. I have here a large number of figures with which I need not trouble the House, but what is going to be the effect of this action which the Chancellor is bound to take? It is going to make the gap still wider, because if the payment for raw materials is going to be increased, owing to the price of non-dollar materials being higher, it will raise the price still more in proportion to the dollar raw material.

So I think we are going to have this position, that our industries will have to manufacture from raw materials more expensive than the dollar countries have to pay, and having done that, we shall still have to face competition from the dollar countries. I do not know whether that is true or not, but we should like to know how far that has been considered by the Government, and what reply, if any, they have to it. I want to give one other example of that. It seems to me that we are in some danger of being involved in a spiral where our industry has got to buy raw materials more expensively than the dollar area, and then to sell our manufactured goods in competition with those of this same dollar area.

For example, supposing we have to buy more Egyptian cotton and for that we have to pay higher prices, is it not going to make it even more difficult to sell British cotton goods in Canada, where already price competition is serious? I should say that the effect of the widening gap between the price levels in what are becoming the free world's two main price areas, the dollar area and the sterling area, will hamper and obstruct trade all over the world.

It seems that we have just the same difficulty in respect of machinery. Last year we imported £43,000,000 worth of machinery, and of that we imported £31,000,000 from the United States—a very high proportion indeed. Are the Government going to tell us that that machinery can be replaced from anywhere else or that its loss is not going to be a very serious handicap to our industries in their production for export? *The Times* had a fair comment on that on Friday, when it said:

'Many would-be exporters have wanted to improve their plant over the last three years and have been held back because the interests of basic industries and development areas have been put first.'

I am not arguing for the moment whether the policy is right or wrong to put the basic industries and development areas first, but what I am saying is that if we cut dollar imports of machinery now following on the long delays which a large number of exporters have had to suffer, it will be a very serious blow to them.

As the Chancellor is aware, a great deal of machinery has been exported, though our industries need it very badly themselves in order to earn the minimum dollars or whatever it may be. There again our industries will be under a handicap if deliveries of machinery are to be further delayed. Then I cannot see how it can be regarded as other than extremely serious for our national position, nor, I must say, after studying the chief Government speeches last Thursday, do I yet understand how the immediate standstill is going to be made effective or how the subsequent cuts are going to be worked out.

The Chancellor said there were to be exceptions. I agree there will have to be exceptions, but how are they to be decided upon? If a company shows that it requires a certain raw material that can only be got from a dollar country, will it have to show that the article that is going to be manufactured as a result is going to be

Domestic Affairs

exported, or will it have to do more than that? Will it also have to show that it is going to be exported to a dollar area, and if so how much percentage it requires of the dollar raw materials and how much of other raw materials? That seems to me to be the kind of problem that will arise.

Last Thursday the Chancellor said that he wanted to carry through this standstill 'In a manner causing the least dislocation'. I am sure he does, but I cannot see how it is practicable to do so. Take again the example of machinery. Suppose a company has got some machinery on order from the United States. Will it have to show that that production of that machinery is to be used exclusively for export to the United States, or that a certain percentage will go to the United States? How is this going to be measured and worked out? We have seen enough in the last few years of the immense difficulties of allocating scarce raw materials between the myriad uses of peace-time industry to be pretty reluctant to add any more to the extension of these practices.

What does this arrangement imply? I think we are all agreed that restrictions on the free flow of trade are generally undesirable, but when those restrictions have to be imposed in this sudden manner without any clear explanation of how they are going to work—and I will admit that any such explanation is extremely difficult to come to—then there is a most undesirable situation for all British industries. The Chancellor in his speech kept referring to the importance of maintaining full employment. We entirely agree with him about that. [*Interruption.*] The hon. Gentleman knows that the White Paper on Full Employment was not the work of one party alone, but was put out in the days of the Coalition Government, and in a moment I am going to say a few more words on this subject in relation to full employment.

We entirely agree with the right hon. and learned Gentleman about full employment, but surely he will admit that over and above the assistance we get from Marshall Aid full employment can be maintained only if we sell our goods in world markets. Again that must depend on the quality as well as the quantity of our

54

Britain's Economic Struggle

products and upon price. I submit that the question of price is going to be further influenced if we have to buy our raw materials in the more expensive markets, and then sell our goods in other markets in competition with those produced from cheaper raw materials.

On this side of the House, we have been challenged whether we are in favour of a full employment policy. I have referred to the White Paper, which represents the views of all of us, but what I am concerned about is that this standstill and these cuts are inevitably going to have an effect on our employment, not at once, but over a period, for the reasons I have given. If, to an increasing extent, we have to buy these raw materials in the more expensive areas, and sell them in competition with those who have access to cheaper raw materials, then inevitably our problem is going to increase to large dimensions. That is why I am distressed that these cuts are going to fall so much on raw materials and machinery for industry.

It seems to me extraordinary that more tobacco is to be bought this year than last. Surely, if we accept the stern realities of the cuts, a further cut in tobacco, grim as it is, should come before a reduction of raw materials and machinery, upon which depends our power to keep our people employed. I cannot see how the Chancellor's proposals measure up to our real dangers. On the contrary, it seems to me that their effect must aggravate them. *The Manchester Guardian* summed up the whole matter last Friday in these words:

'The crisis is not being met. It is bound to get worse.'

I myself cannot see how there is any escape from the truth of those observations, however reluctant one may be to have to endorse them.

Mr. Harrison (Nottingham, East): On the question of tobacco, it appears to everyone astonishing that the Government should propose to purchase more tobacco this year from the United States than we did last year, but is the right hon. Gentleman aware of the fact that we bought hardly any tobacco from the United States last year?

Mr. Eden: I was quoting actually from the Chancellor's statement. Of course I know that we were largely using up stocks last year. The only argument I am making now is that if we have to make these cuts they should first come on articles like tobacco rather than upon the raw materials and machinery which our industries so urgently need. That we should be buying more seems to be strange, even though we bought so little last year.

I want to look at the long-term argument. In my view, there is no long-term solution to this problem unless our American friends do, in one form or another, what we did in the nineteenth century, and that is to make available, by overseas investments or by other means, sufficient dollars to other countries that want to buy American goods. I am laying down what seems to me to be the long-term solution. It is true that we are facing a world problem, the lack of balance of trade between the Eastern and Western hemispheres, made worse by the threat of a contraction of world trade.

Further restrictions of any kind tend in the end only to make matters rather worse than they were before, because they set up a kind of chain reaction—I think that is the correct chemical term—one restriction leading to another. An effective and lasting solution can be found only by more freedom of trade, by moving away from further restrictions and by making it easier for trade and capital to flow from one nation to another. I think we all agree about that. We all wish to see a return to conditions where currencies are more convertible and where exchange rates reflect the realities of world economic conditions and have sufficient flexibility to reflect changing conditions.

Upon one issue I am in entire agreement with the Chancellor of the Exchequer. I have yet to see any convincing argument for unilateral devaluation of the pound sterling. The whole world has to find some means of escape from the present conditions of inconvertibility of currencies and artificially fixed rates of exchange which breed multiple currency valuations and every kind of complexity and artificiality. The worst of it is that we are just adding to those features by this new arrangement. I realize the immense practical difficulties that are involved in trying to obtain freer convertibility in the face of the lack of trade balance between the Eastern and Western hemispheres.

I feel that our American friends can play some part in helping to find a solution to this problem by providing some underpinning for a freer and more flexible system of world currencies. Many suggestions have been canvassed as to how the Americans could do that—by distributing some of the gold they have got or increasing the dollar price of gold—but the point that I make to the House is that these decisions, important and interesting as they are, are for the American people to take and not for us. Our job is to match our policy to the stern reality of the hour, so far as it concerns ourselves.

Meanwhile, the Government say, 'What would you do about it?' I embark upon this aspect of my task in the conscious knowledge that it is extremely controversial, but I think that certain things need to be said. We should try to arrange this standstill and the cuts so that, as far as possible, the burdens fall upon comparatively luxury imports like tobacco rather than on the raw materials and machinery which are indispensable for our national recovery. Our further proposals are more controversial, but they are designed, in our judgement, to tackle the problem of prices and costs, which is fundamental. We should call a halt to all further schemes of nationalization. We suggest that not only because we have no faith in nationalization but because, among other things, we are convinced that nationalization is the most expensive way of producing goods. . . .

Now I would mention another aspect of our exports to dollar areas. I touch for the moment on a personal matter, because I happen to be a director of an insurance company which does business with the dollar areas. It is going to be difficult in any case greatly to increase our exports of manufactured goods in the dollar

Domestic Affairs

countries. We may do something with Canada, but the general trade, and the exchange of manufactured goods between the countries, as United Nations statistics show, do not exhibit much variation, because of the tendency of countries to an increasing extent to build up those industries for strategic or other reasons. I do not think there is great scope there.

There might be something in invisible exports such as in shipping and insurance services. The earnings of insurance companies in the dollar areas are not those against which we have to set any bill for the expense of importing raw materials. They are the earnings of the experience of our own country, and of the confidence which is felt in the way that we conduct our business. It seems strange at a time like this, when the dollar position is so serious, that the Socialist Party should still appear to be contemplating the nationalization of any part of our insurance industry. I know the distinction which can be drawn among the various companies, but the distinction is much easier to draw in this country, where we are used to these issues in the industry of insurance, than it is to people overseas who do business with insurance companies in this country. If the Government want to make one more contribution they should drop any proposal to nationalize any part of the insurance industry. I am trying to be helpful and making constructive suggestions.

I have this to say in conclusion. In our present difficulties we all realize that in some respects these speeches are difficult to make, because no one wants to say anything to weaken sterling, but frankly, I put it to the House, that I do not think it is our speeches that weaken or strengthen sterling particularly or affect confidence. I think it is the action or lack of action by the Government itself which does. If what the Government does is of a nature to inspire confidence in sterling, then the effect of words will not decide the issue.

The published figures of the Chancellor, as indeed his statement on Thursday, have shown that the extent of our increased loss of gold, particularly in the last quarter, has greatly exceeded the

Britain's Economic Struggle

anticipations set out in the Government's own Economic Survey published barely four months ago. I admit that that can be attributed, in part at any rate, to the change from a seller's to a buyer's market, but surely nobody could have been very surprised by that change. Warnings have been given repeatedly by the Government, and indeed by some of us on this side of the House, that that change was inevitable. As *The Times* said so well on Friday:

'In production this country has a fine record, but so have other countries, especially the U.S.'

What troubles me about this situation is that the very steps which the Chancellor has felt compelled to take will have the effect of increasing the costs to our own manufacturers, and will, therefore, make it more difficult for them to compete not only in the United States and with the United States but in the markets of the world in general. To that extent, instead of being a measure to meet our difficulties, these proposals are adding a further burden to the heavily laden animal of British industry which is struggling so gallantly up the hill.

The Chancellor is rich in exhortations and in imprecations. He cracks the whip, but he adds to the burden all the time. Until that practice is reversed and until a start is made with easing the burden which British industry has to bear——

Mr. Stokes: Which burdens?

Mr. Eden: The hon. Gentleman is scornful. I will take up the point about finance. The right hon. and learned Gentleman made the point on Thursday that the taxation of profits was not a burden on industry, but surely all taxation on undistributed profits is a heavy burden on industry, and so is all taxation, because it is only from savings that industry can hope to get its new money. I do not see how the Chancellor or anybody can be complacent in the light of the savings figures which have just been published.

Mr. Parkin (Stroud): Does the right hon. Gentleman suggest that this is a time when an increase in capital investment by private industry would in some way meet our difficulties?

Domestic Affairs

Mr. Eden: I was dealing with an argument of the Chancellor's the other day, that taxation of profits was not a burden on industry. That would be truer if it were a fact, for instance, that all non-distributed profits were not taxed. There would then be a much stronger case for the argument. We all know that the Chancellor has given some assistance in that respect, but it is true, broadly, that taxation is a burden on industry because it is from industry that all our available finance and wealth resources are ultimately derived.

The Chancellor of the Exchequer (Sir Stafford Cripps): I believe that the right hon. Gentleman has misquoted me by inadvertence. What I said was that it was not an element in costs, not that it was not a burden on industry.

Mr. Eden: I give the right hon. and learned Gentleman that. That is technically absolutely correct, but it is only technically correct, and if he would look at it in a broader aspect he would see that it is not true, because the more a company is able to use its non-distributed profits for its own purposes the better it will be able to lower its costs. I do not think that is in dispute? Is that right?

Sir S. Cripps: I think the right hon. Gentleman will agree with me that there is no form of cost accountancy in which one is arriving at net cost on an article which would introduce an element of the profit.

Mr. Eden: No, but the right hon. and learned Gentleman must surely admit this. Suppose a company has made £100,000 in profits, and that, after various reserves, it distributes £25,000. If the remainder were not subject to taxation, that would be, in fact, if not arithmetically, something which the company could make use of, knowing that it had that, in making its own cost arrangements——

Sir S. Cripps indicated dissent.

Mr. Eden: I think that is so. I ask the Government and the right hon. and learned Gentleman to consider it. I repeat that I do not see how anybody else can escape the fact that, broadly, the present

Britain's Economic Struggle

taxation on industry is a matter which affects costs, if not in detail, over the broad field of industry. It must be so. However, if the right hon. and learned Gentleman does not think so, let us see what we can do about getting the taxation down and then see what the effect is.

To sum up, all these tendencies will simply add further burdens, direct or indirect, upon industry. Unless and until the Government reverse that process we shall be getting deeper and deeper into trouble. I have no doubt whatever that that is what the *Manchester Guardian* meant in its summing up the other day. That is what we feel and it is why we view the situation with infinitely more concern than the Chancellor of the Exchequer allowed to appear in his speech last Thursday.

Chapter 3

Iron and Steel

The Iron and Steel Bill was introduced at the beginning of the session, which started at the end of October 1948. Mr. Eden made clear the Conservative Party's attitude to this Bill in his speech in the debate on the Address:

'Should we (the Conservative Party) be victorious at the polls, we should consider ourselves entirely free to repeal any such legislation.'

Mr. Eden had spoken about the steel industry in many of his post-war speeches. He had always advocated that the industry should continue to be subject to Government supervision which had been operated first in 1933 by the Import Duties Advisory Committee and since the war by the Ministry of Supply and the Iron and Steel Board.

A. AGAINST NATIONALIZATION

The following extract from his speech at Reading on November 3rd gives his general argument against further interference with the industry.

The Iron and Steel Nationalization Bill has now been published.

This is the unwanted Bill. It will create widespread uncertainty in a vital part of our national economy. It presents a wholly unjustified menace to a thriving and prosperous industry.

62

Iron and Steel

Whatever test we may take, output, prices, labour relations or public interest, there is no justification for nationalizing this industry.

Take these points in turn. First, output. Production of iron and steel is at record levels. The first Government target of 14,000,000 ingot tons for this year has been surpassed. The second and higher target of 14,500,000 tons also looks like being achieved, and may even be surpassed. Where, then, is the case for nationalization here? How much better for all of us if the nationalized coal industry could attain its pre-war output per man, let alone exceed it and press on to new records.

Next, prices. Prices charged for British iron and steel products at the present day are less than those charged by any major steel-producing country in Europe or in America. The Socialists talk of a subsidy. In fact, a part of this so-called subsidy is devoted to bringing down the cost of imported steel to the much lower price of the home product. Even if the subsidy were wholly abolished, the increase in the price of finished steel would be only from 3 to 5 per cent, and this would still leave the favourable comparison between British and overseas prices unassailed.

Steel prices, according to the Board of Trade Index, have risen by only 70 per cent since before the war. The price of coal has risen by about 145 per cent.

Labour relations in the iron and steel industry are admittedly excellent. There has not been a major industrial dispute this century. Earnings in the industry have risen since 1938 by 107 per cent.

Finally, public supervision. It is generally agreed that in an industry of this significance there must be some measure of public supervision of prices and of general policy. There was, in fact, such public supervision before the war under the Import Duties Advisory Committee. Since the war these supervisory duties have been carried out by the Iron and Steel Board, and the Government have never suggested that the control exercised by that Board was inadequate. Under this system we witnessed a successful experiment in the technique of combining private enterprise ownership and management with public supervision of economic

63

policy. Under this system the record output, to which I have referred, has been achieved. Yet the Government themselves put an end to the Board by insisting on introducing their nationalization measure. There is no argument for nationalization here.

B. THE BILL

The Debate on the second reading of the Iron and Steel Bill was held in the Commons on November 15th, 16th and 17th. The Bill provided for the establishment of an Iron and Steel Corporation, to which would be transferred the securities of companies engaged extensively in iron-ore working or the production of pig iron, or ingot steel or the hot rolling of steel. Subsidiaries of such companies which made such things as umbrellas, tennis rackets and fertilizers were to be nationalized as well. Holders of shares in companies which were to be nationalized would be compensated by British Iron and Steel stock, the amount of which would be calculated by reference to the Stock Exchange quotation on certain stated dates.

Mr. Eden wound up for the Opposition with the following speech.

W e are now in the closing stages of this three-day Debate. I should like to begin my observations, since the Chancellor of the Exchequer has been courteous enough to be here, by making one preliminary observation about compensation. The right hon. and learned Gentleman dealt with that point last night, and deployed all his well-known legal skill to demolish, as I thought, a case which we on this side of the House had never presented to him. So far as I am concerned, he proved conclusively his argument that Stock Exchange quotations are a fair measure of value of individual shareholdings transferred on a given day between a willing seller and a willing buyer. We have no dispute on that point.

64

Iron and Steel

Our argument is that where an entire company is taken over as a going concern, then a whole lot of different considerations apply. When this point was made by the junior Member for the Combined English Universities (Mr. H. Strauss), the Chancellor dismissed the argument as having no logic. Like him I have had enough dealings with some of our continental friends to be sometimes distrustful of logic. However that may be, I think the Chancellor will admit that this argument has been consistently accepted by the courts in considering cases of this nature. I want to refer particularly to the words used by the Master of the Rolls in 1944 in a case concerned with the valuation of certain Stock Exchange assets of a certain company. He said:

'Public market quotations are often related to quite small shareholdings, and isolated transactions are notoriously no guide to the value of investments of this character, particularly when the amounts involved are large.'

That is a very important part of our argument and the Chancellor did not say anything last night to rebut it. Perhaps the Lord President of the Council will have a chance to do so in collaboration with his right hon. and learned Friend.

My main sentiment has been one of very considerable sympathy with the words of the General Secretary to the Iron and Steel Trades Federation in April:

'This is going to be an issue at the next General Election.'

Remarkable speeches have been made by hon. and right hon. Gentlemen on both sides of the House who are in close contact with the industry. I would single out—and I hope I shall not embarrass him—my right hon. Friend the Member for the City of London (Sir A. Duncan), and on the other side of the House—and I hope I may say it without embarrassing them—the hon. Member for East Swansea (Mr. Mort) and the hon. Member for Brightside (Mr. Marshall) yesterday. I should like at once to give one reassurance to the hon. Member for Brightside. He paid a tribute to the quality of the steelworkers in this country, and he used these words:

65

Domestic Affairs

'Those who think that nationalization will make these sturdy steel men into slackers, men who will not pull their weight, have certainly got to think again.'—[OFFICIAL REPORT, 16th November 1948; Vol. 458, c. 277.]

Those were his words, and they were much in the tempo of what was said by the right hon. and learned Gentleman. But nobody in this House does think it, or has even suggested it. Member after Member has paid tribute to the relations which have existed in the industry in the past, despite external problems which might very well have ruined all co-operation. The only discordant note came from the hon. Member for Brigg (Mr. E. L. Mallalieu). He told us that in his view the relations in the industry were worse than at any time in the last thirty years. I am surprised at the diagnosis. It is not borne out by anything I have ever heard said. I was interested to know what one of his constitutents said about his statement. I will read a quotation from the *Yorkshire Post*. The Chairman of the Divisional Labour Party, Mr. Deece, said:

'I am of the opinion that things are probably not all they might be in the industry, but I certainly would not say that the feeling is worse than twenty years ago. I do not believe that is true of this area, at any rate.'

Another even more delightful quotation in the *Yorkshire Post*—a very cautious, a very Yorkshire observation—was by the Chairman of the local Iron and Steel Trades Confederation, a Mr. Lawman Welch, whom perhaps the hon. Gentleman knows. He said:

'Mr. Mallalieu may have been referring to another area— probably South Wales—and not here.'

Very Yorkshire, that one. I hope the hon. Member for Brigg will read the observations of his own constituents. I am sorry that in this Debate he should have been the one hon. Member to state that relations in the industry were worse than at any time in the last thirty years.

Another argument which has been used a good many times in this Debate is about the continuous working week, the existence

66

Iron and Steel

of which I should imagine we all agree is, in itself, a remarkable tribute to all engaged in the industry. We have been told in this Debate, for the first time, that agreement was reached on this only because of the prospect of nationalization. Well, that may be so, but nothing of the kind had ever been said by any member of the industry. We have been told in this Debate—not by the hon. Member for Brigg; it has been argued from the other side—that agreement was reached because nationalization was held out.

I have to point out in reply that the General Secretary of the Union, in his reference to the continuous working week, gave four reasons for it—if I may say so, four very good reasons. They were, first, that it meant reducing the hours for preparatory workers who hitherto had worked in excess of forty-eight hours. Secondly, it was the first stage in the claim for a forty-two-hour week which, in the present economic crisis, was deferred. Thirdly, it was a desire to help the nation and the Government in the struggle for recovery by full utilization of existing plant. I believe that is right. Fourthly, it was to bring our smelting practice into line with every other major steel-producing country. These were the arguments used by the General Secretary and I can only point out that the word 'nationalization' does not occur among them. I hope nobody else will say that the continuous working week worked only because the prospect of nationalization was dangled before the industry. If we agree on that, we are always one step further forward.

I will not deny, in reply to the hon. Gentleman the Joint Parliamentary Secretary, who spent much longer on this point yesterday, that the trade-union leaders of the industry are in favour of nationalization. Of course they are. Equally, of course, many of the men in the industry—maybe the majority of the men in the industry—wholly loyal to their leaders, share their view. But I will add something else: there are others, and there is among many of them a considerable measure of doubt whether the transfer of ownership of the industry from free-enterprise to the State is of itself going to result in greater prosperity for the industry.

There is another argument, and it is a very important argument,

Domestic Affairs

which I have no doubt has had its effect, not only in this Debate but outside in the country. The idea is—we have had it hinted at and, indeed, it has been mentioned tonight—that if the State owns an industry, then in bad times the industry will be carried along, and employment will continue, more effectively than under free enterprise. I think it is fair to say that that is the argument. But is this really true? Does the hon. Gentleman think it is true? In the long run, can the State afford to make losses any more than can private enterprise—this quite apart, of course, from the fact that the Bill forbids the Corporation to make any losses at all.

Let us see what happens. Take the example of civil aviation today. It is not only a Government-owned organization, but also a Government-built organization. What is going on there? Because the nationalized Corporations are running at a loss, the Government have been compelled drastically to reduce the number of men they employ. I am not saying that is wrong. I am only drawing attention to the fact. It is described in the *Daily Herald*. On October 16th, it was said in the *Daily Herald*:

'When the full cuts are in force, 10,000 employees are likely to be on the redundant list.'

That is in a Government-controlled, owned and built organization. Are the workers so sure that when the Government are the sole owners and the sole court of appeal, their employment will be more assured than it would be under any other system? The truth is that Lord Keynes was very right when he demonstrated a long time ago that if the State is to counteract the adverse periods of slump, as we all want it to do, then the way to do that is not by the State's owning the industries, but by the State's trying to ensure that there is a demand for the products which those industries turn out. It was just that world fall in the demand for steel and other products that led to unemployment in the steel trade and other trades in the 'twenties and 'thirties. Everybody knows that is true, and that a nationalized industry would have been affected by those world economic

68

Iron and Steel

conditions just as the privately owned industries were. The demand was not there; that is all.

Indeed, I must remind the House—and some hon. Members here will recall it—that when in 1923 we sought permission from the country to make use of tariffs—I know that hon. Gentlemen below the Gangway disagreed; but Mr. Baldwin, as he then was, went to the country to get those tariffs—so that we could maintain our trade on equal terms with that of other countries that were dumping steel in this country, none was more elequent in denial of that than some hon. and right hon. Gentlemen opposite. When the Chancellor of the Exchequer said last night that the industry had enjoyed the protection of tariffs since 1932, he appeared to regard that as some particular favour for the industry. It is perfectly true that that happened in 1932, and that the industry at long last enjoyed a measure of protection which the industry of every other country had enjoyed before that. I do not think that was so much of a favour. It was certainly a necessity.

I should like to tell the House what I believe to be the mood of the nation today on this subject of nationalization. I submit this to the Lord President, who is acknowledged to be one who has his ear to the ground and knows all about public opinion. I submit this to him. I think that the nation is saying something like this, 'In this one Parliament we have seen a great many Measures of nationalization—nationalization of coal, transport, electricity, gas, Cable and Wireless, and so forth.' [HON. MEMBERS: 'The Bank of England.'] And of the Bank of England. I should have thought that even the most ardent advocate of nationalization would have admitted that in respect of some of these industries, at any rate, the case for the success of nationalization has not yet been fully established. I will not put it any higher than that. It is not necessary to put it any higher than that for the purpose of my argument. There has been anxiety—and I would say to the Lord President that there is anxiety—on many accounts. I here quote—not myself, because the right hon. Gentleman may not think that very good evidence—but the hon. Member for

Domestic Affairs

Walton (Mr. Haworth), who said in the House on November 2nd, in a speech to which I listened and which greatly impressed me:

'On these benches'—

that is, on the benches opposite—

'we have got to admit a disappointment over one of our theories. The hon. Member for Hornsey spoke about the tragedy of a theory killed by a fact. Here is one. I am disappointed at the fact that what I have advocated on public platforms for the last twenty-five years, that if we nationalize an industry the people in that industry would work harder because they were working for the State than if they were working for a private employer, has not altogether worked out. I believed that, as did my hon. Friends on these Benches. I do not know what my hon. Friends feel about it now'—

they got a bit restive I remember—

'but I am very much disappointed that we have not had the results one would expect.'—[OFFICIAL REPORT, 2nd November 1948; Vol. 457, c. 754.]

I would say to the right hon. Gentleman, in the light of that, which I think expresses the feeling of a good many people in the country, that the mood of the nation about nationalization today is this: 'For the moment we have had enough nationalization. Let us see how the existing schemes work out. If they prove themselves, very well, then we are ready to consider and proceed to further measures of nationalization, but, for the moment, we have had enough.' I would say to the right hon. Gentleman that to proceed at the present time against this temper is forcibly to feed the nation on nationalization, and this course, I am confident, the nation will resent and resist. I apologize for making these observations to the right hon. Gentleman because, knowing his political wisdom, I have some suspicion that he has already said something like that to his own colleagues.

The Chancellor of the Exchequer told us last night that:

'The opposition to this Bill stems from two main sources—those who believe that private enterprise and free competition are essentially the best way of serving the national interest and those

Iron and Steel

who resent bitterly this attack upon the citadel of the power of the property owners.'—[OFFICIAL REPORT, 16th November 1948; Vol. 458, c. 325.]

The Chancellor of the Exchequer knows very well that we have never argued on behalf of either of those classes, but I must tell the Government, since they do not seem to know, that opposition to this Bill stems also from a third class whom the Chancellor of the Exchequer never mentioned—those who maintain that this Bill and the Government speeches have so far produced no argument to show that the Bill in any way improves on the present system of free enterprise and management, subject to public supervision and control. That is our case.

Mr. David Jones (The Hartlepools): Why public supervision of private enterprise?

Mr. Eden: Because it seems to work well in this case, and we are willing to accept it. Here is an industry which is producing at an all-time record level and at competitive prices. There is no dispute about that. It is an industry which has embarked on a scheme of modernization approved by the Government. We know that the industry is efficient today. There is no particular dispute about that. But it has yet to be established by any speech from the Government Benches that when the ownership is transferred it will be as efficient as it is today, let alone more efficient. Not one single time has the efficiency argument been used. It is quite true that we are told that the old boards of management are to remain for a time, at any rate; that they are to be responsible not to the shareholders, but to Whitehall; but they will be hedged round with all sorts of restrictions set out in the Bill which, to put it mildly, are unlikely to inspire them to initiative or to take any risks.

The Chancellor of the Exchequer told us yesterday that there is need for foresight and planning. Of course there is, but our whole case against this Bill is that there is not one glimmer of it within its eighty-eight pages. The hon. and learned Member for Kettering (Mr. Mitchison) asked how could we expect to have a plan in a Bill. Perhaps it is a bit old-fashioned to expect a plan in a Government Bill, but if we cannot have a plan in the Bill we should at least have an indication of some sort of plan in the speeches. So far there has not been a glimmer of a sign of that. Personally, I believe that no such plan exists. I have in mind the warning given by the then Minister of Fuel and Power (Mr. E. Shinwell) in another connection—and the right hon. Gentleman must have heard that speech, because it was delivered at the Labour Party Conference. The then Minister of Fuel and Power was in reminiscent mood about the coalmining industry, and he said:

'Unhappily, while the Labour movement is quite properly focused on the fundamental ideals of Socialism, little attention has been paid to the extremely difficult, technical administrative problems which the carrying out of nationalization involves. There has been, I regret to say, very little guidance on detail, and so we have had to improvise in the light of existing circumstances.'

Well, I know that speech got the right hon. Gentleman into trouble somewhere up above; but what troubles me about that speech is that, on the evidence of everything said by the Government spokesmen so far, there is no indication at all that their position in respect of iron and steel is in any respect further advanced than it was in respect of coal. And how disastrous it would be if the right hon. Gentleman's confession about coal were now to be repeated in respect of iron and steel. We are still without any indication that the Government have got any plan for the future of the iron and steel industry when it is transferred to the State.

Now, the Chancellor of the Duchy (Mr. Dalton), whom I am glad to see here, has been making one or two speeches lately. A few nights ago he spoke to the Fabian Society in London, and what he told them interested me very much, because I thought that there I could find the plan I was pursuing. He said that the national interest demanded that we should have an iron and steel industry more efficient, more up-to-date and larger than now, or than its present owners proposed that it should be.

Does the Lord President endorse that? If so, how much larger? The industry, as was explained by my right hon. Friend this after-

Iron and Steel

noon, has now planned—we understand in agreement with the Government—an expansion to 18,000,000 tons in the early 'fifties. What is the expansion the Government have in mind in excess of that figure?—a figure agreed between the industry and the Government. There must be some further figure, or I am sure the Chancellor of the Duchy would not have said that we must do better still. What is that figure? Twenty million? Any advance on 20,000,000? Twenty-five million? I suppose there must be some figure. And I suppose that the Lord President will tell us what it is.

What about the development programme of the industry which the Government have approved? This afternoon we heard from the hon. Member for North-West Hull (Mr. R. Mackay) a lot about finance. I do not think he need really worry about that finance. I will not go into the question of the loan which he mentioned; there were a good many other loans that were not a great success at that time, but they were all under-written and they got the money. On the question of the development programme of the industry I would say that the Government have approved it, and that its finance is assured. I believe that over two-thirds of the scheme has actually been approved in detail.

I want to ask the Lord President this: Do the Government maintain that this development plan, which has been approved by them in detail as to two-thirds of it at least, ought to be larger? Is that what the Chancellor of the Duchy meant? If so, in what respect ought it to be larger? Where are the material resources to come from to enable the industry to carry out this further expansion? We are entitled to know. Here is an agreed plan into the early 'fifties, and here are Ministers saying: 'We must have a larger plan.' Well, what is the larger plan which the Government want? Why is it that it cannot be carried out in the same way as the present one is carried out? Everybody knows that supplies of raw materials are the limiting factor.

Some hon. Members have called in aid Mr. Lincoln Evans, the general secretary of the Iron and Steel Trades Confederation. At Margate in September of this year he made a speech—which

73

Domestic Affairs

right hon. Gentlemen opposite probably also remember—part of which I must read to the House, and particularly the Chancellor of the Duchy, who I know will want to agree with this. Mr. Lincoln Evans is no wicked Tory. This is what he said:

'People talk about expanding capacity. It does remind me of the old saying—"Ignorance is not so much a question of not knowing anything; it is knowing too much." If by some magical means we were able to increase the productive capacity of the industry to 20,000,000 tons next year, can anyone guarantee we are going to supply the 8,000,000 tons of extra coal that will be necessary? Unless you have the raw materials to maintain the capacity in existence, you are simply'—

I am sorry, Mr. Chancellor—

'misleading the public by saying you can produce more steel. The essential question is not that of productive capacity, but the question of raw materials.'

Again, I ask the Government what is their plan, and what is the target of greater production they wish to reach? Have they ever suggested to the Steel Board that the development plan ought to be larger? The Chancellor of the Exchequer said yesterday that the present demand is very exceptional. I agree, but every exception carries with it its own dangers, which I need not emphasize, once the time of exceptional demand, which the Chancellor referred to, is past.

I must say that perhaps the most unconvincing part of the whole of the Minister's speech was his reference to the Steel Board. At no time, so far as we know, when the Board was in existence, did we hear one word of criticism against it from any Minister. If the Government were not satisfied with the Board, or the results the Board produced, why did they not say so? But then, the Minister said, it was always meant to be a stop-gap. If, however, it is producing good results, and if the sole test, as the Lord President has told us, is to be results, surely the life of the stop-gap might usefully be prolonged; its efforts might be encouraged, and even its terms of reference might perhaps be amended. Most

74

Iron and Steel

ludicrous of all is the argument that it was the action of the steel masters that brought the life of the Steel Board to an end. It was the Government's own action in proceeding with nationalization that killed the Steel Board. Let the right hon. Gentleman look at their terms of reference and he will see that it was not only the steel masters, who resigned, but the chairman and all the other members, except the trade unionists. [HON. MEMBERS: 'Oh.'] Naturally—they were pledged to nationalization. Then what about Sir Alan Barlow, a very distinguished Treasury official? Are we going to be told that he was a wicked industrialist in disguise during all the years he has been in the Treasury?

The only criticism of the Board which the Minister of Supply has ever made was in his speech on Monday. I want to quote what he said. I think it is fair criticism. He said:

'Any proposals put up to us by the industry can be vetoed, neither the Board nor the Minister has effective power to ensure that other proposals, however desirable they may be, will be initiated, let alone carried out, if the directors of the individual concerns do not like them.'—[OFFICIAL REPORT, 15th November 1948; Vol. 458, c. 56.]

That is the only reason the Minister adduced, in his speech on Monday, against continuing a system of public supervision of a public-owned private industry, yet that system has worked pretty well over the last two years. It has not been perfect and could be improved, but under this system we have had a record output to which everyone has paid tribute, and under the system two-thirds of the development plans has received approval of the Government acting through the Board. We feel that the Government ought to produce strong, efficient reasons, apart from ideological reasons, if they are to justify their action in breaking up this system and their insistence on replacing it by a State monopoly. Yet the only argument we have had so far is this one which will not bear a moment's examination.

I have searched the Bill—and I ask the Lord President to correct me if I am wrong—and can find nowhere any powers

Domestic Affairs

given to the Minister whereby he can order the Corporation to undertake a specific project. The Minister said on Monday that no controller had any authority to compel shareholders to spend money which he considered it necessary to spend. All right, but what powers has the Minister in the Bill to compel the Corporation to spend money on what they consider to be an unwise project? The Corporation are bound by Clause 29 to pay their way. Has the Minister any right to over-ride that? I cannot find it anywhere in the Bill.

What it means is this: if the Minister cannot give specific directions he must rely on co-operation from the Corporation. The Minister has received co-operation—of which no complaint has been made by anyone—from the Steel Board in the last two years. What justification has he for expecting to receive fuller co-operation than that which he already has had from the industry? I challenge the Minister, or the Lord President, to tell us of any project which the Government have commended to the industry in the last two years, while the Steel Board has been in existence, which the industry has refused to carry out. The truth is, as we believe, that so far from planning and advocating projects, the Government have been unable to make any contribution at all to the broader economic aspects of steel policy.

Our case is this: an evolution in the use of the Steel Board and, if necessary, some amendment, in agreement, of the powers of the Board would be a far better method of ensuring what the Government seek and of maintaining the prosperity of the industry than the abrupt transfer of ownership for which the Bill provides. I must say, in passing, that I do not think the Chancellor of the Exchequer's references last night to strategy were particularly convincing. The right hon. and learned Gentleman drew a parallel between control of the naval dockyards and ownership of our steel-making resources in relation to national defence. If that parallel has any meaning at all, it would presumably apply to a firm like Vickers, whose armaments activities are not nationalized at all.

76

Iron and Steel

As for the ability of the industry to fulfil the orders required of it, during the inter-war years it never failed the Government of the day, so far as I know, in discharging any programme that was put to it. Nor does it lie with hon. Members opposite to suggest that the programme put to the industry ought to have been larger, since they consistently voted against whatever programme there was. The programme is the responsibility of the Government, and the discharge of the programme is the responsibility of the industry. I repeat that in my experience I have never known the industry fail to fulfil the programme put to it.

One of the arguments constantly used in this Debate is that the industry must be nationalized because it is of the utmost importance to our national economy. I should have thought that its very importance makes it all the more necessary that the decision tonight should be taken on grounds of economic efficiency, and not on the purely ideological grounds that Ministers have so far advanced. The fact is that if steel is vital to our economy, or to the defence of the country, then so are a great many other industries—the chemical industry—[HON. MEMBERS: 'Hear, hear.']—that cheer from the benches opposite is what I hoped for—the machine tool industry, the agricultural industry—[HON. MEMBERS: 'Hear, hear.'] Yes, it seems that they all ought to be nationalized, according to hon. Members opposite. So hon. Gentlemen opposite agree with me. Right hon. Gentlemen on the Front Bench opposite do not seem quite so agreeable. Hon. Gentlemen and I agree that if this argument applies to steel it applies to the industries I have mentioned, and to a great many others, too. In logic—an expression of the Chancellor's—it does. [HON. MEMBERS: 'Hear, hear.'] Hon. Gentlemen opposite still agree with me. We are getting to agree on almost too much—apart from the Front Bench. We are agreed that this will lead to wholesale nationalization and to the steady reduction to a negligible proportion of the remaining free sections of our national economy. The Minister of Health (Mr. Bevan) agrees. I thought he might. The agreement is reaching the Front Bench now.

77

Domestic Affairs

Having listened to this Debate, I would say that so far there does not seem to be any agreement on the Government Benches as to the underlying motives behind this proposal to transfer the ownership of the industry. The Minister of Supply wound up his defence of the Measure by pointing to its overwhelming merits and claiming that this great reform removes from the private to the public sector of our economy an industry which is the citadel of capitalism. The Chancellor of the Exchequer took very much the same line in rather more austere language. That is definitely their justification; but is it the justification of the Lord President of the Council also? He used entirely different language two years ago, and the arguments which he used then seemed to me a much more acceptable basis for discussion between us. The right hon. Gentleman said that this was not in essence an issue of party politics at all. He said that it was in essence a matter of business, namely, what was the best course to take in the interests of the community for the handling of this great basic industry? Here is what he said:

'. . . although political theory and party politics are bound to flit across the Chamber'—

certainly they have done that in the last few days and they have bumped against each other once or twice, too—

'and we all enjoy that on all sides, it is really not a party political matter. It is a matter of business, and national business at that.'— [OFFICIAL REPORT, 28th May 1946; Vol 423, c. 1106.]

I think that is the right test to take, because the nation is going to approve those who are least doctrinaire in their approach to the future of this great industry. The nation wants results and it will judge by them. The results today are very good, and it is for the Government to say that the results following upon the transfer of ownership are going to be better than are the results today.

Is the right hon. Gentleman's position still the same as in 1946? If it is, I hope he will give us some practical reason why he thinks that this industry will be more efficient and will better serve the nation than it does at the present time once the ownership has

78

Iron and Steel

been transferred. We have not yet been flattered by one such argument. We have had no indication of the plan which the Government intend to put into effect. Over and over again we have had arguments put forward about how important it is to capture this citadel. I have listened to this Debate and I am driven to this conclusion, that the Government's sole purpose is, by means of this Bill—and the cheers by hon. Members opposite support the view—to bring free enterprise in industry in this country to an end. The Bill gives the State a wide interest in all sorts of activities beyond the primary processes of steel making and steel rolling. The State is going to enter as a competitor into a wide range of engineering, machine tool manufacturing, chemicals, and other activities.

Does anyone in this House really expect that a duality of that kind will last very long? One of two things will happen. Either the Government will become weary of operating these varying activities which they can neither understand nor control, or step by step they will seek to nationalize all those industries in which this Bill gives them some share. If this last is really the Government's purpose, as I believe it is, the voter at the next General Election will have to decide not merely on a change of ownership in the steel industry, but at the same time on a change of ownership in the engineering, machine tool and a whole score of other industries. I will quote the words of the *Manchester Guardian* last Tuesday, which seem to me succinctly to describe the position:

'That that is the natural outcome of the Steel Bill is now becoming convincingly clear. There is no point after this at which the advance towards the extinction of private enterprise in British industry could be halted.'

That is the position. That did not get quite as many cheers from the other side as I should have hoped. As I listened to the Chancellor of the Exchequer last night, it seemed to me that his view of democracy, as he expressed it then, was indeed a very strange one. It seemed to amount to this, 'I am a constitutionalist if the country agrees with me; if not, I am still a revolutionary.'

79

Domestic Affairs

Sir S. Cripps indicated dissent.

Mr. Eden: All right, the right hon. and learned Gentleman shakes his head. I will now ask the Lord President a question in order that we may elucidate this point. At the last General Election admittedly iron and steel figured in the programme, the Socialist catalogue, among many other things. At the next General Election, unhappily perhaps, iron and steel is bound to be a major, if not the major, issue. Supposing that at the General Election our party receives a clear majority from the nation, would the right hon. Gentleman then accept that we have the full right not only in the strict letter of the Constitution but in its spirit also as a free democracy, to repeal the legislation which the Government are tonight asking us to pass, or would he regard that as a provocative act justifying revolutionary action?

We are at the concluding stage of this three-day Debate. So far no single argument has been produced on the grounds of efficiency to show that under this Bill this essential industry will operate more successfully or at a lower cost or with better industrial relations than exist today. At a critical time, when we still depend for our life on foreign help, when we are daily consuming our accumulated foreign assets, the result of the thrift of our ancestors, or, if hon. Gentlemen prefer, the result of the wicked capitalist instincts of our ancestors. [*Interruption.*] They are very glad to consume them all the same. How long have we been eating the Argentine railways? The Government are deliberately taking a gamble with the future efficiency of this industry whose recent record is one in which all sections of this House take pride. In our judgment it is a gamble which no Government would be justified in taking. There was never a case where the onus of proof for change of ownership lay more clearly with the Government that demands that change. There was never one where less evidence has been adduced of any advantage to the nation in such a change. So, therefore, we ask the House to oppose this wanton and foolish step and to reject the Bill which embodies it.

Chapter 4

Agriculture

The Conservative Party's Agricultural Charter was published at the end of June 1948 and received cordial endorsement from the Party Conference at Llandudno in October.

During 1946 and 1947 production in cereals declined by nearly 30 per cent from 1945 and home-killed meat by 10 per cent. In August 1947 the Government announced, as part of the economic crisis proposals, a programme of expansion which aimed to increase home food production by £100,000,000 a year by 1952. This would in fact restore agricultural production to little higher than it stood in 1945, the result of the able direction of the Conservative Minister Mr. R. S. Hudson, supported by Mr. Tom Williams, who became Minister under the Socialist Government.

Socialist policy still wavered over land nationalization which Dr. Dalton and others were known to advocate. Socialist propaganda took every opportunity to falsify Conservative achievement in the past and to misinterpret its policy for the future.

Mr. Eden gave a comprehensive review of his attitude to the importance of agriculture in a speech to the Guild of Agricultural Journalists on 5th November 1948.

The history of our agricultural industry over the last hundred years has not been a happy one. The contrasts have been too numerous and too sharp, and the periods of depression have always lasted longer than those of prosperity. It would be tempting to analyse the past and to weigh up the factors contributing to this instability. Indeed such an analysis is

Domestic Affairs

necessary if we are to devise a policy which will restore stability to the land. But my time is limited and I would prefer this afternoon to start from certain broad conclusions as to the past and then to look ahead to see what the future holds for what is still our greatest single industry.

The agricultural industry has been prosperous when imported food has been scarce. There has been depression when there have been offers of plenty from abroad and no lack of the wherewithal to pay for it. Before the passing of the Corn Laws more than a hundred years ago food imports played a relatively small part in our trade; and as the industrial population expanded, home-produced food was at a premium. When munitions of war displaced food cargoes in the two world wars British agriculture came to the rescue, and farm incomes and wages rose in proportion to the increased output.

In 1846 the Corn Law policy of protection for farmers had to be finally abandoned in the face of insistent public indignation at the levying of the duty on imported cereals. Again after the 1914–18 war the mounting cost of guaranteeing the price for home-grown wheat, barley and oats could not be sustained while there was abundance on the world's markets. And I think it is fair to say that it was largely upon the issue of protection for farmers that the Conservative Party was defeated at the polls in 1923.

All periods of depression on the land have had a common factor: the alternative to buying food at home was that it could be imported more cheaply. These were the conditions after the Treaty of 1815 at the close of the Napoleonic wars. They were still present and were accentuated when the wheat cargoes arrived from the new countries, and they were repeated after the First World War. Are these conditions going to reappear?

Here, in passing, I must make a reference to education. Wise statesmanship will always be needed in this country to lead eighteen million urban electors to appreciate the value of the rural market to their manufactures.

Agriculture

There is also one further qualification. Although it would be unjust to attempt to saddle the consuming public with a heavy load in the form of inflated food prices primarily to preserve a way of life, we must not forget that agriculture has proved itself in two wars to be our fourth line of defence. In these days we are often reminded of the injunction: 'If you wish for peace be ready for war'. I myself prefer another version: 'Trust in God and keep your garners full'. There is plenty of evidence to show that aggressors in years gone by have been influenced in their decision to precipitate war by the prospect of starving this country into submission by the interruption of our food supplies. Fortunately for our survival on these occasions the stamina and resilience of the farming industry prevented these prospects from being realized but it was touch and go at times. That we came through at all was due to the magnificent achievements of all engaged in the industry—farmers, their wives, and the farm workers—who deserve and must receive lasting recognition from the State for the essential part they play in the national economy. And may I say in passing that there is much in the relations between the farmer and his agricultural workers which is a model and an example to others.

An efficient agricultural industry with the land kept in good heart and capable of rapid expansion of production in time of emergency would be a powerful deterrent to aggression. It would also be an insurance against defeat. For this purpose alone a reasonable premium in the form of assistance for agriculture is not merely defensible; it is also common prudence.

This factor, then, was not the least among the motives that actuated the Conservative Government in the inter-war period to bring before Parliament a large number of measures for the maintenance of the agricultural potential. There were altogether nearly thirty of these Acts passed dealing with every aspect and branch of the industry—research, marketing, provision of credit, subsidies, housing, and so on. With one exception, that of extending unemployment insurance to farm workers, the Socialist Party opposed the lot. It seems not unreasonable to recall these things now that the same party presents itself as a historic protector of the land.

Today, however, agriculture as a way of life, agriculture as an insurance against war—important as these factors are—must give way to agriculture as the indispensable means of sustaining life in our people. Our fertile acres and our productive herds, to the extent to which they enable us to feed ourselves from our own resources, make the most direct contribution possible to the solution of our economic difficulties. Do these economic difficulties constitute a short-term problem or a long-term one? Can anyone see an end in the foreseeable future to our battle for the balance of payments? And in this connection I must ask you to recall that we are today not only living on money loaned or given by the United States of America, but we are also consuming at a formidable rate our own overseas capital assets—Argentine railways, Brazilian railways, and so on. Therefore I would say it is a long-term problem with which we are faced, and it is in this sense that we have treated the matter in our Agricultural Charter.

I was very glad that the Minister, Mr. Tom Williams, said the other day that the Government programme was not a stop-gap crisis expedient, but a long-term policy. I also from time to time hear of the Minister of Agriculture complaining that our Agricultural Charter expresses in part, at least, what he is trying to do. That does not worry me at all. I have no objection to agreeing with the Government from time to time. My chief difficulty is that I find so few occasions when I can agree with them. I would not object to a bi-partisan agricultural policy if one could be arrived at, any more than I would object to a bi-partisan foreign policy. But I am bound to say that I see little chance of any such accord being reached in respect of agriculture between the parties and that in particular on account of Socialist insistence on a policy for nationalization of the land.

Not so long ago, in January 1947, we had the warning of the Chancellor of the Duchy of Lancaster: 'We are moving towards the

Agriculture

nationalization of the land and not by slow steps.' And his warnings never fall on inattentive ears.

Our principal criticism of the Government today, however, is the lack of unanimity in the actions and the words of certain Ministers in their dealings with the land. We have had consistent promises of more supplies of the vital feeding stuffs and equally consistent disappointments. While the Minister of Food was talking on Monday of the great increases in rationed feeding stuffs provided this year for pigs and poultry, the Parliamentary Secretary to the Ministry of Agriculture stated in a written answer to a Parliamentary Question that in fact the total supply of coarse grains available to farmers was 300,000 tons less in the 1947–8 crop year than it had been in 1946–7. Last year Mr. Strachey told us that he was negotiating a contract for feeding stuffs with Jugoslavia, but all we have received so far has been poultry and eggs produced in Jugoslavia on the feeding stuffs we were promised for our own hens. In July he was excusing his policy of buying finished products instead of feeding stuffs on the grounds that they were so much cheaper—an argument which we demonstrated to be completely fallacious and which he did not venture to repeat or defend. On that occasion he concluded his speech by saying that so long as we had an industrious population producing manufactures we could feed ourselves. In other words, in Mr. Strachey's opinion we could rely on our exports to produce the food we needed. In view of our present balance of payments that is indeed an assumption which I would not dare to put forward.

It is at this point that the policy of our Agricultural Charter and the Government's policy part company. The target of 50 per cent higher production than before the war is the same in each case; but whereas the Socialists have given no indication of what lies beyond 1952 and have laid down no specific long-term target, we have carefully examined the future position of the country's food supplies and put the permanent contribution to our requirements as at least 50 per cent more than before the war, or at about two-thirds of our total needs. Few today will question the immediate

85

danger of food shortage. The popular term for it is the food 'crisis'. The word 'crisis' is misleading. It is, in a sense, almost comforting. It suggests something that is temporary and will therefore soon either pass away or be overcome, and this, of course, has some truth in a country like France, which, unlike ourselves, is normally to a large degree self-supporting. But we are not self-supporting or anywhere near it.

What are the factors on which we justify our policy? First, world population is increasing rapidly—by twenty millions a year —and all over the world there is a demand for higher standards of nutrition. More of the food produced in the New World, in Africa and the Far East will in future be consumed by the local population. As industrialization spreads in these areas labour is being drawn to the towns from rural communities. There are more food consumers and fewer producers. In every area not devastated or disorganized by war, consumption of food per head has increased. Although less fats and oils are being produced, the countries that produce them are keeping and consuming more than ever. It is, for instance, largely her increased consumption that has taken India entirely out of the export market. We have to ask ourselves for how long shall we get for ourselves all the new groundnut oil from East Africa? Meat consumption in the United States is up by 23 per cent. As wages rise in every country, both white and black, as health improves and infant mortality declines in primitive countries, as the general feeling against exploitation and in favour of greater independence and self-government grows, exportable surpluses must continue to decrease in quantity and increase in price.

Secondly, due to our own changed economic circumstances we can no longer command food supplies at bargain prices from all quarters of the world. Countries which formerly relied on exporting food to Britain to pay interest on loans have now cleared off their debts and are developing industries of their own with products which compete with our exports. Canada and Australia continue for their own very good reasons to build up their secondary

Agriculture

industries. South Africa and South Rhodesia are doing [the same. The Argentine between 1935 and 1946 decreased her labour employed in agriculture by 11 per cent and transferred it to industry.

Thirdly, it is obvious that if, on a long-term basis, world demand for food is likely to exceed supply, world prices will tend to remain relatively high and will not drop to the very low levels experienced between the wars. Another important factor, as well as increased demand, will also tend to keep world prices up. The cheap food we imported from abroad in the seventy years before 1939 was cheap because it was the result of the exploitation of the natural fertility of millions of acres of farmland in the New World. The era of such 'Wheat mining' is now over. There is today a general tendency among farmers in the great grain-producing areas towards mixed farming on the British plan in order to maintain soil fertility. This means crop rotations and more varied systems of agriculture. Even when world food prices fall from the present levels, have we the resources with which to pay? Where are our reserves of foreign exchange?

Lastly, increasing mechanization and scientific advances have increased—and in the next few years will still further increase—the efficiency of our own production relative to other countries, thus further narrowing any possible gap between the cost of home production and of imports. And if there is a gap, as there may be from time to time, then that is the insurance premium that we are prepared to pay for our fourth line of defence. These are the grounds on which we look forward with confidence to more stable conditions for rural Britain. It is because we believe that the long-term need for a fully productive agriculture is in line with the economic position both today and for the future that the Agricultural Charter received such overwhelming support at Llandudno last month.

At the same time, it is impossible to be dogmatic about the future course of world production, of prices, and so forth. We have had enough experience to know that. For this reason I draw

87

Domestic Affairs

attention to the special importance of the undertaking given in the Agricultural Charter to our producers that: 'We will reserve first place in the home market for the British farmer and second place for the Empire producer.' This is a new departure as a statement of our policy.

Similarly in respect of horticulture, which has made such rapid expansion in recent years and is capable of considerable further development and which must be a permanent part of our economy, I draw attention to another passage in the Charter which runs: 'Safeguards must be introduced to protect British horticultural producers from the dumping of foreign surpluses.' If you want a case in point the answer is onions. Our proposals must not be regarded in the same light as temporary proposals to give a fleeting measure of protection. They are an attempt to lay down a national policy to feed the people and to raise the standard of life in these islands.

I have said enough to show that the key to the future prosperity of agriculture is in our hands. But confidence is needed to turn the key. The object of our Charter is to provide that confidence—continuity in the system of guaranteed prices and markets on the well-tried system of the February review, instituted during the war by Mr. Hudson, continuity in the county committee system, but there is no sense in encumbering these county agricultural committees with too many officials.

I am told that the staffs of the Ministry of Agriculture including technical staffs of county centres, now number 17,765 and that they are still mounting. Certainly it takes an awful lot of paper to keep a pig and a complete volume to kill one. And finally we require effective priorities for the essential capital needs and feeding stuffs.

Given these things, I believe that all who live on or by the land can build a certain future and that happiness can gild their way of life.

Chapter 5

The House of Lords

Since the Parliament Act of 1911 Bills which were passed by the House of Commons in three successive sessions, whether by the same Parliament or not, would, with certain exceptions, become law even if rejected by the House of Lords in each of these sessions, provided that two years had elapsed between the date of the Second Reading in the Commons at the first of these sessions and the date of the Third Reading in that House at the third session.

The Act of 1911 envisaged reform of the House of Lords in due course. In 1918 and 1922 the Coalition Government made proposals for reform which were not followed by any Debate in the Commons. In 1927 Lord Cave, the Lord Chancellor, made further proposals, following which the Socialist leader, Mr. Ramsay MacDonald, moved a vote of censure in the Commons on the grounds that it was an outrage on the Constitution that proposals outlined in the House of Lords for its reform should be brought forward without a mandate from the people. The proposals were dropped in the absence of the Labour Party's approval.

In 1933 a Bill for reform was brought forward by the Marquis of Salisbury, but it made no progress beyond a Second Reading in the Lords, where it was bitterly attacked by Socialists.

In their 1945 declaration of policy 'Let us Face the Future' the Socialist Party had said: 'We give clear notice that we will not tolerate obstruction of the people's will by the House of Lords.'

During the first two sessions of the post-war Parliament the House of Lords had improved many Bills by amendment, but had rejected none. In the Coal Industry Nationalization Bill they proposed ninety-five amendments, all of which were accepted by the Commons. The same service was done to other major Bills in the first session. In the second session their critical examination

Domestic Affairs

of Bills was all the more valuable because of the guillotine procedure forced on the Commons by the Government. In the Lords Ministers had paid tribute to the Tory Opposition for its help in enabling the Upper House to perform its proper function as a Second Chamber.

But when it was decided not to introduce the iron and steel nationalization measure in the 1947–48 session, the Government determined to reduce the suspensory powers of the Lords in case they rejected such a Bill. They therefore brought in an amending Parliament Bill early in the 1947–48 session to reduce the length of time that must elapse between the first Second Reading and the third Third Reading to one year and reduce to two the number of consecutive sessions in which the Commons would have to pass the Bill. Such an amending Bill if it was rejected by the Lords, as it was, could become law by the end of 1949. By its terms it operated retrospectively so as to affect any Iron and Steel Bill brought forward in the 1948–49 session. The Bill did not cover the composition of the House of Lords.

Mr. Eden spoke last for the Opposition in the Second Reading Debate, which was concluded on 11th November 1947.

The Parliament Bill was given a Third Reading by the Commons after a division—Ayes 340, Noes 186. During the Second Reading debate in the Lords Lord Salisbury, the Opposition Leader and son of the Lord Salisbury who had introduced the Bill for the reform of the Lords in 1933, appealed to the Government to discuss with the leaders of all parties a comprehensive scheme for reform to cover composition as well as powers. The Debate was adjourned and discussions took place over the period of 19th February to 4th May 1948, when it was announced in a White Paper embodying an Agreed Statement that the talks had broken down. Mr. Eden was present at the discussions and joined with his Conservative colleagues in refusing to consider any period of delay less than eighteen months from the first Second Reading in the Commons or twelve from the first Third Reading.

The following is the main part of his speech in the Second Reading Debate in the Commons.

The House of Lords

We are drawing to the end of a two days' Debate which
was opened by the Lord President of the Council (Mr.
H. Morrison) yesterday, and it will be appropriate if I
begin by making one or two remarks on the Lord President's
speech. His particular argument about this Bill was the need he
felt, and I am sure he felt it or he would not have said so, to
prevent a constitutional crisis. Like the right hon. Gentleman, I
have been the Leader of the House of Commons, and I can quite
understand that instinctive concern to prevent a constitutional
crisis arising, for that is the last thing which a Leader of the House,
who wants a smooth passage for Business, ever wants to see. I
would have understood, and even supported, the right hon.
Gentleman's anxiety if anything during these last two years had
given a shred of evidence to show that there was the least danger
or likelihood that the action of the House of Lords would create
any kind of constitutional crisis. I could not help feeling, as the
right hon. Gentleman worked himself up to this part of his case,
that he was just putting up an Aunt Sally for the fun of knocking
it down, or perhaps it would be fairer to say for the fun of trying
to knock it down, and I hope he enjoyed that.

It is generally accepted by all Members of this House, wherever they sit, that the House of Lords have not been obstructive.
Does anyone deny that? I never thought they would be, because
the curious thing in that respect, as in so many other respects, is
that the House of Lords is a typically British institution. It is no
use the hon. Gentleman opposite shaking his head. He had better
read the speeches of Members of his own Government. They have
all said it. It adapts itself, as British institutions have a habit of
doing, to the tempo of the times. I say to the Prime Minister
tonight, deliberately, that in the words of his own 'Let Us Face
The Future,' the Government have not got a mandate for this
Bill. The right hon. Gentleman told the country, and I do not

Domestic Affairs

complain of it, that if his party had a majority, and there was obstruction from another place, the Government would not tolerate it. There has been no obstruction. The right hon. Gentleman does not deny that. The right hon. Gentleman the Lord President said that there might be obstruction. Is that a new parliamentary doctrine, a sort of general preventive arrest lest anything should happen, in which case I do not know where any of us find ourselves? It is not at all a doctrine which smacks of the ordinary creed of the Prime Minister, but if it is not a preventive arrest, why is this being done?

I say to the Prime Minister—I believe he knows it to be true in a much wider sense—that he has no mandate for this Bill at all. It is not an issue today upon which there is any vestige of popular support. I ask hon. Gentlemen who go round their constituencies, is there anywhere any indignation, real or simulated, about the way in which the House of Lords have used their powers in the last two years? We know perfectly well that there is none at all.

I have here a quotation, not from a Tory newspaper, because I would never quote that in this House, but from a newspaper which, in the early days of the life of this Government, gave it the most ardent support—more ardent, indeed, than the great *Daily Herald*. I refer to the *News Chronicle*—[*Interruption*]—do not spurn all your supporters or there will be none left. I was horrified to hear the Lord President turn down the *New Statesman* yesterday. It is very serious. It is the only weekly which the party opposite have left. If hon. Members start turning down the *News Chronicle* I shall be really apprehensive. They cannot hold the Press by turning them down every day. The *News Chronicle* is a great friend of theirs. Listen to what they say:

'Here the Government are inviting trouble. They cannot put the Upper House on trial, for the Lords have done nothing which can be charged against them. All the world knows that their work since Labour came to power has been concerned with wise and singularly unpolemical amendment to very hasty legislation.'

I say to the Lord President, 'Please note.' The quotation goes on:

92

The House of Lords

'By thus brawling with phantoms the Labour Ministers may find that they have arraigned themselves before the bar of public opinion. In attacking imaginary abuses, they may find themselves called upon to defend their own competence, to cope with the national problems which are real.'

How very well said by a newspaper that does not always agree with the Tory Party.

No one has been more eloquent in support of the work done by the House of Lords than the Members of the Government themselves. There are many quotations which I could give from speeches by Ministers. I do not want to repeat them. I am going to quote only one because to me the name is attractive. I hope that the Lord President of the Council will regard it as deep calling unto deep. It is Lord Morrison in another place. One never knows what may happen. I ask the right hon. Gentleman to take heed. Fate plays strange pranks with us sometimes. This is what Lord Morrison had to say on July 31st last—almost the last meeting of their Lordships' House:

'After many strenuous days and sleepless nights in another place, an abnormally large number of Bills came to your Lordships' House. I must admit that the reasonable consideration given to these Measures in your Lordships' House, and the alterations made therein, appealed to me very much . . .'—

That is to say, they appeal to Lord Morrison—

'Indeed, I think the majority of the Bills which came to your Lordships' House returned to another place in an improved condition.'

That was said by Lord Morrison. The Lord President of the Council should have a friendly feeling for that quotation. I would say to the Prime Minister when he talks about the mandate for this Bill, that at the last Election I think that his party secured about 11,000,000 votes. Anybody can make their own estimate, but I would say that not a score of those who voted for the Government thought that they were going to introduce legislation to curtail the powers of the House of Lords. I do not

Domestic Affairs

believe that it was an issue in any of the speeches or election addresses of hon. Gentlemen opposite. [*Interruption.*] Well, all right. I say that, as far as I am aware, the matter was not an issue at all; and neither is it an issue now.

The people are worried about much graver problems than this. If the Prime Minister could tell us tonight, 'There is a situation of growing tension between us and the House of Lords. Here is the gravest economic crisis we have ever known. I, the Prime Minister, as head of a Socialist Government, want to pass this, that and the other Measure and the other place will not let me'— if the Prime Minister said that, I could understand his demand for this Bill. I could understand that, but here is no issue of that kind at all. There is no issue in which the Government wish to do something in connection with the economic crisis which another place prevents them from doing. I think myself that the Government do not do anything about the economic crisis at all. Hon. Gentlemen opposite have addressed a number of meetings in the country during the last month, and so have we. When one is in Opposition, one has more time to do this than when in Office, and I have myself addressed meetings and have been asked hundreds of questions about all sorts of things. I have been asked about food and no doubt I shall be asked about potatoes. These are not the only things about which I have been asked. I have been asked about houses, where they were and why the Government were not building them. [*Interruption.*] Oh, yes, I have. I have been asked about clothes, I have been asked about the basic petrol ration, and so have all hon. Members in all parts of the House been asked scores of questions about all sorts of things. I have never had one question about the House of Lords. Has any Minister been asked that? [Hon. Members: 'Yes.'] Well, what answer did they give then?

I would make another criticism of this Measure. I would ask the Prime Minister himself to consider what to me is a very objectionable aspect of this Measure—that it once more embodies this practice of retrospective legislation. I think that all parties—

The House of Lords

I do not care of what political view—ought to be on their guard against this. I know that in wartime, when the Prime Minister and I were in the same Government, we used it, but it is most objectionable to make that kind of legislation permanent in time of peace.

I want to deal now with something which the right hon. Gentleman said in his speech and which has been discussed a good deal in this Debate, and that is the question of the effect that this reduction of a year will have on actual legislation. I think my right hon. and learned Friend the Member for West Derby (Sir D. Maxwell Fyfe) dealt with that very effectively. It is the length of the delay which now remains for public opinion to crystallize on any issue, should this Bill be passed into law, and it seems to me a very important aspect of what we are discussing. The hon. and learned Member for East Leicester (Mr. Donovan), in a well-argued speech, made certain calculations of his own, and I do not quarrel with them. With these calculations, the hon. and learned Gentleman showed that there might be six months from the moment when a Bill became an issue between the two Houses up to the time when it received the Royal Assent as a result of the final approval of this House. This six months would be all the time which the nation would have to consider the matter. I want to put this quite fairly. It is quite true that the period from which the Bill is introduced into this House is longer than that, but I submit to the House that the period when it becomes an issue before the country is the period in which it becomes an issue between the two Houses, and that, under the existing Parliament Act, is admittedly eighteen months, but, under this Bill, that period becomes six months. I say to the Prime Minister that that period is altogether too short on any submission or on any argument.

I come now to another argument. There are some hon. Members who have spoken in this Debate—and all kinds of points of view have been expressed—who clearly were against any Second Chamber of any kind. The hon. Member for South

95

Domestic Affairs

Ayrshire (Mr. Emrys Hughes), whose speech I have here, is one of these. Of course, it is a point of view that has existed in every country, a point of view that is being made very vocally at the present time by the Communists in France. Those who take that view are against any hereditary peers or, indeed, any live peers, or any form of Second Chamber. They remind me, if I may say so, of a doggerel I used to hear in my childhood about murderers and their habits, which I must paraphrase to meet the present situation. It runs something like this:

> 'They slit his throat from ear to ear,
> His brains they battered in;
> His name was any goddam peer,
> They swore they'd do him in.'

That is a perfectly possible and legitimate point of view towards another place. It is not the point of view of most hon. Members opposite, but it is at least a point of view which is intelligible. But there is a second category which seems to be a much larger category at the moment.

Judging by the speech of the Home Secretary, and of others on the Front Bench opposite and on the Benches behind, there are those who believe that there should be a Second Chamber, but who are not content with its composition as it is today. Let us have a look at it. I do not deny that there is room for an issue in connection with the composition of the House of Lords; but it is essentially not an issue about its powers; it is an issue about its composition. I put this to the right hon. Gentleman the Lord President: if there were today on his side of the House a general acceptance about the composition of the Second Chamber, there would not really be any argument at all——

Mr. H. Morrison: I want to make it perfectly clear to the right hon. Gentleman that, whatever is done about the composition of the House of Lords, it is our view that the extent and the degree of its power is the first thing to deal with, and that is what we are doing.

Mr. Eden: Then I say to the right hon. Gentleman that he is running absolutely counter to all other experience in dealing with

The House of Lords

the Second Chamber, as I will show in a minute. I think there is a case to be made out about the composition of the hereditary Chamber but there is no case for assuming that a Second Chamber when reconstructed is going to be so ineffective as the right hon. Gentleman wants it to be. I think it would be most unfortunate if events so turned out, and I am going to show him some examples from very recent history in our own Empire of what I mean.

Let us try and discuss for a moment the question of composition, because it does bear on our discussions. I know that it is a very complex question; I have sat on some of the committees which examined the composition of the House of Lords a great many years ago. But I am equally certain that if we want to—and I suppose that even the right hon. Gentleman would wish to—at some time resolve the problem of the composition, as opposed to the powers of the Second Chamber, we will never really do that successfully unless we have an all-party agreement. The right hon. Gentleman the Prime Minister made the point quite fairly the other day when he asked why, during all the time that we were in power, we did not attempt to do it. I will give the right hon. gentleman my answer.

Mr. H. Morrison: The party opposite did not know what to do.

Mr. Eden: I will put it a little more politely, and I will give two reasons why we did not do it. The first was that, so far as I am concerned—and I speak for myself—that particular problem never seemed to me a desperately urgent one. [*Laughter.*] I hoped I would get that reaction; it was just what I was looking for.

Mr. H. Hynd (Hackney, Central): It was because the right hon. Gentleman had a single-Chamber Government.

Mr. Eden: Of course, I understand the hon. Gentleman— because the House of Lords had a Tory majority. It was because I was absolutely convinced that the House of Lords as the Second Chamber would adapt itself to whatever the political situation of this Chamber happened to be. That is why. Was I not right? What is the right hon. Gentleman complaining about? The House of Lords have not taken action in respect of this Government

Domestic Affairs

different from that which they have taken in respect of the Government of which I was a Member—[*Interruption.*] I cannot pick out of that muddle any coherent argument; if so, I would reply to it. I did not believe that if there was a Socialist Government the House of Lords would so abuse their powers as to create a constitutional challenge, and they have not done so. What has happened is that the Lord President of the Council creates this bogey because he is so worried about other things, and wants people to forget them.

The right hon. Gentleman said that we never made any attempt to handle this. We have made attempts to handle it, but on every single attempt that we have made we have been opposed by hon. Members opposite. I heard with amazement the speech of the hon. Member for Central Bristol (Mr. Awberry), who expressed approval of certain proposals for the reform of the House of Lords made in 1927. I remember that very well, and probably the Prime Minister remembers it. I remember something else—the then leader of the Labour Party coming to the House and saying that in no circumstances had the House the slightest right to discuss the reform of that Chamber. He claimed that these reforms were brought in by the House of Lords to reform themselves. Yet here the hon. Member for Central Bristol complains that we did not carry out these proposals. What was the use of asking us to carry out those proposals against the wish of the then leader of the Labour Party?

Mr. H. Morrison: Had he the power of veto?

Mr. Eden: The right hon. Gentleman is not being quite reasonable, even for himself. The hon. Gentleman objected to us for not proceeding with the reforms of 1927, and I was reminding the right hon. Gentleman that the Labour leader of that day moved a Vote of Censure on the House of Lords for having raised the subject at all, and I told him we were right in not trying to proceed without seeking some form of unity on the constitutional issue, as he would have been well advised to do instead of trying to use this issue to cloud his failure on every other issue.

The House of Lords

I believe there is a case for a Second Chamber. I think it is indispensable. In most democratic countries today they have a Second Chamber. The argument is overwhelming, and what we have experienced in this House in the last two years of the spate of legislation makes a Second Chamber far more necessary than in the days gone by. This afternoon the Home Secretary said that that was all right, but that what was wanted was political equality, where his party would have an equal chance. Of course there is a case for that, and we on these benches say there is a case for that. But that is a case for altering the composition of the Second Chamber, not for changing its powers.

May I give the Prime Minister a word of warning? Supposing we did happen to have a Second Chamber with a closer balance of parties than there is today, does the Prime Minister think that it necessarily follows that that Second Chamber would be more subservient to the views of this House than is the present hereditary Chamber? Earlier tonight we had a very sincere speech by the hon. Member for Stoke (Mr. Ellis Smith) about the kind of Second Chamber he wanted constituted, with doctors, scientists, and all sorts of people in it, but only a small minority of the wicked politicians. Let it be argued that there is a case for that. Do not let the Government think that a Chamber of that kind will be more subservient to this House than is the present hereditary Chamber.

I would go even further and say to the Government that once they have got rid of the hereditary principle they may find the Second Chamber far less ready to pass their iron and steel Bill than even the present House of Lords. The Government would be wise to look where they are going. The hon. Lady the Member for Epping (Mrs. Manning) told the same story. She wanted all kinds of new constructions of the Second Chamber. Do not let this House have any doubt as to what the consequences of that might be. If the Prime Minister wants an example, let him look to Australia and observe what happened in Victoria. Let him look to the *Times* article yesterday which says this about the election there:

Domestic Affairs

'The election was forced by the Legislative Council to enable Victorian electors to express an opinion on bank nationalization.'

There was no hereditary Second Chamber there. Yet they cruelly embarrassed the Government of the day and they defeated them. I think I hear the Lord President muttering in his rage, and I can understand it.

I would say this to the Prime Minister: The real trouble is that you simply cannot deal with this matter piecemeal. Everybody has always recognized that fact. The Parliament Act recognized it. The problems of composition and of powers are one. They cannot be kept apart. The only people who do not seem to realize that are the Government, who illogically complain about the composition of the House of Lords and then try to amend their powers. I myself do not think that this is a good time to tackle the problem because the Government ought to have their minds full trying to promote the national effort. They ought to have in mind the words of the Minister for Economic Affairs (Sir S. Cripps), who only the other day in this House told us:

'We shall find our way through to a brighter and more prosperous future all the quicker if we devote ourselves single mindedly to our country's interests.'—[OFFICIAL REPORT, 23rd October 1947; Vol. 443, c. 294.]

I think that is right.

Mr. H. Morrison: Will hon. Members opposite do so?

Mr. Eden: We will. If the Government want to attack this business, let them examine it in the spirit of what the Minister for Economic Affairs said. Let them set up a proper body for this purpose. This Measure—and the Prime Minister knows it quite well—does not really satisfy anybody. It does not deal with the real issue. It creates a bogey of the House of Lords which does not really exist—a bogey of obstruction—and, at the same time, it diverts the attention of the nation from the immediate need. Perhaps that is what the Government want to do; I am beginning to think it is. They seem to be transferring their affection—

The House of Lords

particularly the Lord President—with almost indecent speed from the economic crisis, which is now the business of the Minister for Economic Affairs, to this topic which they find more alluring, on the principle, I suppose, of the popular song:

'If I'm not near the girl I love, I love the girl I'm near.'

I say there is no opposition in any part of the House to the consideration of the reform of the composition of the Second Chamber so long as such reform will fit it better for the purposes of its constitutional functions. If the Government want to set up machinery to deal with that I am quite certain that all parties will do their best to work to make that result successful. But if they feel that work of that kind would distract the public mind at the present time—as well it might—from the economic crisis, I say that the same applies to this Bill which they are bringing before the House. If they think they ought not to distract the public mind, why bring in this Bill instead of concentrating on the economic crisis?

I would finally say this to the Government, and to the Prime Minister particularly. It may be that in many respects on paper the present system is not a very defensible system because we on this side of the House have a large majority in another place. We know that profoundly well. Yet, you know, Sir, the queer thing is that in this country of ours sometimes things, though not very orderly on paper, have the habit of working out pretty well. The Prime Minister knows that, too. In other countries where things are pretty good on paper they have the habit of not working out at all. I just wonder whether it is wise to create this upheaval, because we cannot really deal with a part of this problem without raising issues covering the whole of it. I doubt whether it is wise or necessary to do that at the present time. Many harsh things have been said about the House of Lords, but the queer thing is that it works, on the whole; and has worked. In the lifetime of this Parliament it has worked.

We are living, all of us now, in a shattered world where many traditions are broken. I say sincerely to the right hon. Gentleman if I were he I should leave this subject alone, unless he really feels that he can deal with it as it should be dealt with—as a whole—and present us with a plan, or discuss with us a plan. We have our sharp parliamentary differences; and yet sometimes it happens that there are issues that are bigger than party. The future constitution of this country—it is an unwritten constitution—is really bigger than party. It would be good if we could deal with it on those lines, if we have to deal with it at all. I am bound to tell the right hon. Gentleman that, in my judgment, this Bill deals with a grave constitutional issue in the wrong way and at the wrong time. It is really a fundamental lesson on statesmanship that one should not deal with a large issue in a small way. This is just niggling. It seems to be a murky and miserable little Bill, bred by dissension out of despair. It contributes absolutely nothing to the major economic perils that confront us. It cannot stimulate the nation. The Prime Minister knows that. It cannot inspire any part of the country to a greater effort than it would otherwise have made. Well, Sir, I believe it to be the clumsiest blunder this Government have yet committed. I still hope the Prime Minister will say that what we need is, not this Bill, but a consideration of the constitutional problem which exists, and no doubt there is much contribution that could be made. But to this Bill we must offer unshakable opposition, and I trust that the House will overwhelmingly support our Amendment.

Chapter 6

Socialist Policy and Nationalization

The Socialist Party in its 1949 pamphlet *Labour Believes in Britain*, on which their leaders were to base their programme for the next General Election, held out further threats of nationalization.

Of the two industries nationalized in 1946, the coal industry had cost the taxpayer £22,000,000 and the Civil Airways £25,000,000 by the end of 1948. Coal prices rose 4s. per ton in 1947 and a further 2s. 6d. per ton in 1948 for the home consumer and by no less than 25s. per ton for export coal.

Electricity and Transport had been nationalized in 1948.

Both in the coal industry and in the railways unofficial strike action had been taken since nationalization, and in the summer of 1949 the National Union of Railwaymen in pressing a demand for 10s. increase in wages threatened nation-wide go-slow action.

For the economic background, see Chapter 2, D.

Mr. Eden went to Scotland for the week-end after Whitsun 1949 and spoke to a Unionist meeting of 14,000 people at Westgate Park, Dalkeith. In the course of his speech he stated the Conservative policy towards nationalized industries.

There is throughout the British Isles an awakening to the magnitude of the problems that now confront us. That is healthy, for while no problems, however formidable, can daunt us, there is always danger in the masking of unpleasant truths.

For the last year or two, while our export trade has made a remarkable recovery, upon which all concerned are to be warmly

Domestic Affairs

congratulated, certain favourable factors have tended to disguise stern realities. First, the devastation and dislocation of war created a situation in which the peoples of the world were hungry for goods —any goods from any quarter—to replace the shortages of the war years. That period is over. Henceforth there will not be the same eager rush to buy. We must, therefore, expect to meet increasingly keen competition in every market. Our ability to sell our goods overseas, upon which our national life depends, will be determined by their suitability, their quality and their price.

Secondly, we have been enjoying Marshall Aid, which has been an essential factor in our recovery. On the admission of Ministers themselves, without Marshall Aid we should have had today anything up to two million unemployed. And this aid is due to come to an end in 1952. By that date we must be able to maintain our own economic life, and that means that we must be able to sell enough to foreign lands, including the dollar countries, to buy the food we need and the raw materials, without which our industries cannot keep going. This last factor is a new element in our situation as compared with the years between the wars. Serious as the recession of trade and unemployment could be then, we had always sufficient reserves to enable us to buy from abroad the raw materials which our industry needed. Our difficulty, then, was not to pay for the raw materials but to find a market for our finished goods. Today, if we fail to find continuing markets for our exports at the necessary level, we shall find the whole momentum of our industrial life slowed down and our standard of life endangered.

I don't believe that anyone would dispute the analysis which I have just made. Indeed it is in accord with much that the Chancellor himself has said. The Jekyll Cripps would surely endorse it. It is against this background that we must analyse what seem to me to be disturbing elements in our political and industrial life today.

First of all, we are still taxed up to the hilt and beyond it. Our national expenditure is about £3,000,000,000 a year, that is to

Socialist Policy and Nationalization

say, three times what it was before the war. An average of 8s. in
the pound is taken by the Government out of the nation's earnings. That is much too high a proportion and allows no room for
manœuvre in emergencies such as may arise. There is no further
taxable margin available. If anybody thinks that profits could be
more highly taxed, as the Hyde Cripps is apt to do, the answer to
that is that there is nothing to be got out of such a course except
to impose further burdens upon industry. The truth is that industry needs every penny of relief we can give it to enable it to
re-equip itself and hold its own in competition in world markets.

It is extraordinary how confused the Socialist mind can be
about this matter. The latest pamphlet issued by the Fabian
Society and written by Professor G. D. H. Cole contains, among
other things, this sentence: 'That is why many of us, though we
recognized the dilemma in which Sir Stafford Cripps was placed,
could not stomach a Budget which simultaneously made concessions to capitalism and reduced even by a little the working-
class standard of life.' What were those concessions to capitalism
which Mr. Cole could not stomach? The most important was the
increase of the allowance to industry for the provision of new
machinery. What is such a concession except a help, and not a
very generous one, to our export industries to equip themselves so
that they can continue to compete in foreign markets? For unless
our industries are able to do so, we cannot hope to maintain our
standard of living, nor meet the cost of those social services to
which we, just as much as Professor Cole, attach so much importance. In other words, the concessions to industry given in the
Budget were not a help to capitalism, as Professor Cole dubs them,
but a help to the nation.

The second aspect of our national affairs which must cause us
all concern is the increasing evidence of the liabilities of nationalization. Now it is quite true that many sincere people in this
country earnestly believed that the nation would benefit by the
nationalization of all the means of production, distribution and
exchange, as the Socialist creed has it. We, as Unionists, never

believed that, but we can, none the less, feel sympathy and understanding for the disappointment and sense of frustration which has been clearly shown to exist in some of the nationalized industries. In respect of the railways the position was well exemplified by a Gallup poll taken among their members by the N.U.R. last December. After a year's experience of nationalization, the N.U.R. put a series of questions to the railway workers. The answers showed clearly enough that, whereas 88.7 per cent of them had supported the original plan to nationalize the railways and were, therefore, certainly not prejudiced against it, nearly half of them now find the position more frustrating than it was before nationalization.

To judge by the experience of some industries, at least, nationalization is in many ways multiplying the problems of relationship between employer and worker. The size of the nationalized corporations is apt to make employers, and even trade-union leaders, more remote from the rank and file union member. As a result, negotiations seem more drawn-out and more frustrating. And it is certainly profoundly disturbing to find any trade-union leader of the present day maintaining that former trade-union leaders, who now sit on the boards of the great State-controlled industries, 'have passed over to the other side'. What we need, above all, is a spirit of partnership. Surely the time has long gone by when anyone can afford to talk about having two sides in industry.

Another certain result of nationalization which the whole nation has observed is the increasing cost which it inevitably entails. This is an issue of national importance at a time when keener competition is beginning to confront our export industries.

In such conditions it really seems incredible that the Government should persist with the nationalization of iron and steel and, in its new programme, catalogue a whole list of further nationalization proposals, which have nothing in common except that they are all ill thought out, ill co-ordinated and damaging to our economy.

Socialist Policy and Nationalization

Let us for a moment look at the record of the iron and steel industry. Here we have the highest output in all its history; the targets set by the Government itself have been surpassed. The output for the month of May was an all-time record. Moreover, steel is being produced here more cheaply than anywhere else in the world, except in Australia, where certain special advantages exist, and where, incidentally, the industry is also run by free-enterprise. Why in the name of all common sense can the Government not leave this industry alone? But this assurance I can give you. If we win the next General Election the threat of nationalization will not be fulfilled.

Now let us turn to the other industries that are threatened by the Socialists with the same melancholy fate.

First, the sugar-refining industry. Apparently the Socialists suggest that nationalization will make sugar cheaper. Why in the world should it? The precedents are all against it. Has nationalization made your coal any cheaper? or better in quality? Has it made electricity, gas or rail transport any cheaper? True the sugar-refining industry has made profits in the past. What an unforgivable sin. So far as I am aware no one has ever suggested that the profits have been made by exploitation. They have, in fact, been made as a result of efficiency and of a conservative financial policy. And it is out of profits, let me remind you, and out of profits alone, that industries can grow and develop. Presumably refining here is well and cheaply done because we re-export sugar on a large scale. Tate and Lyle, the very efficient firm, who, in the words of the Socialist Party pamphlet, dominate the sugar-refining industry, last year exported to various countries no less than 10,000 tons of refined sugar every week, nearly one-third of their total output. This was done in the face of keen competition from all the sugar-refining countries, including the United States.

And then there is the example of cement. Here again let us take the test of price to the consumer. The price of cement has gone up only half as much as that of building materials generally. Or, to

Domestic Affairs

give you another contrast, it has gone up only one-third as much as the price of nationalized coal. In any case, every increase of price which has been made from the outbreak of war to the present day has required and received the assent of the Ministry of Works. As for the charge that the industry needs to expand, the obstacles to expansion are not the unwillingness of the industry, but the control imposed by the Government upon development and capital investment. I am not for the moment arguing whether this control is right or wrong, but it is obviously ludicrous to complain that an industry does not develop faster when the speed of its development is directly controlled by the Government itself. In contrast with other building materials, the average output per month of cement is now well above what it was in 1938, and enables us to export over twice as much as we did before the war. That is a pretty good record. Whatever reasons the Socialists may have for deciding to nationalize the cement industry, the reasons they have given are clearly not convincing.

The proposal to nationalize certain insurance companies and societies because they are engaged as part of their business in industrial assurance, must surely seem the most fantastic of all. There can be no dispute that insurance as a whole is one of our most valuable export industries. Its annual invisible export earnings to the nation can be put at about £33,000,000. Most of this is in hard currency, which fact is in itself a remarkable tribute to the standing of British insurance companies. It is quite true that the Socialists propose to nationalize only those companies which are engaged in industrial assurance business, but if part of our insurance industry is nationalized our foreign customers may be forgiven if they find it difficult to see any reason in principle why the rest should not be nationalized also. Confidence will thus be weakened and the damage will be done. What makes the whole of this proposal so incredible is that these particular invisible export earnings, with the invaluable hard currency they bring, call for no corresponding import of raw materials. They are a free gain to our balance of trade which is at present in deficit to the

Socialist Policy and Nationalization

tune of at least £200,000,000 a year in respect of our dollar earnings. Moreover, Sir Stafford Cripps was warning us only last Thursday that the dollar gap was widening rather than narrowing.

And the Economic Secretary said yesterday: 'I doubt whether the public has even yet understood how serious and threatening is our dollar gap.' Why then jeopardize any part of our invaluable dollar earnings?

Now you may say to me what is the Unionist Party's attitude in respect of nationalization?

First, we would call a halt to all further schemes of nationalization.

Second, if steel has been nationalized by the date of the General Election, we shall take steps to denationalize it if we are returned to office.

Third, where it is practicable we shall seek to denationalize other industries, and this applies, for instance, to large sections of the road transport industry. Where it is not practicable to denationalize we shall decentralize. It is our belief that the interests of this country will be best served by restoring free competitive enterprise on the widest possible scale. But the fact must be faced that in the case of certain industries which this Government has nationalized this will not be possible. For one reason it is highly unlikely that private capital would be prepared to return to such industries as coal mining. Moreover, it would clearly be greatly to the disadvantage of the country if basic industries, such as coal and railways, became political shuttlecocks tossed to and fro between nationalization and private enterprise with the changing fortunes of political parties. We do not, therefore, propose to denationalize the coal-mining industry or the railways.

But we shall have a great deal to do to improve upon their present operation. The fact is that the form of nationalization that the Socialists have imposed upon these industries is far too rigid and far too centralized. We intend to decentralize in both cases and to reduce the excessive authority given to central bodies. We intend to restore more authority and responsibility to the

Domestic Affairs

managements on the spot. It is only by this process of spreading responsibility that the present rigidity, indeed ossification, of the nationalized industries can be cured. Beyond this we shall have many changes to make in the industries which remain nationalized, changes which have been outlined in the opposition that we have offered to the nationalization measures as they have passed half heard and half considered through the House of Commons.

For example, we will give more effective protection to the consumer, and will increase the opportunities given to the House of Commons to conduct searching and effective enquiries into the operation of these boards. In these and other ways we will certainly improve upon the present operation of the industries that must remain nationalized.

I don't conceal from you my belief that even these measures, effective as we may hope to make them, are a second best, a poor substitute for free enterprise. Because we say that denationalization in certain cases will be impossible does not mean for one moment that nationalization was wise in the first place. Far from it. The practical difficulties of denationalization make it all the more vitally important to ensure that further nationalization measures, such as iron and steel nationalization in particular, are not allowed to be put through, because the damage that will then be done to our whole economy may never be fully repaired.

Few problems of policy have caused us more anxious thought than those which have arisen in relation to the effect of Socialist legislation on the Scottish national life. Each measure of nationalization has carried a double penalty for Scotland. First of all, the penalty which the whole nation shares of increased centralization, reduced efficiency and increasing costs and charges. But there is a second penalty peculiar to Scotland. For nationalization inevitably means control from London. And that means, in many cases, that decisions on problems which should properly be decided in Scotland are taken in Whitehall. And so today I think it is true to say that there is here in Scotland a wider interest in

Socialist Policy and Nationalization

the practical issue of how administration is to be decentralized, than there has ever been for very many years.

I need not again rehearse the proposals for dealing with the nationalized industries which Mr. Churchill put before you in his speech at your Glasgow Conference. These proposals will bring considerable relief, and a much wider measure of local responsibility. But we do not pretend that they are the whole answer. Let us be very clear on this point. The concentration of all power at the centre, the denial of effective action to any authority other than the central one, these are symptoms of the disease of Socialism. And the cure for that disease is a Unionist victory at the polls. If Scotland is to have, to regain, a more decisive voice in her affairs, the first step is to elect a new Government. Another Socialist victory, another five-year period of Socialist power, the further measures of nationalization which have been threatened, all these taken together would seriously imperil the structure of the national life of Scotland.

A political philosophy which denies individuality either in man or in nations cannot, I believe, for long retain its hold on this island. But while we are striving for that victory, we are not content to wait until it comes to produce proposals for the future of Scottish affairs. We are now, with the very active help of the Scottish Unionist Members, examining this problem to see— apart from our general proposals—what immediate practical steps can be taken to enable Scotland to enjoy a larger measure of control over her own affairs.

Chapter 7

The Conservative Alternative

INTRODUCTION

The speeches in the earlier chapters contain examples of the way in which Mr. Eden constantly put to the Government his remedies for the solution of their problems. From time to time during these years, when making a general review of the nation's problems, he set out the policy which the Conservative Party would pursue in those circumstances.

The general background to these speeches is to be found in earlier chapters.

A. OUR POSITION

Mr. Eden spoke at the Conservative Party Conference at Brighton on 2nd October 1947. The following are supplementary notes to the general economic background which was given in Chapter 2.

Capital Expenditure. On October 23rd, three weeks after Mr. Eden's speech, Sir Stafford Cripps announced that cuts totalling £200,000,000 were to be made in the annual expenditure on capital construction at home.

Food Subsidies. In 1947 these subsidies were estimated to cost £392,000,000 per year. The Chancellor of the Exchequer had said: 'I intend to find that sum this year, but in present circumstances it would be impossible to justify a further increase.'

By July 1948 they were running at the rate of £470,000,000. In his 1949 Budget Sir Stafford Cripps announced that the maximum total annual cost of food subsidies was to be restricted to

The Conservative Alternative

£465,000,000 per year and that some food prices would have to be increased.

Imperial Trade. Negotiations were in progress in Geneva between twenty-three nations on international trade and tariffs. An agreement was signed on October 30th whereby in return for restrictions in American import tariffs Britain and other parts of the British Commonwealth agreed to make large concessions both in tariff rates and Imperial Preference margins. Conservatives took the general view that we had been required to make greater concessions than the U.S.A. and urged the Government not to subscribe prematurely to a policy of non-discrimination in tariffs.

Nationalization. The records of nationalized industries in 1947 were: COAL—£23,250,000 (deficit). The price of coal had risen since nationalization by 6s. 6d. a ton. CIVIL AVIATION—£10,000,000 (deficit). CABLE AND WIRELESS—Profit of £1,750,000 compared with £3,500,000 the year before.

In the summer months I have been spending some time addressing meetings in different parts of the country, and in the course of those meetings it has fallen to my lot to criticize the Government's handling of the present economic crisis; but today I do not want to do that—tempting as it is. I want to concentrate in the main upon our position as a party.

Of course, it is impossible in examining the Conservative policy entirely to ignore the Government's contributions to the crisis. We have a Socialist Government. Nobody is in any doubt about that. It is very close to us all. It goes to bed with us at night in the form of outworn and tattered sheets. It gets up with us in the morning when we find that the electric stove has shed its load. It accompanies us wherever we go, when, for instance, we buy our four-page newspaper. It is a cadaverous ghost at every meal. We are hardly to be blamed if the embarrassing intimacy of this spectre occupies quite a lot of our thoughts. Nor, I think, ought the Prime Minister to complain if we talk about it from time to time.

113

Domestic Affairs

But my task today is a different one. It is to examine our own views rather than the shortcomings of the Government. I am well aware that many members of our Party have been reluctant to issue any declarations. We are properly suspicious of detailed future policies. We know that no set of complicated remedies can be devised in advance for the treatment of ills that shift and change their course from day to day. The nation, in fact, is now suffering from this Government's too rigid commitment to doctrinaire policies. At the same time we know, you and I, that it is impossible to go up and down this country without hearing on all sides: 'What would the Tories do about it?' It seems to us to be our duty to answer this question. Therefore, in respect of the immediate situation, 'What would we do?' I say, first of all: True Leadership. We could quarrel with the Government about policy, but even that is not our main criticism. True leadership means foresight, courage and single-mindedness. We had such leadership in the war: who can say we have got it today? You could not attribute foresight to a Government which includes Mr. Shinwell—political courage to a Government which includes Mr. Alexander, or single-mindedness to a Government which carries Mr. Barnes.

The public does not yet understand the true nature and full implications of the present crisis; and this is not the public's fault; it is the Government's. In the war we had, under Mr. Churchill, true national leadership that took the public into its confidence and gave a lucid exposition of our problems and our prospects. We must have such leadership again.

Secondly, immediate steps to stop inflation, which is playing havoc with all our other plans. Inflation is getting worse. It is bound to continue to go on getting worse as a result of Sir Stafford Cripps's export drive, however desirable that may be in itself. As a result of that drive there will be less goods coming into the shops, and therefore more money chasing less goods. How is this inflation to be dealt with? I would suggest to you two ways. First, by a really balanced budget, and by this I mean a budget which is not merely

The Conservative Alternative

balanced but balanced at a level which this country can bear; and by a capital expenditure programme which instead of being based, as it has been hitherto, on the unco-ordinated appetites of individual Ministers, bears some relation to the nation's capacity in men, money and materials. Such a budget would have to include a reduction of Government expenditure, and particularly of the present high cost of the machinery of government.

As to capital expenditure, the Government have been trying to do too much at once. Now, admittedly, cuts in capital expenditure involve some most unpleasant decisions. Hospitals, schools, public works, houses, the re-equipment of mines, of agriculture, of railways and of industry as a whole, all these things we all of us desperately want to see. If we cannot have them all at once—and unhappily we know that we cannot—then an order of priority must be established. There is really no escape from that, and if only the Government had faced up to this reality when we warned them more than a year ago, much waste would have been avoided and much work, now half completed, could have been finished. Already inflation has raised prices, particularly for the old age pensioner, for children and for the lowest scale of wage earners. The benefits of the new social services, which we all supported —and some try to take all the credit—are being rapidly dissipated.

More than a year ago the Chancellor warned Parliament of the heavy financial burden of the food subsidies, but the Chancellor of the Exchequer is not a gipsy who can be content merely with a warning. He should be a great officer of State responsible for action. What does he mean? If the burden of these subsidies is one which the country can and should bear, why does he warn us? If it is too great for us to bear, then warning is not enough: action is what is needed, and if action is unavoidable and should the subsidies now be cut, account must at the same time be taken of the special hardship such long-delayed decisions will inevitably inflict on certain sections of the community. It would, in our judgment, be necessary to make some compensating increases in certain of the

Domestic Affairs

social services and to reduce taxation, particularly on the lowest incomes.

Thirdly, our Imperial heritage. The Conservative Party has a vigorous and abiding faith in the future of this country and in the future of the British Commonwealth and Empire, or it is nothing at all.

These are not just questions of economics, important though economics are today. Foreign policy, defence policy, all these matters have to be thought out in Imperial terms and not in those of our island alone.

As regards defence policy, I have been disturbed at the extent to which the propaganda of the extreme Left has concentrated on this particular part of our national expenditure. Any reduction in that sphere should be part of an agreed Empire plan. No one would deny at this time that we have to make reductions in expenditure upon the fighting services to the minimum consistent with efficiency. We must go on constantly combing the tail, as we did in wartime. But we must not allow our forces to fall into a condition in which they are incapable of meeting our international commitments. That would be disastrous. And then there is the economic aspect of Empire policy. It is impossible to exaggerate the significance of Empire trade. Before the war 49 per cent of our exports, as you know, were sold to the Empire. We as a party are proud that through long years we have played our part in that carefully contrived system of Imperial preference, which reconciles the ideal of unity with the aspirations of free and independent nations. We maintain that within a system of preferences there are immense opportunities for the development of the resources of the Empire. Empire policy cannot be a makeshift policy. It must be a permanent policy. Therefore, we welcome any recruits, wherever they may come from and however raw and confused their thought! Of course, we are delighted to hear that the Empire, for which a few years ago some who are now Ministers could only 'blush', is now one they are prepared to bless. But we cannot forget, at the same time, nor, I think, should others forget, that ours is the Party

The Conservative Alternative

which has borne the heat and burden of the day. I know all about rejoicing in the sinner; but I have always felt a bit of sympathy for the other ninety and nine.

Fourthly, an intensive drive to develop our production. You will notice I say our production and not our exports. It is not that I minimize our need for exports. All of us, Tory or Socialist, employer or worker, all of us realize that our standards of life, indeed our life itself, depend on our ability to export. Even Mr. Aneurin Bevan has perhaps learned that by now. But our aim should and must be not merely to distribute to the world the greater part of our scarcity, but to distribute to the world part of our plenty. We cannot continue for ever consuming nothing and exporting all, nor, let me add, can we expect other countries to be prepared indefinitely to take what we send to them while we refuse what they want to send to us. But certainly we as a party would do, and will now do, all we can to develop overseas markets. For the problem of finding markets for our exports is perhaps the most formidable of all. Government arithmetic alone is not going to find us markets. There is nothing incompatible between what I have said about Empire trade and the importance of plans with our Western neighbours in Europe for greatly increased production and a mutual exchange of goods. Indeed, it is indispensable that we should do this if markets are to be found for our exports. The two conceptions, Empire trade and Western European trade, are, in fact, complementary and must be worked out together. Indeed, in this respect we have a special responsibility, for we are the bridge between these great new countries of the Commonwealth and our neighbours in Western Europe. We should do everything in our power to further the constructive efforts of the Committee of Sixteen Nations in Paris.

Fifthly, the intensive development of our own agriculture. You might perhaps say I have covered that point by what I have already said with regard to production. But I look on agriculture as something standing by itself—not only because of the character of this industry but because of the importance of the results. Cuts in the petrol ration, the abolition of foreign travel, less flicks and less fags (to use the elegant language of the Chancellor of the Exchequer), all these things added together will only save a fraction of the dollars that would be got by the restoration of the level of agricultural production to where we left it in July of 1945. But you cannot get increased production just by setting increased targets, nor even just by giving increased prices. It is no good giving the farmers the job unless you also give them the tools. Therefore, we must give them priority in machinery, priority in spares, priority in houses, priority in imports on which alone an increased meat and poultry production can be based. These are the things the farmers need. No one is in a better position than the farmer to know that fine words butter no parsnips, and up to now he has had little except fine words.

Sixthly, no more nationalization.

Let us unite and not divide the nation on economic policy. You will remember, perhaps, that earlier in my speech I mentioned the qualities of leadership, and amongst them that of single-mindedness. By that I meant that our rulers should abandon all thought of party advantages or political slogans. Their thoughts ought to centre only on those things which promise relief from our present difficulties. Even the most ardent supporter of nationalization—the man who goes furthest in those claims which we dispute for its long-term advantages—would say that the result which he expects can have no possible effect on the present situation. We believe that the immediate results—the complete changeover from one system to another—must lead to disorganization, confusion and loss of efficiency. This is what we as Conservatives have preached in the past as a matter of theory. Today we can claim it as something which has been proved in practice. We have now, which we had not at the last General Election, nearly a year's experience of nationalization in the coal-mining industry.

The other day there was a meeting, not of the wicked Tory Party, but of the National Association of Colliery Overmen affiliated to the T.U.C. At that meeting it was said that 22,000

The Conservative Alternative

were employed in salaried positions in the industry compared with 15,000 in 1935, and that the administrative cost of raising coal, which in 1935 was 2½*d*. a ton, is now, in the great new bureaucratic paradise of Mr. Shinwell, no less than 1*s*. 8*d*. a ton. Now I ask you: Is this dreary process to be repeated with railways, road transport and other activities? Is that great industry of iron and steel to follow the same road?

Finally, there is the question of controls. We all admit that there must be some controls while raw materials are scarce. But let the Government concentrate on the main essential controls and relax the vast network of detailed controls. They do not really work. They only frustrate, and much time and labour are wasted in form filling. The Government themselves have now taken our advice about building materials. Let them follow on with other branches. In all these matters much excellent advice, they will find, is given in the Industrial Charter, a piece of work which I must say, in my judgment, reflects the greatest credit on its authors. I am sure that you will be glad to hear that similar statements of policy are being prepared in respect of other spheres.

Let me, then, summarize what we think should be put in hand at once.

First, let us have real leadership showing foresight, courage and single-mindedness.

Second, stop the inflation by a properly balanced budget and a programme of capital expenditure which puts first things first and then gets them done quickly.

Third, let us think imperially in foreign policy, in defence, trade, and indeed in every question that affects the life of this island.

Fourth, let our exports come out of greater production so that we share in plenty rather than in scarcity.

Fifth, give our farmers the tools to do the greatest dollar-saving job of all.

Sixth, no more nationalization.

Seventh, streamline the system of controls.

Ladies and Gentlemen, there are some thoughts for you. If

Domestic Affairs

you will give me five more minutes, there is something else I want to say. Will you? [*Applause.*]

I want to add this: Beyond all these considerations is the great divide between us and the Socialists. There are only two directions in which our country can develop. One is Socialism, which means in effect that industry becomes one giant State monopoly, or a series of State monopolies. The other is what I called at Blackpool last year a nationwide property-owning democracy. The latter, I maintain, is in the true tradition of our Party and our race. We do not want a Britain where a soulless State presides over and determines every single movement of our lives. Nor do we want a Britain of extremes of wealth and poverty. We want to see ownership widely spread. We want the farmer to own his farm, the working man his house, the artisan to have an interest in the work he does, with liberty and justice and opportunity for all.

This is the time to state what we really stand for, and not just what we have come to be associated with. For four hundred years Toryism, or Conservatism—call it what you will—has played a part in moulding the destinies of our country. Other parties have come and gone, as they will come and go again. Conservatism will remain because it is based on certain fundamental principles, and not on a rigid formula applicable only to a single generation. Take nationalization away, and what remains of British Socialism? Precious little. The great principles upon which our Party bases its conduct generation after generation go deeper than an economic doctrine. They do not deal only in production and wages and profits. All these are important limbs on the body of its political thought, but they are not the heart and soul of it. At the core Conservatism stands for liberty of the individual, his right to liberty, to justice, to respect for his own distinctive personality. It regards the family as the basic social unit, and the sanctity of family life as vital to the health of the State. It does not regard the social centre, valuable as it can be, as a substitute for the family. Conservatism asserts that the duty of government in this country, where the Christian virtues are still venerated, is to guard and

The Conservative Alternative

encourage those virtues. You cannot have an efficient working nation when you put temptation in the way of individual honesty and create a paradise for the spiv. We are not a party of unbridled, brutal capitalism, and never have been. Although we believe in personal responsibility and personal initiative in business, we are not the political children of the laissez-faire school. We opposed them decade after decade.

Where did the Tories stand when the greed and squalor of the industrial revolution were darkening the land? I am content with Keir Hardie's testimony: 'As a matter of hard dry fact, from which there can be no getting away, there is more labour legislation standing to the credit account of the Conservative Party on the Statute Book than there is to that of their opponents.'

Now, finally, these truths we must expound throughout the land. Our creed is a mobile and living force which must impress the spirit of each unfolding age or perish. I have said repeatedly for years past that the problem confronting every age is how to reconcile freedom with order. 'Laissez-faire' remembered freedom and denied order. Socialism remembers order and has to deny freedom. The message of Conservatism to a generation growing up in a regimented age is this. Our faith is freedom within the law for all men. Come, help us to reconcile this with the order which the modern world must have.

B. POLICY RESTATED

On 23rd July 1949 the Conservative Party published a re-statement of policy, entitled: *The Right Road for Britain.* The reactions of the National Press to this statement, in general, followed party lines.

On the afternoon of July 23rd Mr. Winston Churchill addressed a meeting of 40,000 people at Wolverhampton. In the evening, after the News, Mr. Eden spoke on the Home Service of the B.B.C.

Domestic Affairs

A few weeks ago I was speaking to you on my return from a tour of the British Commonwealth and Empire. I brought you a message of affection and encouragement from our kinsmen overseas.

Tonight I have to speak to you on a more controversial subject. I want to set before you the policy of the Conservative Party, which has been published today. It is called *The Right Road for Britain*, and I want to show you the choice that you, as electors, will have to make between Conservatism and Socialism.

Both parties largely agree about the stern realities of our national situation. As the result of two world wars we have spent a large part of the savings which our ancestors built up and invested overseas. As a nation we are not living within our means. We are not paying our way. For the time being our American friends are assisting us with loans and Marshall Aid, while Canada and the other overseas Dominions have been most generous to us.

Despite all this, our gold reserves, which are not only ours but those of the whole sterling area, have fallen to a point where the Chancellor of the Exchequer has thought it necessary to enforce a standstill on present purchases from dollar lands. We are consuming more than we are earning. On the admission of Ministers themselves, without Marshall Aid we should have at least a million and a half more unemployed in this country.

About all this there can be no dispute. It is a situation of the utmost gravity and a challenge to our statesmanship. What must we do?

We must earn our own livelihood. Unless we can sell our products in foreign markets at competitive prices we shall suffer unemployment and will not be able to maintain our standard of living or our social services.

This Government has proceeded on the basis of the mandate it received from the electorate to nationalize a large section of

The Conservative Alternative

British industry. The Socialist Party now proposes to extend that field still further. We are told, for example, that sugar, insurance and cement are to be the next instalment. I am sure that that way disaster lies. Nationalization has meant higher costs. It has neither increased efficiency nor created content within industry itself. It has been expensive, rigid and clumsy. In many instances the workers have found their Government employers at once more powerful and more remote than those they had known before.

Do you think it is entirely an accident that recent industrial disputes, of which we have had so many, actual or threatened, have all taken place in Government-controlled industries?

Yet the Socialist programme is for still more nationalization. They propose to interfere even more in the day-to-day management of industry with their inflexible and frustrating methods.

We Conservatives believe that Socialists, by their nationalization schemes, by their heavy government expenditure and high taxation, are adding to our difficulties and multiplying the crises.

We shall reverse that process. We believe that the nation will never meet the present challenge nor attain its former greatness until each of us is inspired with the determination to sterner effort.

Everybody, whatever his or her position may be in industry and trade, must have the opportunity and an inducement to make that extra effort which alone can give Britain her future of wealth and happiness. A sense of personal responsibility and self-sacrifice will triumph over all difficulties.

What we have to do today is to make the fullest use of our productive resources in the most efficient way. To do that we must reduce Government expenditure and get taxation down. I know that this is difficult, but it must be done.

Industry and Agriculture must be given the chance to install the most modern and efficient plant. Every product and process which can contribute to our earnings must be worked up to the

123

Domestic Affairs

full. We must increase our valuable invisible exports such as shipping, banking and insurance.

We will undertake no further nationalization. We will restore free enterprise where that is practicable. We will free iron and steel from the threat of State ownership. We will restore road transport to private and municipal operation.

Where we have no alternative but to leave some industries nationalized, we shall radically overhaul their administration and seek to make them more efficient, less centralized and more human.

We believe that there must be the closest collaboration between Government and industry; not that the Government should own and run industry. Free enterprise should be humanized and not nationalized.

We must not think any longer of industrial relations in terms of two sides, with interests which are permanently opposite and inevitably conflicting. The truth is that both management and labour have the same interest in the prosperity of their industry. Their relations should be based on the knowledge that all are engaged on a common task and that the prosperity of employers and employed is indivisible. You cannot enforce the spirit of partnership by law, but the Government should give a lead in securing the establishment of the idea of a common interest in a common enterprise. There are many means to this end. Piecework, profit-sharing, promotion by merit, joint consultation and co-partnership; these are among the proposals we make in our Workers' Charter. The Charter offers security, incentive and status to the individual. In giving effect to it we will work out its application with trade unions and employers and we will extend it to agriculture wherever we can.

We shall encourage equal pay for men and women doing equal work.

We regard the small individual trader and manufacturer as a most valuable asset to free society, and we shall do all we can to help them.

The Conservative Alternative

Our proposals for agriculture seek to restore a proper balance in the industry by encouraging the raising of more livestock and the improvement of conditions in rural areas. We will prevent the unnecessary loss of good farming land for other purposes. We will guarantee prices and markets for the food that British farmers can produce up to our general target. The market gardener and the fruit grower will also be protected from foreign dumping. We will give British farmers first place in the home market and Empire producers the next. I am convinced that with the full development of home and Empire production we can go far to meet our most urgent needs.

We shall give the necessary priority to houses for the agriculural population. We shall also press forward with the reconditioning of dwellings in the countryside, which the Socialists have failed to do.

We want to see every family in the land enjoy a separate and good home. Though we know the difficulties, we will do all we can to extend timber supplies and encourage a substantial increase in the rate of house-building. We intend to help those who want to own their own homes.

We realize that Scotland has her special problems which nationalization and control from Whitehall have intensified. We have set up a special committee which will report about these to us in the autumn.

The recent developments in our social services are, for the most part, based on legislation and White Papers of the Coalition Government, in which Conservative Ministers had a majority. We shall endeavour to maintain the range and scope of these services and the rates of benefit. Today the real threat to our social services lies in the pursuit of policies which may prevent Britain from surmounting the present crisis and earning her own livelihood.

There is, I am convinced, no future at all for this country as a Socialist State with its rigid and costly centralized control of our national life. In *The Right Road for Britain* we have sought to set before you an alternative of freedom and enterprise.

Domestic Affairs

Only on such foundations can we hope to build a way of life which will withstand the onslaught of the materialistic creeds of our time.

Communism today suppresses the freedom of worship and every other freedom wherever it can seize power. Communism is ruthless in its methods and world-wide in its activities. We in Britain have a special opportunity to guide and keep the world in the true path of freedom. We are not only a European power. We are the heart and centre of a great Commonwealth and Empire, which is faced with the same problems and inspired with a like faith. If we really work together there are no limits to our joint endeavour. There are no difficulties that we cannot overcome.

We have to solve our problems at home if we are to fulfil our responsibilities in the world. Unless we can build in the world a strong front against Communism there can be no sure defence for our way of life at home. And so it is that we can only hope to meet this challenge by a true faith in our own ideals. Our way of life will only work if control and direction from the centre are reduced to the minimum needed because of our economic plight.

The Socialist Party is far too much given to control for the love of control. So in restricting liberty in small matters they are playing into the hands of those who would suppress liberty in the greater things of life. The more we are conditioned to control, the weaker becomes that sense of personal responsibility that in the past has been our strength as a nation, enabling us to overcome difficulties and dangers as great as those that confront us now. With faith, freedom and responsibility as our watchwords we can win through, with endurance for ourselves and hope and confidence for the generations that are to come.

PART TWO

THE BRITISH COMMONWEALTH

INTRODUCTION

In the third week in January 1949 Mr. Eden, accompanied by Commander Allan Noble, M.P., who had acted as his Parliamentary Private Secretary for the past three years, left London for a Commonwealth tour.

In recent years Commonwealth leaders, both members of their Governments and leading citizens outside them, had paid many visits to Britain, but few leading British statesmen had visited Australia and New Zealand. Since 1945 there had been two conferences of Prime Ministers in London. Mr. Eden had himself attended the previous conference held in London in May 1944. At the second of the post-war conferences, held in October 1948, the Prime Ministers discussed and agreed to the part Britain was playing in Western Union and European recovery. The Prime Ministers expressed themselves as anxious to maintain and to extend methods of consultation between their Governments, and recommendations were being considered by them. By mid 1949 no steps had been taken to introduce any machinery for economic co-ordination similar to that established in Paris between the sixteen nations participating in Marshall Aid, or for defence co-ordination similar to the Brussels Pact Defence Council and the Committee under Field-Marshal Montgomery.

When Mr. Eden started his tour it was known that a further conference of Prime Ministers was shortly to be convened to consider India's position as a member of the Commonwealth in the light of her expressed intention to adopt a republican constitution.

H.M. the King, who had been to Canada in 1939 and in the Union of South Africa and Rhodesia in 1947, had arranged to go to Australia and New Zealand early in 1949. On the instructions of his doctors, this last visit had to be postponed and the peoples of the two Dominions felt not only the sympathy and concern which all his subjects showed at the news of His Majesty's illness, but a keen sense of disappointment.

Chapter 8

Canada, the British Commonwealth
and the World

Mr. Eden arrived in Canada on 22nd January 1949. Mr. St. Laurent, who had succeeded Mr. Mackenzie King as Prime Minister, had taken the lead the previous summer in calling for an Atlantic Pact, negotiations for which were still in progress in January.

Canada had generously given Britain a million-dollar credit in 1946. Canada herself had her own economic troubles after the war, of which shortage of U.S. dollars was among the most pressing. Her geographical position required a close trading relationship with the U.S.A.; her position as a member of the British Commonwealth made her anxious to play her part in the economic unity of the Commonwealth. In defence matters, also, the closest co-ordination of weapons and methods with the U.S.A. was essential to her, and yet she played her part in the Commonwealth defence arrangements.

Trading difficulties had recently arisen between the Canadian and the British Governments. The cancellation of contracts for newsprint in 1947 and the limitations forced by currency shortages on Britain's purchases of food from Canada had inflicted hardships on Canadian industrial and agricultural interests, particularly upon the latter, who had built up their production to supply Britain with food in the war and who knew that Britain was now short of food. The problem remained: how could Britain build up her exports to Canada to earn Canadian dollars to pay for these things? Bilateral trade agreements with eastern European countries, including Poland and Russia, whereby Britain promised to sell machinery and steel manufactures in return for food, timber and feeding stuffs alienated Canadian opinion, since it was thought that Canada could supply the same things in exchange for steel, primary raw manufactures and machinery. Steps had only recently been taken to encourage British exports, especially textiles and machinery, to Canada, but British prices were still high.

The exchange question was in danger of bedevilling the relations between the two countries, but both their Governments were now pledged to do their utmost to solve the problem.

On January 24th Mr. Eden spoke at a dinner given in his honour by the Board of Trade of the city of Toronto. 1,400 people were present and the address was broadcast from coast to coast. As was his custom when outside Britain Mr. Eden avoided all criticism of the Socialist Government.

TORONTO BOARD OF TRADE

I am indeed grateful to the Toronto Board of Trade for the compliment they have paid to me in inviting me to address you tonight. This throbbing and thriving city holds so eminent a position in the industrial and commercial life of Canada that any visiting Englishman must consider it a privilege to be your guest. I congratulate you upon the vigour of your organization and upon the distinguished contribution which you are making to the life of this city and to the welfare of Canada, and I wish all possible success to your future efforts.

I know you will agree with me that a special tribute is due to your President, Mr. Lawson, for his services to this Board over so many years, for his wise guidance of its affairs and, may I add, for the brilliant organization of this evening.

It is a real pleasure to be in Canada again, to enjoy your generous hospitality and to be refreshed by the enterprise, courage and vitality of the Canadian people.

If anything could add to my sense of gratification tonight, it is the fact that my colleague and friend of many years, Mr. Vincent Massey, has introduced me to you. It would be presumptuous of me to attempt to pay tribute to the invaluable services he has rendered to our two countries and to the British Commonwealth. His period of service as Canadian High Commissioner in London was one of unsurpassed distinction, for which neither you nor we can ever cease to be grateful. I feel sure that he has yet further service to render to his fellow men in the years that lie ahead.

I realize, of course, that tonight I am speaking not only to you in this room, but to a wider audience in their own homes, each of whom it would be a pleasure to meet personally.

And now, may I add a word of greeting to my French Canadian friends among our radio audience.

J'espère que vous me permettrez de vous saluer tout particulièrement, mes amis canadiens de la langue française. Vous devez savoir combien je respecte et admire vos traditions et votre langue incomparable. Ici, au Canada, vous avez démontré, par un exemple vivant, ce que peut accomplir l' amitié de deux peuples. Vous êtes le modèle parfait des relations internationales. Puisse le monde entier suivre vos pas!

We live in a world of international tension. Wherever we look, in Europe or in Asia, in Berlin, in Malaya or in China, the two opposing ways of life confront each other. Sometimes there is open conflict. Sometimes there is what is called cold war. But the challenge is always there.

To me there is something tragically reactionary in the Communist creed and in the rule behind the iron curtain. As man has continued his age-long struggle, it has been increasingly his ideal to create conditions of government which give the widest scope for freedom and for the development of individual personality. Indeed, the extent to which, in any state, we can combine freedom with order is the measure of human progress. It is all these values that are now threatened by Communism. Under this deadening dogma men are not encouraged to think for themselves. On the contrary, the whole insistence is upon a common pattern. We are all to be stamped alike. When one says turn, we are all to turn.

Not only does Communism discourage individual independence of thought: it positively forbids the exchange of opinion across the frontier, between lands behind the iron curtain and ourselves. Moscow only propagates distorted messages which give a fantastic caricature of the conditions in which we live. No outside air is allowed to circulate, and that, no doubt, for reasons that are clear enough. The breath of sanity would sweep away too much of that dense fog of suspicion and mistrust in which Communism thrives.

The Communist tragedy has this at least in common with that of Hitler: it forbids all contact with the outside world. This, if the Soviet peoples understood what was happening, would be frustrating to themselves; it is menacing to others. For a free exchange of thought between nations is in itself an aid to peace. Where countries are boxed off and the lid is slammed down tight, foul pests breed and putrefy the body politic.

What makes this practice so pernicious internationally is that it marches with a blind faith that the Western democratic way of life, or, as the Communists prefer to call it, the capitalist way of life, is tottering to its doom. We know the folly of such beliefs, but it is dangerous in a world where international authority is weak that any one great power should base its policies upon assumptions that are fundamentally in error in respect of others. That is precisely what Soviet Russia is doing today.

If anyone doubts the truth of what I am saying, let him refer to the latest exposition of Communist philosophy, as set out by M. Dimitrov in Sofia. I admit that this is not an easy thing to do, for M. Dimitrov spoke for eight hours, and full accounts of the speech are, perhaps mercifully, difficult to obtain. But M. Dimitrov is important, for he has always been accepted as one of the most authentic exponents of the Communist creed, and this time he told us that he had received Stalin's personal advice and guidance. I have no doubt that this was true. Dimitrov did not conceal the fact that what he calls a people's democracy is 'completely different from and antagonistic to the Western democracy'. Equally he made it clear that the success of Communism is dependent upon Soviet power. There is no pretence that in the countries which

Canada, The British Commonwealth, The World
have recently acquired the blessing of such rule it in any way
represents the will of the majority. In the coalition governments,
which paved the way in many lands for the present single-
party dictatorships, the Communists were in every instance in the
minority.

For Dimitrov Communists everywhere are the interpreters of
the Soviet instruction. There is no other thought or law. For him
there is one Communist front which accepts one Communist
guidance, that of Stalin. Any who attempt to divert, even by a
hair's breadth, from such command fall at once under the ban
of the most violent Muscovite denunciation. The experience of
Marshal Tito illustrates this vividly enough.

Such a doctrine and such methods are the negation of all that
free men have sought to achieve by the practice of toleration and
goodwill. Here is no live and let live, no birth of thought, no gleam
of grace or humour; just the despot and the slave.

What can we do, we the free nations of the British Commonwealth, to strengthen the causes that work for peace? First, we
must have faith in ourselves and in our destinies. In a world where
much has gone awry, we can, without conceit, point to our Commonwealth as an unrivalled example of the capacity of free
nations to work together for a common end. We have our way of
life to which we hold, and which we will not yield up. We believe
in government by consent and that the individual personality
should be encouraged to live and grow. Our relations with one
another, as countries of the British Commonwealth, are based on
no written constitution. They have grown through confidence in
each other. When disagreements arise, as from time to time
they must, discussions take place within our family as to what we
can do to make our co-operation closer still and of truer significance to ourselves and to the rest of the world. I am sure that I can
speak for the people at home in Britain when I say that we are
eager at all times to consider with the utmost goodwill any project and any responsibility which will foster our unity and
strengthen our purpose.

133

The British Commonwealth

The tradition which is part of the life of our British Common-wealth has been a natural growth. The well-tried methods by which our mutual relations have evolved make us perhaps a little chary of any elaborate new machinery. Yet it is likely enough that we could improve upon the existing methods of consultation. At any rate, we should always be on the look-out to do so. Because methods work reasonably well today, that does not mean that they could not be bettered for the future.

Secondly, we must work together with those who are like-minded with us to build up our moral and material strength. We say this in no aggressive mood, but simply because it is our inten-tion to defend our way of life. Certainly every effort was made during the war years, and since, to meet the Soviet Union in a spirit of true comradeship and as the allies of a common battle-field. All those endeavours have been repulsed, and the work of U.N.O. has been largely stultified by Soviet abuse of the veto. Only one course, therefore, remains. The free nations on either side of the Atlantic must work and plan together to the fullest extent in their power, in the political, the economic and the mili-tary spheres. The closer they are collectively, the safer will they be individually.

We in Britain have all noted with admiration the statesmanlike lead which your Prime Minister has taken in respect of the Atlantic Pact. We wish all success to that endeavour. This at least is certain: if we can once establish closely united and strongly based arrange-ments for joint effort and mutual help between the free countries on either side of the Atlantic, we shall have taken the most effective step in our power to improve international relations and to main-tain peace. And then, maybe, we shall be able to negotiate with the Soviets on the only basis which they understand, negotiation from strength. When that hour comes we shall need to show both audacity and restraint.

If we are agreed upon the policies which I have outlined, then I submit that we must pursue them with the utmost energy and resolution. We must not underrate the challenge. We are dealing

Canada, The British Commonwealth, The World

with a dynamic and fanatical ideology in which Communists believe with a fervour that is almost religious. If we are to prevail, we must match their frenzy with an even deeper devotion to the faith we hold.

And now I would like to speak to you about my own country. Britain has to meet the challenge of the post-war world in conditions of comparative impoverishment. Nothing could have exceeded the generosity which you in Canada have shown to us financially and materially also, both during the war and since. But for that, our fate would be hard indeed. The fact remains that during two wars waged in one generation our small island has spent itself, jointly with you, in life and in treasure. It is in life that the toll is most heavy. Nothing can replace what we have lost. The loss is not only in numbers, but in quality as well. It is of the material cost, however, that I must speak to you now, for it is relevant to the problems that confront us.

Before the war of 1914 Britain lived to a very large extent upon the interest on her investments overseas, and upon the services she rendered to the world in shipping, in finance, in insurance and in countless other ways.

The prestige of London as the financial centre of the world has matched the fame of British shipping as the carriers of world trade. By performing such services for other lands, and by the export of manufactured goods which have poured from our country in the last hundred years, we were able to build up valuable investments in many countries and in every continent. The income from these investments has stood us in good stead ever since. Even in the period between the two wars nearly a third of everything we imported into Britain was paid for by our overseas investment income and our invisible exports. The cost of the second world war has drastically transformed all this. The year in which we and you and the sister nations of the British Commonwealth and Empire stood alone together saw the exhaustion of the larger part of our own accumulated investments. And so we are compelled today to view our problems in a new and, in some respects, a grimmer context.

The British Commonwealth

Unhappily these exchange difficulties have created very serious commercial problems between us. We must all deplore that, and it is clearly the duty of everyone, in government or outside of it, to do everything in his power to ensure that these unpleasant realities shall be as little harmful as possible to the good relations, indeed the deep and abiding affection, that exists between our two countries. Unfortunately our capacity to buy from you is inescapably influenced in general by the impoverishment created by two world wars, to which I have referred, and in particular by the shortage of dollars. This is not the time to enter into so complex an issue in detail, even if I had the technical information or the detailed knowledge, which is in fact only at the disposal of governments. But this I will say, that all sections of the British people would be deeply unhappy if they thought that this hampering exchange question could cloud the horizon of our true friendship or weaken the family ties that unite us.

We cannot, in present conditions, buy from you and pay you except in the goods that you will buy from us. We hope, of course, that you will buy from us all that you can and thus help us to buy from you. In return we must see to it that we do not pledge ourselves by bilateral agreement to deliver to foreign countries the goods that you would buy from us.

You in North America and we in Britain are in an uncomfortable currency jam. In fact one might say it faces us with a sixty-four dollar question. You in North America are supplying us with generous quantities of goods and raw materials, in part in recognition of the need which the war has imposed upon us, and in part in the expectation that our position will thus be so strengthened that normal trade between Europe and North America may be resumed. We are deeply grateful for this help and our desire to see normal trade restored is not less than yours. Nonetheless, we find ourselves today sometimes in the position where by reason of our shortage of dollars we are compelled to trade with other countries rather than with you in North America.

This problem of exchange is really an old problem with a new look. But there are ways to meet it. May I suggest one? In the nineteenth century Britain supplied the world with goods to the value of thousands of millions of pounds, for a large part of which she took payment by investing the proceeds in the country concerned. If now North America were prepared in like manner to make investments in the sterling area this would be an important contribution to restoring the balance of payments with all that this entails.

Maybe that in this way we could help to revive that wider exchange of goods and services with third parties which was an essential element in Anglo-Canadian trade in pre-war years.

Everyone, in government or in commerce, each of us in our daily life, must do everything in his or her power to help to explain, to minimize and, where possible, to remove any obstacles that now exist. The more real the problems that beset us, the greater the need for the practice of patience and courtesy, that we may understand each other. I can only tell you that the love for Canada at home, always strong, has never been truer or more heartfelt than it is today.

One of the risks attendant upon state trading is that negotiations between Governments upon commerical matters may foster ill-will which would never arise if the transactions were diversified through merchants. A misunderstanding between two merchants from two different countries need have no more significance internationally than a misunderstanding between a buyer and seller at home. But a misunderstanding about trade between two Governments, with all its attendant publicity, can all too easily foster mutual irritation between two nations. It is essential that no such misfortune should cloud relations between our two countries. Our balance-of-payments difficulties are indeed formidable; they are beyond dispute. They are a challenge which we must face together as friends.

But I would not have you think that on account of these problems of the balance of payments there is among our people any sense of helplessness or despair. The British people have their

The British Commonwealth

faults, I hope that we know that, but a rigid unadaptability is not one of them, and our industries and our people have applied themselves with vigour and ability to the challenge of the changed circumstances of today.

As you may perhaps have heard, we have some political differences at home. We are not all of one party. Rumour has it that the same applies here in Canada. You won't expect me tonight to comment on our political differences. Those are for domestic consumption; one has enough to say about them at home. But I think it would be fair and true to say that the overwhelming majority of our people hold tenaciously to our free way of life. We dispute our differences on the public platform, in the Press and over the B.B.C. We think our thoughts to ourselves or exchange them with others if we so prefer. We cast our votes in the secrecy of the ballot. All these things the British people are not prepared to change. All of them are threatened or doomed in the lands behind the iron curtain. Our traditions have roots that strike deep, and there is today a wide and firm determination that the faith of free men, for which the flower of two generations has given its life, shall not yield to any totalitarian tyranny.

The message that I bring you, therefore, about our own country is one of measured confidence: a conviction that, despite the difficulties, the formidable nature of which may not yet be fully understood, our people will win through. Their qualities of character are unchanged since the dark days of 1940. Many of you saw and knew them at that time, as we saw and welcomed your gallant Canadian troops, then the buttress of our island defence. The conditions of today are a challenge to inspire us; they are not a threat to daunt us. Together we can, I have no doubt, repel the dark forces that would enmesh us. This grand old British race, intrepid in war and amiable in peace, has yet some more to give to a world in need of guidance and of faith.

Chapter 9

New Zealand and the British Family

Mr. Eden reached New Zealand on February 3rd. Again he spoke on several occasions of the Commonwealth and the world. Large audiences came to listen to him and he was given a warm welcome, as indeed he had been during the rest of the tour.

On the day of his arrival he took particular pleasure in his visit to Auckland, and when he attended a civic reception given that evening in his honour, he started his speech to 3,500 people with a reference to the Earl of Auckland and the Eden family connection with the city.

I am deeply grateful for your welcome and for the kindness of the Prime Minister and the Government of New Zealand in inviting me to be their guest while in your happy and glorious country.

I hope that you will allow me to say that to arrive in Auckland gives me truly a sense of coming home. I am very proud of my family's connection with your beautiful and thriving city. As I have seen it today, Auckland is indeed the queen of the sun-kissed bays. When George Eden, Earl of Auckland, as First Lord of the Admiralty a century ago, helped Governor Hobson in his expedition to this country, he can hardly have imagined what a wonderful future he was helping to open up. He can hardly have dreamt that so fair and famous a city would one day bear his name. To

139

The British Commonwealth

requote to you the famous Kipling lines which are so familiar to you and to me:

'Last, loneliest, loveliest, exquisite, apart,
On us, on us, the unswerving season smiles,
Who wonder 'mid our fern why men depart,
To seek the Happy Isles.'

On February 11th, towards the end of his stay in New Zealand, Mr. Eden attended a State lunch in Wellington at which the Prime Minister, Mr. Peter Fraser, presided. Afterwards Mr. Eden spoke to the assembled company which included leaders of all political parties and the Diplomatic Corps, amongst whom was the Soviet *Chargé d'Affaires.*

D uring the time that I have been in your beautiful land you have made me feel more than ever how close and affectionate are the ties that bind our two countries. I understand, of course, very well that the wonderful greeting which has been extended to me here and throughout New Zealand is not offered to me personally, but falls to my lot simply because I happen to be for the moment a visiting Britisher. I assure you that I shall faithfully record all this when I reach home and tell them that in the surge of problems of the modern world they have no more generous and understanding friends than here in New Zealand. You are generous in your comments when we are right, and, what is much more remarkable, you are tolerant and understanding in your criticism when we are wrong.

Then there is the undying memory of the war years and of the ordeal which we endured together. We in Britain received from the New Zealand Government and people unswerving help and

New Zealand and the British Family

support from the first hour of the war until the last. No comrade-ship could have been more heartfelt, no loyalty more true. You never wavered, and you never failed. There were times of acute anxiety and difficulty. Together with the sister countries of the British Commonwealth and Empire we sustained for a year alone a challenge as stern as ever faced a freedom-loving community. Inevitably the price was heavy, in life and in material sources, but not one of us considered the alternative for one moment.

Many heroic deeds might be singled out from New Zealand's own record. I will mention just three that come immediately to my mind: the gallant part of your pilots and air crews from the Battle of Britain until VJ day; the action of H.M.N.Z.S. *Achilles* at the River Plate; the unsurpassed record of your New Zealand Division.

During the war years the allies built together and maintained a strong comradeship of the battlefield. Many of us hoped that the unity thus accomplished would be carried through into the years of peace. It was certainly in that spirit that we began our work at San Francisco. I felt then, and I feel now, that if the four great world communities—the United States of America, the Soviet Union, the French Republic and the British Commonwealth and Empire—could accept and maintain between each other an abiding friendship, then the world might reasonably look forward to a prolonged period of peace. It was in this spirit that we laboured at San Francisco. Our Charter was not a perfect document—no human achievement ever is. I know that your Prime Minister, amongst others, would have liked amendments which maybe in my heart of hearts I would have welcomed too. But at least the Charter did represent the greatest measure of common agreement available at that time, and at least it did set out rules of international conduct which, had they been observed in the spirit and in the letter, would have made their contribu-tion to the establishment of international law. Until the world is prepared to accept the rule of international law and abide by it, there can be no enduring peace.

The British Commonwealth

Unfortunately the hopes which we cherished while we laboured at San Francisco have not been fulfilled. It is not for me at this moment to comment in detail upon why this has been, but this I feel compelled to say, I do not believe that meetings between statesmen, however illustrious their positions, will of themselves bring about any lasting improvement in the state of international relations. Something much more than that is needed. Confidence, in the world as it is today, cannot be restored by words alone. Only deeds will do that. If we can once reach the stage where nations are prepared to contribute by their own actions, to restore international good faith, then we may all be surprised by the extent to which confidence will gather momentum. A few hours of agreeable discussion, a few phrases of general agreement, are only illusory, and will in fact do more harm than good if after they are over we find ourselves once again in a period of disputed pledges and hostile propaganda.

The disappointment which all of us felt at the comparative failure of the United Nations has strengthened the demand for regional arrangements, yet this was, in any event, a natural development, and was of course specifically provided for by us when we drew up the Charter at San Francisco. Indeed, it is necessary to emphasize that the conception of a Western Union, that is to say a closer relationship between the countries of Western Europe, is not a new one. Still less has it been brought into being by events which have occurred since the war. The project for a Western Union was informally discussed between us while the war was still in progress and while I was still Foreign Secretray. Our Eastern allies knew all about it then and raised no objection. On the contrary, comments were favourable, which was natural enough, for it cannot surely be said that it is right to have mutual treaty arrangements between the countries of Eastern Europe and wrong to make similar arrangements between the countries of Western Europe. It is my own belief that closer relations, in a political, economic and a

New Zealand and the British Family

military sphere, between ourselves in Britain and our neighbours in Western Europe can be of benefit to peace. But there is here an absolute condition for all of us at home. We should not be prepared at any time to make arrangements with any foreign country, however friendly, which in any way cut across the mutual interests of the British Commonwealth of Nations. For us the Empire ties must always come first. But in point of fact I see no reason why there should be any conflict of interests here. In two world wars you have seen yourselves engaged loyally and heroically in a conflict which has arisen in Europe. If, by a Western Union, we can help to create more settled political conditions on the European Continent, that will be a contribution to the peace of the world. If we are able, by arrangements between ourselves, to co-ordinate our defensive military arrangements, such plans threaten no one and can in themselves create a sense of confidence between us. Again, if in the economic sphere we are able to improve the standard of life of Western Europe, this again cannot fail to advantage other great world producers, and particularly the nations of the British Commonwealth. To widen the area of prosperity must clearly benefit all.

As I have said, these projects for a Western Union were under discussion during the war years. One of the reasons why they were not carried to fruition at that time was that some of the allied Governments in Western Europe felt that they had not the necessary authority to pledge their countries until after their liberation and the holding of elections. This seemed reasonable enough, but the point is worth marking, that the Western Union as it is now being worked out is merely a continuation of projects prepared in the war years with the knowledge of all concerned and without complaint from anyone.

More recently we have the project of the Atlantic Pact, which seems to me a desirable and necessary corollary of Western Union. This is one of the three great unities of which I spoke in Britain some time ago: the first is unity within the British Commonwealth; the second is the unity of Western Europe; the third

The British Commonwealth

is unity across the Atlantic. Such arrangements cannot conceivably be regarded as aggressive moves by the Western Powers, or as a menace to peace. On the contrary, the conclusion of an Atlantic Pact would, in my judgment, create the best possible conditions for the discussion of peace. My advice would therefore be to go ahead firmly and without delay with the policies upon which we are now engaged. It is by such means that we can best hope to bring a sense of confidence and security to a world that yearns so earnestly for peace.

The achievements of your own country have many lessons for the outside world. Here you do in truth practise tolerance. Here the Maori and the Pakeha live happily side by side. Here you set an example of which you may well be proud. Everything in our experience points to the need for closer collaboration between the nations in the modern world.

The whole tendency of recent scientific development has been to make the world physically an ever smaller place. Indeed, scientific discovery has outpaced man's political development, with the result that there are now forces loose in the world which we find it difficult to command.

Moreover, this scientific progress has had another consequence. The improvement of communication has sharpened the reaction to world events. A century ago mere geographic space and the absence of news was, in itself, a shock absorber. Some events might take place in a part of the world remote from either London or Vancouver and we might not know of it, still less feel its political consequence, until such consequence had almost ceased to exist.

Today, all that is different. Any political happening of any significance in any part of the world has its reaction at once in all other parts of the world.

All this emphasizes that, in this contracting world of ours, there must be a system of world order if we are to enjoy lasting peace and security. The nations must accept and abide by a rule of international law.

New Zealand and the British Family

A final word about ourselves, the British family. In the family of the British Commonwealth what is the spirit in which we should approach our problems? I would recall here a quotation from the meeting in London in May of 1945 of the Prime Ministers of the British Commonwealth. Your Prime Minister will recall that event as clearly as I do. These were the words of that declaration:

'We the King's ministers of the United Kingdom, Canada, Australia, New Zealand and South Africa. . . . In a world torn by strife we have met here in unity. That unity finds its strength not in any formal bond but in the hidden spring from which human action flows. We rejoice in our inheritance, loyalties and ideals, and proclaim our sense of kinship to one another. Our system of free association has enabled us, each and all, to claim a full share of the common burden.'

These words apply as truly to the endeavour to win the peace as they did to the endeavour to win the war. I can assure you that we in Britain, although of course we have our party differences as you have here, are ready and eager to play our full part. The British Commonwealth, which can claim for itself to be the one really successful experiment in international co-operation, can help to lead the world to a future free from the constant menace that has shadowed our own time.

Chapter 10

Australia—The Land of Opportunity

During his tour of Australia Mr. Eden spent a short time in each State and saw conditions in the towns and the country. He made many speeches, in which he declared his faith in the unity of the British Commonwealth and told his audiences of the inspiration his tour was giving him. He thanked the Australian people for their help in sending parcels and in the aid to Britain.

On his return to England he wrote a series of articles. The following is one of these articles.

Australia is a land of giant distances which embrace every variety of climate and opportunity. The last twenty-five years have not witnessed any startling growth in population or development, but they have been years of consolidation. Australia has built herself into a nation. There is today a sense of unity and confidence, of national solidity, which certainly did not exist a generation ago.

Only the advent of the aeroplane has made it possible to grasp an impression of the size and scope of the country in less than a year's travel. In four weeks we flew more than 7,000 miles, and yet there were wide areas which we had to leave untouched.

The mere question of size creates a multitude of problems. As I reflect upon them, my strongest sentiment is one of awe at the courage and determination of the early pioneers. What is

146

Australia—The Land of Opportunity

astonishing is not what remains to be done, but what has been accomplished in so short a span as a hundred years.

The first need of Australia is for population. This is fortunately not an issue of political controversy; it is now universally understood and accepted. The present immigration system is based on nomination, and it achieves the purpose which I advocated over twenty years ago, that every immigrant should have a 'private citizen to whom to turn in time of difficulty or of need'.

An Australian nominates and undertakes to care for the intending migrant, who is given an assisted passage. The nominator is expected to provide accommodation until the migrant can establish himself, and, owing to the housing shortage, this may take some time. Camps have been built and these are especially useful for those with a long journey to undertake into the bush before they reach their host and his home.

There is much to be said for this system. It results in the new arrival being able to rely, as it were, upon a godparent who accepts a certain responsibility for him in the early days of settlement.

While in Australia I received many letters from recent arrivals who, having found for themselves the work they wanted, are making arrangements to nominate in their turn some of their relatives or friends at home. This type of scheme depends, of course, upon its own success for its momentum. It seems to work very well. All the signs are that it is gathering speed and that shipping capacity is likely to be the present limitation.

At the same time, plans are being made for the movement and absorption of a considerable number of displaced persons. Australia has agreed with the International Refugee Organization to take 12,000 of these people a year. They are housed initially in reception centres, and they seem to be learning the ways of their new country with energy and content.

The most stubborn obstacle to the acceptance of larger numbers of migrants is Australia's housing problem. It is true that, except in Darwin, the Commonwealth suffered no blitz, but

The British Commonwealth

for the six years of war housebuilding was virtually at a standstill. In every State vigorous efforts are being made, by a wide variety of methods, to combat this shortage. In the meanwhile, intending migrants should bear in mind that it exists.

I found that the 'White Australia' policy is fundamental to the faith of almost every Australian. By their action in the acceptance of newcomers from Europe, and by their plans for agricultural development and industrial enterprise, Australians are doing much to justify their policy before the world. They are acutely conscious of the racial problems which confront countries like South Africa, and recent outbreaks there have strengthened the Commonwealth's determination to preserve a 'White Australia'.

Australians are proud of their British origin and they certainly hope to see a British majority among the newcomers. This, however, does not prevent them from welcoming other settlers of European race, whose capacity for hard work has won them praise.

The openings in this new land are many and varied. They range from clerical work in the city banks and offices to the primary opportunities on the land itself. Australians have made great strides forward on their own account even though there is a shortage of manpower everywhere on the sub-continent.

Queensland, for instance, despite its sub-tropical character, has little over a tenth of its land unoccupied. This is a tribute to the energy and determination of a remarkable people. But it does not mean that these hundreds of square miles are all employed or developed to the fullest extent, or anything like it. It does mean that a start has been made throughout this huge territory, and the nature of the task can be judged by the fact that Queensland is nearly eight times the size of Great Britain.

It is in this State, too, that an agricultural experiment on a national scale is being carried out. At Peak Downs work has started on the growing of sunflower seed for export to Britain and of sorghum as food for pigs. This enterprise aims to cover 250,000 acres of land. It is a daring project, and the experience gained from it should have many valuable lessons for us all.

Australia—The Land of Opportunity

I thought that the Northern Territory presents the most formidable problems, and perhaps the richest opportunities. Here are some of the far-flung cattle stations which look so vast to European eyes. I motored all morning over one, 1,300 square miles in extent. We failed to find the owner and he failed to find us. No unusual occurrence, and despite our experienced guide we were ourselves for a few minutes 'bushed', which merely meant that we took the wrong turning where there are no turnings.

Yet by no means all this territory is desolate. We were fortunate enough to see the area round Alice Springs soon after the rain. The rolling country, the trees and shrubs and flights of parrots were beautiful to look upon, and the transient green freshness of pasture bore no resemblance to the popular conception of the dead heart of Australia.

But in reality life in much of this Northern Territory is pretty tough and solitary. Nothing has done more to alleviate danger and loneliness in the outback than the Flying Doctor Service. This has been an inestimable boon. It was visualized more than thirty years ago by Pastor John Flynn, who was less appalled by the difficulties of giving spiritual comfort to his scattered flock than by the possibility that neglected illness and accident might almost extinguish it.

A man kicked by a horse, a woman with fever, or a boy with meningitis, had to travel perhaps 500 miles slung between two horses, to the place where they could wait for a train—due maybe a week later. No wonder Flynn observed that for those in the outback it was 'an aeroplane or a grave'.

Now, any one of the outback stations can call up its base on the pedal wireless and consult the Flying Doctor, who will prescribe treatment or, if necessary, fly to it and bring back the sick or the injured to hospital. There are now seven Flying Doctors. There is even one Flying Dentist. In time there may be Flying School-teachers, who will supplement the only education these isolated children now know, which is by correspondence course.

Some attractive inducements have wisely been put before the

The British Commonwealth

Australian who may be tempted to try his chance in the Northern Territory. Here the primary producer pays no income-tax, and if he has luck he can make quite a fortune for himself. He deserves it.

I came across men who know the Northern Territory and who are convinced of the substantial contribution it can one day make to the world's supply of meat, and of the decisive part that it can play in Australia's future. I share their views.

But all this is long-term stuff. Some of this territory cannot to-day carry more than five cattle to the square mile. It must be developed, and this involves heavy expenditure upon roads, railways and harbours.

It is invidious for a visitor to attempt comparisons between the States; nor, in a single article, can one give any account of them. Each has its special features and specific appeal.

Victoria has its sense of stability and blend of charm and progress. New South Wales is a miniature of all Australia with its vigorous life expressed in every branch of farming and of industry. Southern Australia has its graceful, friendly capital and smiling countryside, and Tasmania its balanced agriculture so reminiscent of Normandy.

One of the most attractive is certainly Western Australia, the only State I had never visited before. The agricultural lands that surround Perth are fertile and prosperous with their crops of grain and flocks of sheep, and I have seldom travelled through more alluring country than that which stretches south-west from the State capital to Bunbury.

In climate it has something in common with California, and the people everywhere are among the friendliest, even in Australia. I think that of all the States, Queensland and Western Australia provide the widest scope for an increase of population in the next twenty-five years.

The leitmotif dominating the concert of Australian effort is the opening up of their country, through agriculture, through projects to combat the ravages of drought and flood, and by some measure

Australia—The Land of Opportunity

of industrialization. The driving force behind much of this endeavour stems from Australia's sense of unity with, and devotion to, the British Commonwealth.

I felt that this good will towards Britain is probably greater than it has ever been. It is seen, for example, in Australian attempts to increase food production. Some of the schemes may not come to complete fruition for a decade. But Australia's inalienable kinship with the mother country is symbolised now by the gifts of food and parcels that her people generously send to that land, Britain, which so many of them still call home.

The government and institutions of Australia are British in origin. They preserve and enhance what are perhaps the leading British political virtues. They are flexible and adaptable. They can challenge new conditions and absorb them, and yet still retain the original thought and tradition from which they stem. Australians are proud of their British heritage; we in Britain are honoured in our Australian family.

Chapter 11

My Commonwealth Tour

Mr. Eden arrived back in England on March 30th, having travelled 40,000 miles since the middle of January. He summed up his impressions to an *Evening News* reporter in these words: 'I found unity.'

He had been to India and Pakistan in addition to Canada, Australia and New Zealand.

Whilst in Malaya, he visited British troops, rubber estates and saw much of the country. He broadcast a message of good wishes and tribute to British planters, the Armed Forces, the Malays and the Chinese.

In India he stayed with the Governor General and had friendly talks with Mr. Nehru, the Prime Minister, and Sardar Patel the Deputy Prime Minister. He spoke to the Indian Council of World Affairs and had the honour of addressing a special private meeting of the Constituent Assembly.

In Pakistan he saw the Governor General at Lahore, visited the Khyber Pass and at Karachi met Liaquat Ali Khan the Prime Minister.

On April 27th the Commonwealth Prime Ministers announced in London that an agreement had been reached whereby India accepts H.M. the King as the Head of the Commonwealth and will remain a member of the Commonwealth after assuming the status of a sovereign independent republic. Mr. Eden, speaking two days later, said he agreed with Mr. Churchill who had given his general approval to the agreement whilst deferring final judgment. Mr. Eden added:—

"It is early to judge what the final effect of these events may be; but this I do believe from my own recent experience in India and Pakistan brief as it was. There is, in both countries, a deep, and I believe sincere, desire to co-operate with us and our partners

My Commonwealth Tour

in the Commonwealth. In my judgment, this tendency can be expected to live and grow. If so, how infinitely beneficial that must be, not only to all of us working together as members of the Commonwealth, but to the world at large."

On April 27th he broadcast a brief account of his tour over the Home Service of the B.B.C.

Twenty-five years ago I was lucky enough to have the chance to travel round the world to Canada, New Zealand, and Australia, and back by Ceylon, Aden, and Gibraltar. All these territories formed part of what in those days we called the British Empire.

I have often wanted to repeat that journey. The Prime Minister of New Zealand had been kind enough to urge me more than once to re-visit that lovely land. And so when the opportunity came this winter to couple with such a visit a journey to Canada and Australia, I was happy to seize it. But this time I came back via Malaya, India and Pakistan. I thought you might like to hear my impressions of the trip.

The King's illness had caused infinite regret throughout His Majesty's Dominions, but especially so in Australia and New Zealand which had been busy making such eager preparations to welcome him. Everywhere I went I was asked to deliver the same message: I was to tell the King how deep was their disappointment and how keenly they hoped that His Majesty would one day be well enough to visit them with the Queen, and see for themselves how strong is the affection in which they are both held.

Commander Noble was my indispensable colleague throughout my travels. We flew altogether some 40,000 miles in a little over two months.

We did not have much time in Malaya, but it was long enough for us to understand what good work is being done there under

The British Commonwealth

difficult conditions, by all sections of the community, Malay, Chinese, and British. Planters and tinminers, troops and police, they are all having a pretty tough time, and the bandits are giving much more trouble than either their numbers or efficiency would warrant, because the country might have been designed for ambush. The position is bound to be serious for some time to come, but the forces of law and order grow stronger month by month, and the bandits should be steadily driven back to the more inaccessible parts of the jungle. The cost of living in Malaya is high, even in cinemas and beer, and the troops naturally feel this. They find the climate trying, too, but their morale is very good.

In India and Pakistan we were received with much kindness. Whatever the future holds, I hope and believe that it will be possible to strengthen the friendly understanding that today undoubtedly exists with both these new dominions.

In Delhi I was asked to speak to the Indian Members of Parliament, a memorable experience for any English visitor. They made me feel quite at home. In Pakistan we travelled through the picturesque Khyber Pass up to the Afghan frontier. As I looked back across the Peshawar Plain, it seemed to me that their crops were doing well.

In Australia and New Zealand we were able to make a longer stay. There we met and spoke to tens of thousands of people, not only in the big meetings, but more informally on the farms and cattle stations, in factories, on the beaches, at cricket matches.

I think I enjoyed the informal contacts most of all, for our kinsmen down under are very ready to talk about their country and their plans. I remember one day in Sydney I had swum out to a raft, when two young Australians joined me. At first they did not know that I had anything to do with politics, and talked away about their hopes for the future, their views of Australia, and the home country from which their parents had come. When they did identify me I was afraid that they might be put out of their stride. But not at all. We just sat there discussing everything from politics

My Commonwealth Tour

to cricket. It is this warm-hearted friendliness which is my first impression as I look back on those strenuous weeks.

I heard many complaints while I was in Australia and New Zealand that people from home do not come to see them often enough. This is true. There is too much one-way traffic in visits at the present time. Nor do the Dominions know each other as well as they might. This applies not only to men in political life, but in every sphere: universities, commerce, and the professions. The more we know each other the more effectively can we make our influence felt.

And yet in spite of this physical lack of contact, that family feeling is very real between us. The strongest impression of my whole tour was that of the underlying unity. We resemble each other so closely; there are such strong family traits, whether in Toronto, or in Auckland, or in Adelaide.

I'm going to give you just two examples of what I mean. On the morning that I was leaving Vancouver, I was asked to look in at the University of British Columbia on my way to the aerodrome, to speak to some of the students. I gladly accepted, because it is always stimulating to meet the younger generation. I thought there might be a hundred of them. Instead of that, there were six thousand standing packed in what they call their Armoury, and hundreds more outside. I shall never forget that experience. I have never spoken to a more inspiring audience in my life. On these occasions, when one is deeply moved, the words do not always come easily. Yet my task should not have been difficult, for what these young people wanted to know was just how things were working out in the old Country, and what the chances were for future peace and co-operation between the nations of the world. Many of them had fought alongside some of you who are listening to me tonight. They were your comrades in the victories of the battlefield. They were wondering, no doubt, what were the chances that those victories would really bring enduring peace.

For my second example, I will take you to another scene, perhaps six thousand miles away, to Queensland, where we travelled

155

The British Commonwealth

to the lovely country known as the Darling Downs, probably the richest wheat-growing land in the world. We spent. the day exploring it, and as the afternoon wore on we were to call in at a place called Picnic Point, a little way outside the town of Toowoomba. The view is one of the finest anywhere on earth. The plan was that we would meet there the Mayor of Toowoomba and the Mayor of the neighbouring Warwick, some sixty miles away, which has many links with the Warwick I have the honour to represent in our own Parliament. Actually, when we got there we were rather taken aback to find an assembly of some five thousand people and a welcome that would have warmed the heart of a stone. Here, once again, the people of Toowoomba and of Warwick, Queensland, were so like, say, the people of Taunton and Warwick, England.

I believe from my experience of this journey that the invisible ties that unite the nations of the British Commonwealth are stronger today than they were a generation ago. The kinship seems somehow more natural and accepted, more a part of our lives at home and overseas. Or perhaps it is what we have endured together that now holds us so close. That year when we stood alone, we and the sister nations of the Commonwealth. That is a year as fresh in the mind of a citizen of Wellington, or Brisbane, or Winnipeg, as it is for anyone here in London. Although it is true that except for Darwin they were never blitzed themselves, they knew all about it and were sadly troubled. They had confidence that we would win through. They were our comrades in arms, and did all they could to help us in every way. To this day you will find any audience in any part of our Commonwealth overseas ready and eager to hear stories of the blitz. I remember one Sunday afternoon I promised to speak at a chapel in Melbourne. I asked what topics they wanted me to talk about. High upon the list were, any memories of 1940, any stories of Mr. Churchill. I was happy to do both, for I never think of 1940 without imperishable memories of Mr. Churchill.

It is difficult for me to give you a picture in a few minutes of

My Commonwealth Tour

the way of life down under. It is a full and varied life, and the range of opportunity is wide. It is impossible to generalize about climate; I found it almost everywhere abnormal, at least, so I was assured. Britain is not the only country where the visitor is told: 'Oh, you should have been here last month.' But in a country the size of Australia any intending settler can virtually choose the climate he wishes, from the semi-tropical in the north of Queensland to the contrast of Tasmania, which is more like Normandy or even Scotland. There is wheat-growing country and sheep country and cattle country and forest and bush in plenty, and the great desert of the Nullarbor Plain.

New Zealand, more compact in size, is perhaps nearest to us in her natural features. But the thought I want to leave with you is this dominating impression; how closely so many of the people in all those countries, Canada, New Zealand, or Australia, resemble each other and resemble us; our family likeness is very strong.

What is the lesson from all this for us? It is surely that in a world so much at odds, where there is stress and strain, and some bad temper, too, this British family of ours has a special message to give. We are not bound together by any precise code of rules, or by any elaborate constitution. We have our kinship and devoted loyalty to our Sovereign. But for the rest, the bonds are not those of script or of law. They are natural friendships and affinities, and the stronger for that. We think alike and we have the same traditional faiths and hopes. We believe in government by consent, and that the individual human personality should be encouraged to live and grow. We resemble each other, but we do not want all to be stamped in the same pattern by command. We wish to live and let live, and we do not think that this tolerance is just laziness; it is born of a respect for the way of life of others.

It is in no burst of conceit that we can claim that the British Commonwealth is the one wholly successful experiment in international co-operation that the world has yet seen. I sometimes think that there is a very interesting contrast between this family spirit of the British Empire and the aggressive philosophies of some

The British Commonwealth

other countries. The Governments of some countries have evolved a way of life which they seem determined to impose on everyone, like the governess in the *Punch* cartoon dragging the child by the hand and saying: 'I brought you out here to enjoy yourself, and enjoy yourself you shall.' We in the British Empire have no set philosophy—no doctrine to preach; we have simply grown up together through weal and woe and we have found that 'live and let live' is the essence of family life.

Which of these is going to be the real evangelism of the future, which is going to be the true gospel of community life? Which of these will illuminate or darken the paths our children will have to tread in the future? I don't know, but I think sometimes that from this family spirit there might grow the sense of brotherhood so that in time we might merge into the wider citizenship of a united world and enjoy a lasting peace.

And, meanwhile, the prairies of Canada, the dairy farms of New Zealand, the cattle stations of Australia, all send you the same message: one of love and loyalty for the old land which so many of them still call home; one of unbroken trust in that British family which has yet leadership to give to a world in need of guidance and of faith.

Good night to you all.

PART THREE

FOREIGN AFFAIRS

INTRODUCTION

Throughout this period Mr. Eden gave his general support to the foreign policy pursued by Mr. Ernest Bevin. From time to time he criticized the detailed application of foreign policy and made it clear that he would have handled certain situations in a different way. Throughout, he was at pains to show up the absurdity of those who campaigned for a "Socialist" foreign policy. But over the aims and principles of British foreign policy there was broad agreement between the Foreign Secretary and his predecessor, with whom he had, of course, discussed many of the post-war problems in Mr. Churchill's War Cabinet.

In the following pages an attempt has been made to give a brief survey of the background of the more important world events against which the selected speeches were delivered. These notes are far from being a short history of the period. Many events and changes which Mr. Eden had in mind are not recorded. For example, the notes do not include any account of the struggles in Indonesia, Indo-China, Malaya and China. Mr. Eden often referred to these and other matters, but these speeches are not among the selection that has been made.

For convenience, the selected speeches and activities have been divided into three chapters. They form only a small part of those which Mr. Eden made on foreign affairs during this period, but they contain statements of the principles which guide him in his attitude to international problems and examples of the constructive proposals which, although in Opposition, he constantly contributed to the national discussion of foreign policy.

Chapter 12

World Affairs 1947 to May 1948

INTRODUCTION

The Council of Foreign Ministers met in Moscow in the early part of 1947 to discuss the preparation of peace treaties for Germany and Austria. The session which lasted from March 10th to April 24th produced no agreement, but many considered it had served a purpose in revealing the sharp cleavage of opinion which existed between Russia and the West over reparations, the future of the Ruhr, the level of German industry, the economic and political future of Germany, the Austrian Treaty, the territorial claims of Yugoslavia and the problem of German assets. The Russians, who constantly reiterated the need to uphold the Potsdam Agreement of 1945, had by their action in the Control Council in Berlin, by their despoliation of the Eastern Zone of Germany and by their proposals at the Council of Foreign Ministers, made impossible the economic unity of Germany which was the basis of that agreement. But the Moscow talks had a more important message for the world. They showed that the Russians were not seeking agreement with the West; they were attempting to dictate terms. During the session Mr. Marshall, the new U.S. Secretary of State, proposed a Four-Power Treaty pledging joint action against German rearmament for a period of forty years. M. Molotov refused to discuss such a Treaty unless it were broadened into a joint peace settlement to include concessions already refused by the Western powers. Mr. Bevin also discussed with Generalissimo Stalin the possibility of revising the terms of the Anglo-Soviet Treaty which Mr. Eden and M. Molotov signed in 1942, but nothing came of this.

The Council met again in London on 25th November 1947. The British Government pursued its aim of German political and

Foreign Affairs

economic unity under allied control. The conference ended on December 15th without reaching agreement. It had, in truth, broken down and no further meeting was arranged. Britain, France and the U.S.A. decided to go ahead without Russia and to secure the unity of their three Zones of Germany. For this purpose discussions were started in London early in 1948 between the three great Powers and the Benelux countries concerning the inclusion of Western Germany in the European Recovery Programme, international control of the Ruhr and the establishment of a West German Government.

EASTERN EUROPE

Meanwhile the Russians were extending their control of the countries of Eastern Europe. Albania was ruled by a firmly entrenched Communist and pro-Russian Government; Marshal Tito in Yugoslavia still appeared to be supporting the Russian policy, but by the beginning of 1948, his relations with Moscow were strained. Russian troops remained in Poland, and the Communist Party, aided by the majority of Polish Socialists, won the elections at the beginning of the year by terrorist and other irregular methods. By the autumn the position of M. Mikolaczyk, leader of the Polish Peasant Party and war-time leader of the Polish Government in London, had become impossible and he escaped from Poland at the end of October. 12,000 members of his party had been arrested before the election.

Treaties had been agreed at the beginning of 1947, settling the future of Bulgaria, Rumania and Hungary, and giving the Western powers equal rights with Russia in the fulfilment of the Treaties. But the Russians used the power that geography and the presence of their armies gave them to force Communist Governments on these countries. In Bulgaria the Communists, under M. George Dimitrov, secured a majority and set about the liquidation of opposition parties. Of these the most important, the Agrarian Party, was dissolved in August 1947 after M. Petkov, their leader, had been found guilty of 'preparing for an armed *coup d'état*'. He was hanged on September 23rd—a judicial murder if the word judicial can be used for his fabricated trial.

The same process was completed in Hungary by September. Following reports of an alleged plot to overthrow the Republic, the Socialist Vice-Premier had demanded the arrest of M. Bela Kovacs, Secretary General of the Smallholders Party, of which the Prime Minister, M. Nagy, was the leader. Kovacs was in fact arrested by the Russian military authorities without reference to his rights as a Hungarian citizen. Though the Communists had only 79 seats in the legislature out of about 440, they had as usual, secured, through Russian pressure, the key position in the Cabinet—the Ministry of the Interior. Later, again following the intervention of the Russians, M. Nagy himself was charged with being involved in the conspiracy with M. Kovacs. After M. Nagy's enforced resignation, the Smallholders Party broke into two parts, of which one supported the Communist bloc.

In Rumania the elections held at the end of 1946 were, in the words of the British Government, neither 'free nor fair' and resulted in a Communist-controlled Government, but 66 opposition members were elected to the legislature out of 434 members. Early in 1947 many members of the opposition were thrown into prison, and in July M. Maniu, the leader of the anti-Government National Peasant Party, was arrested and later sentenced to solitary confinement for life. His party was dissolved on July 28th. By the end of the year the Communists were powerful enough to force the abdication of King Michael.

Meanwhile Russia was strengthening her position by other devices, by the inauguration of the Cominform and by a series of mutual assistance pacts interlocking the States of Eastern Europe. The Cominform was inaugurated at Warsaw in October 1947 to provide an instrument for the co-ordination of Communist Parties in Eastern and Western Europe.

The methodical political conquest of Eastern Europe threatened Czechoslovakia throughout 1947. Its Coalition Government was headed by a Communist and included Communists as Ministers of the Interior, Labour and Finance, but their party had only won approximately one-third of the seats in the Legislature at the 1946 elections. Dr. Benes was still President. A sudden crisis developed in February 1948. The methods were familiar. The Communists accused the non-Communists of plotting to break up the Coalition, and the Minister of the Interior, who was building up an all-Communist police force, refused to halt this process. The non-Communist Ministers resigned, and armed 'workers' militia' appeared in the streets. M. Jan Masaryk fell to his death from his Foreign Office window. In April the Communist and Socialist Parties agreed to amalgamate on the

Foreign Affairs

basis of Marx, Lenin, Engels and Stalin. Dr. Benes continued as President until June 7th, when he was succeeded by M. Gottwald, the Communist leader.

WESTERN EUROPE

On his way to Moscow in March 1947, Mr. Bevin signed at Dunkirk the Anglo-French Treaty, which was designed to prevent a renewal of German agression rather than to unite the economic and military strength of France and Britain with a view to the unity of Western Europe. In 1946 Belgium, Holland and Luxembourg agreed to work for an economic union amongst themselves. At this time Mr. Bevin appeared to be reluctant to form any wide union of Western European countries for fear of antagonizing the Russians. Such a union had, in fact, been discussed by Mr. Eden during the war and he had advocated it in November 1945 when he had said:

'Many times Russian statesmen have spoken to me of their need for security and the necessity they feel for friendly relations with their neighbours. We have never disputed that. Any arrangements that may be made in Western Europe are for precisely the same purpose, and will be complementary to the arrangements made by Russia in the East.'

In February 1946 he spoke again of the importance of some form of closer understanding between the countries of Western Europe, and said:

'It is only fair that I should add that, so far as I can remember, no statesman of the Soviet Union has ever raised to me any objection to such a course.'

He continued to hold the view that a closer Western European association at that time would have met with much less Soviet opposition than it met later and would more quickly have built up Western economic, strategic and political strength.

The Government was in difficulty with some of its followers over foreign policy. Fifty-seven Labour Members, led by Mr. R. H. S. Crossman, had tabled an amendment in November 1946 calling on the Government to recast its conduct of foreign affairs. Resolutions on foreign policy hostile to Mr. Bevin were moved

World Affairs, 1947 to May 1948

and defeated at the Socialist Party conferences in 1946, 1947 and 1948. In May 1947 an official Labour Party pamphlet, *Cards on the Table*, published apparently without Mr. Bevin's approval, contained the following statement, in addition to some strongly worded criticisms of Russian and American policy:

'We (the Labour Government) have resisted every temptation to regard Russian policy as final. In particular, when the Tories have continuously pressed us to recognize the permanent incompatibility of the democratic and Communist systems, to make a final decision about the policies of each and to build up an entirely independent Western bloc, we have fought doggedly to prevent the crystallization of zones of influence behind rigid ideological barriers.'

These words contained a complete misrepresentation of Conservative foreign policy. Mr. Eden had repeatedly said that in our foreign policy we should not distinguish between forms of Government:

'Nobody in this country contests the right of the Soviet Union to any form of Government she likes. . . . There is no reason why the two ideologies should not live together in peace if both will accept not to back their fancies in every other land.'

But events and public opinion were stronger than the vociferous back benchers of the Labour Party, and by the end of 1947 the British Government was working to achieve a union of Western European countries. Of these events the most important were the breakdown of the Council of Foreign Ministers, the Soviet aggression in Eastern Europe and their known support of Communist Parties in their strikes in France and Italy, and, above all, the famous Marshall offer of economic aid to Europe delivered by the U.S. Secretary of State in a speech at Harvard on June 5th. Public opinion owed much to Mr. Churchill's speeches at Fulton and Zurich in 1946. In the latter he lit the torch of the United Europe movement which has done so much to hasten the fulfilment of Western Union.

The Communist *coup* in Czechoslovakia was perhaps the most profound shock Western Europe had suffered and shortly afterwards, on March 17th 1948, the Brussels Treaty of Alliance, which Mr. Bevin had initiated, was signed by the U.K., France, Belgium, Holland and Luxembourg.

165

Foreign Affairs

GREECE

The civil war in Greece, which had continued with only short respites since December 1944, was intensified during 1947. During the latter half of 1946 well-armed Communist guerrillas, reinforced and supplied across the northern borders, carried out a dangerous offensive in northern Greece, and the Greek Government brought before the Security Council proof of intervention by Yugoslavia, Albania and Bulgaria. A United Nations Commission to investigate the position was appointed in January 1947 by the Security Council.

Meanwhile the Greek economic plight was growing worse. U.N.R.R.A. supplies would shortly cease. The British Government could afford no more help.

On March 12th President Truman asked Congress to grant 400,000,000 dollars for the assistance of Greece and Turkey and put forward what came to be known as the 'Truman Doctrine':

'We shall not realise our objective unless we are willing to help free peoples to maintain their free institutions and their national integrity against movements that seek to impose upon them totalitarian regimes.'

The civil war continued. Intervention from Greece's northern neighbours continued. But action on the report of the U.N. Commission was prevented in July by the use of the veto by the Russian representative on the Security Council. The Greek question was transferred to the Assembly, which set up the Balkan Commission to work in the field. But the work of this commission was boycotted by Yugoslavia, Albania and Bulgaria.

In this atmosphere of international frustration the civil war reached one of its climaxes on Christmas eve when 'General' Markos, the rebel leader, proclaimed a 'free Greek Government' and simultaneously launched a mass attack on the border town of Konitza. This attack was eventually beaten off and the rebels retreated, most of them across the border to Albania.

But the intensity of rebel action in the north and in the Peloponnese was not relaxed. A successful campaign of abduction of children to the northern countries spread terror and despair. The Greek Army of 150,000 men could not defeat the 30,000 rebels who were always able to seek sanctuary and supplies across the northern borders. Meanwhile the Greek economy was hampered and overburdened by the demands of military operations and the ever-increasing number of refugees.

ITALY

The peace treaty which was signed with Italy in February 1947, though not ratified until the autumn, provided that if the four Foreign Ministers could not settle the future of the Italian colonies within a year of the treaty coming into force the problem should be submitted to the United Nations. To help the Foreign Ministers a Commission was set up to visit Tripolitania, Cyrenaica, Eritrea and Somaliland and report to the Council. There was no agreement either in the Commission or between the Foreign Ministers and the problem was therefore referred to the United Nations Assembly at its 1948 session.

Italy was governed between December 1945 and May 1947 by an all-party coalition under the premiership of Signor di Gasperi, leader of the Christian Democratic Party. In January 1947 Signor Nenni, the leader of the Italian Socialist Party, advocated fusion with the Communists, a course to which the majority of his party agreed. Signor Saragat strongly resisted this move and formed an independent Socialist Party. The division in the Socialist ranks was one of the factors which ended the coalition. From May 1947 until the General Election in April 1948 the coalition was carried on without the Communists or the Nenni Socialists.

Mr. Morgan Phillips, Secretary of the British Labour Party, went to Italy in March 1948 with the aim of persuading Signor Nenni to withdraw from his electoral alliance with the Communists. Having failed, he sent Signor Saragat a message of warm support. But his lead was not followed by all Socialists. On April 17th, on the eve of the elections, a telegram of encouragement was sent to Signor Nenni and this was reported to have been signed by thirty-seven British Socialist Members of Parliament. It was later announced that fifteen of these had never consented to their names being put on the telegram. Mr. Platts-Mills, M.P., who had organized the telegram, was expelled from the Socialist Party.

On March 20th the Western Powers proposed a revision of the Italian peace treaty so as to restore Trieste to Italy. Mr. Eden had

Foreign Affairs

never liked the compromise solution adopted in the treaty by which Trieste became a 'Free Territory'. He said that 'it savoured too much of the Danzig plan after the last war, and asked too much of international tolerance to be workable under present conditions'. The Russians, who had previously proposed the return of the Italian colonies to Italian control in order to encourage Communist support in the Election, now refused to reconsider the peace treaty. But the final result of the elections was that Signor di Gasperi's Christian Democrat Party won a complete majority, though he continued to lead a coalition in which the Saragat Socialists participated but not the Communist-Nenni Socialist bloc.

U.S.A.

It was clear before the beginning of 1947 that the U.S.A. had no intention of returning to an isolationist policy. A bi-partisan foreign policy was being developed between the two great parties, and most of the Republicans in the Senate, under the leadership of Senator Vandenberg, were giving full support to the Democrat Administration's policy.

The 'Truman doctrine' for Greece and Turkey was announced on March 12th, and three months later Mr. Marshall made his famous offer to Europe. The U.S.A. Government gave its full support to the United Nations, whose headquarters was established in New York.

A. UNITY IN FOREIGN POLICY

Mr. Bevin returned from the abortive Moscow conference, and reported to the House of Commons on May 15th in a full Debate, in which Mr. Eden took a leading part. After this Mr. Bevin went to the Socialist Conference at Margate on May 29th to face the critics in his own party, whom he roundly accused of having stabbed him in the back.

The pamphlet *Cards on the Table* was accepted in general by Dr. Dalton for the Party.

At the end of April the Secretary for Overseas Trade had entered into trade negotiations with the Soviet Minister for Trade in Moscow. He made a second visit to Moscow in June, but the

World Affairs, 1947 to May 1948

discussions were broken off when it became impossible to reach agreement over the terms of repayment by Russia of the 1941 credit. (An agreement was eventually signed on December 27th 1947.)

Mr. Eden spoke at Leamington Town Hall on June 7th. During the same day he received the Freedom of Warwick, one of the four men to be given this honour in the last hundred years. The following is the part of his speech in which he referred to foreign affairs.

I have always felt it to be an immense national advantage if British foreign policy in its broadest lines can be above party controversy. One of the reasons why American foreign policy after this world war has been both strong and decisive, whereas after the last world war it was weak and negative, is that President Truman has continued the system inaugurated so wisely by President Roosevelt during the war whereby foreign affairs are conducted on a non-party, or rather, as our American friends call it, on a bi-partisan basis. At most of the major conferences since the war the United States have been represented by Republicans as well as by Democrats.

Since the advent to power of the Socialist Party we of the Conservative Opposition have, therefore, been glad to find it possible to give Mr. Bevin a very large measure of support in his foreign policy. In many respects as regards world affairs it has differed little, if at all, from the policy which we would have pursued. Nor is this surprising, for during the war years we worked together as a War Cabinet, comprising members of all the parties and pursuing a foreign policy upon which all were agreed. We sought then to maintain the unity of the Allies against a common enemy, and to use that unity to lay the foundations of peace. We wished to translate into the period of peace the mutual understanding that we had won in war. In this sense, therefore, it is, I think, fair to say that the present Government has been following

Foreign Affairs

the same objective. I should be the last to deny the difficult conditions in which they have to do so when discussions round the conference table succeeded to joint Allied effort in pursuit of victory.

It is, therefore, all the more astonishing to read in the recent Labour Party pamphlet, *Cards on the Table*, a series of statements which not only totally ignore the support which our Party has given to the Government in their foreign policy, but which even suggest that, had we been in power, we should have pursued totally different aims. It is suggested, for instance, that a Conservative Government would have refused to contribute financially and in other respects to U.N.R.R.A. and the reconstruction of Europe. The pamphlet accuses Mr. Churchill of cynical selfishness in seeking to maintain a proper level of nutrition in this country at the expense of the rest of Europe. How ungenerous this is and how foolish when you consider that U.N.R.R.A. was set up largely as a result of British initiative at a time when Mr. Churchill was head of the British Government and I myself was Foreign Secretary.

The same Socialist document also suggests that if the Conservative Party had been in power we would have responded to the Albanians' mining of British destroyers by a naval bombardment instead of by appealing to the Security Council. There is not the slightest justification for this statement. Faith in the United Nations and a determination to keep faith with the Charter is not for us a party issue. The first agreement to build a United Nations Organization was reached at the Moscow Conference in 1943 by Mr. Hull, Mr. Molotov and myself, and consistently received the strong endorsement of the then Prime Minister, Mr. Churchill, and of all our other colleagues. It was also my privilege to head the delegation at San Francisco, which drew up the Charter. Equally fantastic is the charge that we should have sought an exclusive Anglo-American alliance expressly directed against Russia. We would have done no such thing. What we worked for in the war and what we should have worked

170

for in peace was the widest possible measure of understanding between the great Powers who were Allies on the battlefield. Here let me add that criticism of Mr. Churchill in this respect seems to me monstrous, because there is no man who contributed more by his individual courage and genius to promote Allied unity in war and thereby to make possible Allied unity in peace.

Perhaps one should not attach too much importance to this extraordinary document, *Cards on the Table*. Issued as an official Socialist Party statement, with great fanfares of publicity, it had apparently never been seen by the Foreign Secretary, and was only later approved by the Executive Committee of the Labour Party at its Margate conference. With its brutal frankness towards the Soviet Union, with its patronizing criticism of the United States, and with its wholly unwarranted attacks on the Conservative Party, it is surely a remarkable example of a new method of diplomacy by universal insult.

We have all of us regretted the failure of the Moscow Conference, and there have been some developments since then which must also cause grave concern to all observers of the European scene. I am referring, in particular, to the latest developments in Hungary. As far as we can judge from the reports in the Press, this appears to be an example of open and cynical interference by a great Power in the internal affairs of a small neighbour. Whatever the record of the Hungarians may have been, the fact remains that the present Hungarian Government of Smallholders was elected in the autumn of 1945 in a free election by the votes of 50 per cent of the electorate. The action recently taken by the Soviet authorities results from attempts on the part of the Communist minority to undermine and overthrow the majority party. As a result of this the Secretary-General of the Smallholders Party was arrested three months ago by the Soviet authorities and has evidently been subjected to a long interrogation. He was arrested on a charge of espionage against the Soviet army, after the local Communists had failed to secure the waiver of his Parliamentary immunity. The confession which he has now made is said to implicate the Prime Minister and other leading members of the Party, who are being accused of conspiring to overthrow the State.

In the absence of full information it is impossible to pronounce final judgment on the case, but it seems clear that it is a move designed to secure the establishment of a Communist-controlled regime before the entry into force of the Treaty of Peace and the ultimate withdrawal of the Soviet troops.

To those of use who have been looking and hoping for the development among the Central European countries of political and economic ties with Western Europe, as well as with their great Eastern European neighbour, as part of the general reconstruction and pacification of Europe, this development is inevitably a matter of deep regret and anxiety.

There is one other aspect of Anglo-Soviet relations to which I must refer. We were all glad to hear the account recently given in the House of Commons of the opening of trade negotiations with Russia, and we wish every success to these negotiations. There is no reason to lose all hope of success on account of political difficulties alone. On the contrary, economic progress is one of the surest remedies for political aches and pains. There can be no doubt of the resources of the Soviet Union and also no doubt that in respect of certain commodities, such as timber, she could make a valuable contribution to our most urgent needs. But if an agreement is to be of real value, then the contributions must be mutual and immediate. By this I mean that we cannot be expected to make deliveries to the Soviet Union now in return for deliveries from them in a vague and unspecified future.

B. FOREIGN POLICY IN EUROPE

By the beginning of June, Press reports from the capitals of Eastern Europe created great anxiety in Britain. On June 5th Mr. Marshall had said:

World Affairs, 1947 to May 1948

'It is evident that before the U.S. Government can proceed much further to alleviate the situation and help start the European world on the way to recovery, there must be some agreement among the countries of Europe as to the requirements of the situation and the part those countries themselves will take in order to give proper effect to whatever advice might be undertaken by this Government. It would be neither fitting nor efficacious for this Government to undertake to draw up unilaterally a programme designed to place Europe on its feet economically. This is the business of Europeans. The initiative must come from Europe. . . . It is logical that the U.S.A. should do whatever it is able to do to assist in the return of normal economic health in the world without which there can be no political stability and no assured peace. Our policy is directed not against any country or doctrine, but against hunger, poverty, desperation and chaos.'

In the House of Commons on 19th June 1947 Mr. Eden opened a Debate on 'Foreign Policy in Europe' by outlining the position in Europe, and ended on a note of hope by discussing the Marshall offer. Mr. Bevin, who had been in touch with the French government, followed with a short statement, which is given at the end of Mr. Eden's speech.

Mr. Molotov attended the meeting in Paris, but after discussion he refused to participate in a European economic plan and on Russian instructions the Eastern European satellites, some of which had at first accepted the invitation to co-operate, withdrew from the plan. Mr. Eden reinforced his advice to the Government by an appeal at Leeds on July 5th:

'In these circumstances the duty of our statesmen is clear. They must go straight ahead in collaboration with our French friends and all the other nations who are willing to come in and make a plan in response to Mr. Marshall's historic offer. The essential is that the response to the offer should not be delayed.'

Foreign Affairs

Every Member of this Committee who has been studying recent developments in the international sphere, whether here in Europe or in the Far East, must have have felt increasingly concerned at the trend of events. We in this country have consistently felt that the only wholly satisfactory basis for international peace was close friendship and collaboration between the great Powers whose joint action brought victory on the battlefield. On that issue there is, I think, no dispute anywhere in the Committee. That policy was pursued by the Coalition Government and by the so-called Caretaker Government, and I have no doubt it is being pursued with equal sincerity by the present Government. That was our objective; I think I could say it was our national objective. To an increasing extent we have failed to realize it, and that failure to reach constructive Allied agreement has paralysed European recovery.

The Yalta decision, the Potsdam Declaration, the Charter of the United Nations, the Armistice terms and the Peace Treaties so recently concluded are all based upon the assumption that the victorious Powers would work together and that they would pursue a common policy towards the smaller nations, whether those smaller nations were liberated Allied states or former adversary satellites. For instance, the Yalta Declaration pledged the signatories, all of us, to promote free elections and to allow the nations to choose their own forms of Government. We undertook to help the liberated nations and former Axis satellites—if I may quote:

'to solve by democratic means their political and economic problems.'

The Armistice terms signed with the defeated satellite Powers set up Allied Control Commissions, and by the terms of those various agreements the Allies have obligations to keep each other informed of events in the respective enemy countries. For example, when the right hon. Gentleman the Foreign Secretary asked the Soviet Government the other day for information in respect of recent events in Hungary, he was not merely exercising his own undoubted right under the Armistice terms, but he was also reminding the Soviet Government of what it was that Government's duty to do without being asked. Those facts need to be borne in mind.

I would ask the Committee to look for a moment at the contrasting position in Italy, where the forces of occupation are Anglo-American—whereas in Hungary they are, of course, Russian—and we have always sought to keep the Soviet representatives informed. So far as I know, that has been successfully accomplished. Certainly, I cannot recall any single occasion when the Soviet Government asked for information and were not given it. As I have mentioned the example of Italy, perhaps I might refer to the great pleasure with which I think all Members of the Committee have seen the final conclusion of agreement for the withdrawal of British troops from Italy after the entry into force of the treaty. I think that step is a real contribution not only to Anglo-Italian friendship which we all wish to see restored, but to the recovery and stability of Europe as a whole.

In contrast to those events, I must ask the Committee to look for a moment at what is happening, as far as we are able to judge, in Eastern Europe. . . .[1]

Now a word about Austria. There we saw an ugly political crisis flare up suddenly on the report that the Communist leader, Herr Fischer, had been holding meetings with the leading members of the People's Party—the People's Party which headed the poll in the general election of 1945. Here we are dealing with an ex-enemy country under Four-Power occupation, and so, of course, a different technique is involved, a technique using internal rather than external pressure. But we see this result. It

[1] Mr. Eden went on then to a full analysis of the position in Bulgaria and Rumania, briefly summarized above.

Foreign Affairs

appears that the Chancellor, Dr. Figl, was pressed to reshuffle his cabinet on a basis more favourable to the Communists, who at present, I think, hold only four out of 165 seats in the Austrian Chamber.

If I assume that the pressure comes from the quarter I named it is because it has done so in every country in Eastern Europe. Is that an unnecessarily rash assumption? I leave the Committee to judge. But wherever it came from, the point that I am making is that the Communist Party, which, as I say, holds only four out of 165 seats, is, in fact, in Austria a fragmentary one—not unlike the Communist Party, in point of fact, in this country. The pressure there is for enlargements of the Communist membership, apparently—here again I am only estimating—but apparently in return for some prospective Soviet concessions in regard to reparations and the signature of the treaty. That is what I think is happening.

For the moment the situation appears to be held. But coming so soon after the Hungarian *coup*, these events can hardly fail to cause further apprehension. Where is the next move to be? Will it be Finland, hitherto comparatively free from external pressure, but where already there are rumours of threats against the Right Wing Agrarians and, to a lesser degree, against the Social Democrats? Or will it be in Italy, where the present Christian Democratic Government is wrestling valiantly with a severe financial crisis and a heavy burden of unemployment? We do not know. We cannot say. Hon. Gentlemen may retort to me: 'If you have not certain knowledge you should not throw out these dangerous suppositions.' I would reply that, by making it clear that we are under no illusions that such attempts may be made His Majesty's Government can best contribute to forestalling them.

But the realities have to be faced, and I believe that in the long run we do not do any good to Anglo-Soviet relations if we pretend to accept replies which, in our heart of hearts, we find it impossible to believe. We have to face this fact, that ratification

World Affairs, 1947 to May 1948

of the peace treaties with which the right hon. Gentleman struggled for so long a period, is taking place in conditions of considerable cynicism, and the concessions for which he fought hardest—and all honour to him for doing so—such as the human rights clauses, with their safeguards of such very simple things as the right of free speech, are being flouted in many lands before the ink on the document is dry.

Wherever we turn we see, too, delay in reaching vital agreements. Six months ago I was happy to congratulate the right hon. Gentleman—and rightly so—on the Trieste solution, yet what is happening there? Today there appears to be deadlock over the choice of Governor. I must say—and I choose my words—that the effect of all this is, unhappily, to undermine confidence between the victors in the late war. That is deplorable, and there is no one in this Committee who does not regret it. But for those of us who do really want to see Anglo-American-Soviet friendship, it would be hypocritical to pretend that confidences are unshaken, or that good relations are unimpaired. I must add one personal word on this. I do not forget that a little more than twelve years ago I was the first British Minister to go to the Soviet Union after the revolution; I do not regret that in the war years I saw, as did some of my colleagues, the Russian battlefields. I know something of the terrible price Russia paid in life for the Allied victory, and there is in our minds always—and it is true today that there is still—an immense fund of good will in this country towards the Soviet Union, but that good will can now be evoked only on the basis of sincere partnership and mutual respect. There is really no other way.

If that was all I had to say to the Committee this afternoon I should feel that the outlook would even justify Dr. Johnson's inspissated gloom. Happily that is not so, and for a very few moments more I want to refer to Mr. Marshall's recent initiative. That momentous offer by the United States Secretary of State, made in his Harvard speech, has brought new hope to Europe and to the world. It is, indeed, a generous action, and one which

177

Foreign Affairs

deserves to rank with 'the most unsordid act in history'. The offer is not only important in so far as it affects the economies of both Europe and the United States; it is not merely that dollars may be made available to countries whose economies are now dying for lack of dollars or what dollars can buy, although that is important enough. This offer can mean much more than that. It can mean that European countries are going to be stimulated to agree upon common economic measures for their joint salvation. Such, indeed, is the first step towards that united Europe which my right hon. Friend the Leader of the Opposition has so much at heart.

In the Foreign Affairs Debate in this Committee in November 1945, I made a plea for a transformation of relations between nations, and for the consequent modification of some of our conceptions of sovereignty. Since then, I have on several occasions, both in this Committee and outside, urged the Government, so far as I could, to take steps to secure closer co-operation in economic matters with our Western neighbours, and particularly with France. All this is, of course, wholly compatible with the progressive development, which we all want to see, within the Empire, both for the Dominions and for the Colonies. If the Committee want an example of that they have only to look at what has been done, on a smaller scale, in this sphere in the Benelux Agreement between Belgium, the Netherlands and Luxembourg. By the end of this year, in spite of all the difficulties which had to be overcome—and they have been formidable—these countries will have established a complete customs union between them. I think that one of the results of that will be that this group of small countries will then become probably the third trading power of the world; that is, with their overseas partners, of course. Admittedly, such negotiations take time, and I am not saying that there is a solution of Europe's difficulties, because time is just what we cannot afford. We, the countries of Europe, as I see it, have to meet an economic crisis which will reach its peak in the next twelve months—perhaps in the next six months.

World Affairs, 1947 to May 1948

Mr. Marshall, in putting forward this offer, has, quite rightly, made it clear that while the United States Government are prepared to help, it is for the European countries themselves to agree as to their requirements, and as to the part which they can and will play in making the best possible use of America's assistance. Mr. Marshall, I have no doubt, has memories—as have the right hon. Gentleman and the Prime Minister—of the Combined Chiefs of Staff and the Combined Food Boards in Washington during the war. It would seem perhaps that, according to his experience then, he now wishes to know what Europe's requirements are. He will wish to satisfy himself, and the American people will wish to satisfy themselves, that those requirements have been properly examined, analysed and pruned, so that the American help, whether in dollars or in commodities, can be made available in the right place and in the proper quantity. There may be some hon. Members who say—and it has been said to me already by others not in this Committee—'But are you sure that our American friends are really going to go through with this plan?' Well, I would reply to that, that the best contribution we can make to winning a favourable answer to that question is to prepare a plan with which they can go ahead.

I will mention one other aspect of this question which has to be remembered. The importance to a creditor nation, and especially a creditor nation on the scale of the United States, of restoring the prosperity of Europe hardly needs any argument. I think I am right in saying that last year the United States had a favourable balance of trade at the rate of more than 5,000,000,000 dollars a year. I understand that that figure is now probably much larger. If the United States is to continue as a great exporting nation, then clearly it is of the first importance to her to try to build up European prosperity, and that cannot be done quickly. Perhaps it could never be done at all if the shortage—indeed, the famine—in dollars is not relieved.

So I come to put one or two questions to the right hon. Gentleman, and I leave it to him whether he feels he can answer now or on some later occasion. What organization, what machinery, will have to be set up to enable Europe to put forward her requirements? Is it possible to adapt any existing machinery for this purpose? Can we make use, for instance, of the Economic Commission for Europe, or do we require some special organization for this immediate purpose? On these points I am not prepared to be dogmatic, but I should think it likely that the urgency of the present task might well call for special handling. In any event, it is important, and I should have thought desirable, that the Economic Commission for Europe, set up by the United Nations, where decisions are taken by a majority vote, should be associated with this work in some way.

In my view it was correct that the right hon. Gentleman should make the first approach to our neighbour, France. Here, our relations are always close and intimate. At the same time, I was glad to note that he made a similar approach to the Soviet Union. In any plan, the needs of Germany must, of course, be taken into account, but whatever machinery may be employed, it is essential that the work shall be done with speed. We hope that all will join to help in this work, but if, unhappily, some countries should not wish to participate, it is still our duty to go on with those who will. I believe—and I say this in all sincerity to the right hon. Gentleman—that in this way we shall not only best serve those countries who do join, but also any countries, if there be any, who do not join, for by creating a prosperous and integrated association of countries in Europe, we shall provide not only a message of hope, but a magnetic attraction for all. In any event, the door will always be open, and if any will not come in now, they may do so later.

It is in convincing all concerned that the European system is strong, that it is not going to fall apart, that lies the best argument against the continuation of the present deadlock in European political affairs. No one will seek to minimize the difficulties which confront the right hon. Gentleman in reaching agreement on these issues, but at the same time the opportunities are immense, and, indeed, are unparalleled. We must not let them slip. We have, here in our hands, the possibility of creating a new era for our tortured Continent. Here is an absolutely free choice for East as well as for West. Here is that second chance that so rarely comes, and when it does come, has the nature of a miracle.

The Secretary of State for Foreign Affairs (Mr. Ernest Bevin): It may be for the convenience of the Committee if, at this stage, I make a very short statement—I shall, of course, be replying to the Debate later on. As the Committee will be aware, the French Foreign Minister and I have had preliminary contact on the subject of the United States Government, set forth in the speech of the American Secretary of State at Harvard on June 5th. We decided last night in Paris to propose to the Soviet Government that a meeting of the British, French and Soviet Foreign Ministers should be held during the week beginning June 23rd, in order to discuss these problems as a whole. The reply of the Soviet Government is awaited, and the Committee will understand that until it is received there is nothing I can usefully say on the subject today. I know the greatest interest of the Committee in the United States' proposal, and wish very much that it were possible to say more about the position. All I can do now is to repeat that we regard Mr. Marshall's offer as a great opportunity for Europe. It is a chance that His Majesty's Government will not miss. I have promised that we, for our part, will seize this opportunity and try to turn it to the greatest possible account. I think that so far we have lost no time in getting things started. We shall continue pushing ahead with all possible energy.

C. THE UNITED NATIONS

The second Regular Session of the United Nations Assembly began in New York on 16th September 1947. The events recorded above show how the relations between the great powers had deteriorated in European affairs. In the proceedings of the Security Council Russia showed the same refusal to co-operate in the

Foreign Affairs

re-establishment of peaceful conditions in Indonesia, in the establishment of a Commission for Control and Inspection of Atomic Energy, in the preparation of a military force to work under the Security Council and in the settlement of disputes referred to the Council. Whenever a decision was about to be reached which went against his instructions, the Russian representative used the veto. Thus the Security Council was unable to take any action over the mining of two British destroyers off Albania, nor over the Greek civil war, about which a United Nations Commission had reported cases of flagrant intervention on the side of the rebels by Yugoslavia, Bulgaria and Albania.

This use of the veto had reduced the Security Council to impotence in all important matters. Various opinions were held on the steps that should be taken to enable the United Nations machinery to be effective. Some had considered the abolition of the veto; the U.S.A. put forward the suggestion that the veto should only be used in certain circumstances; eventually a standing committee of the Assembly was set up, known as the 'Little Assembly', in which the veto did not operate, so that discussion could continue even when Russia did not want discussion.

Mr. Eden wrote the following article, which was published on 16th September 1947.

In these days international confidence is not robust, and that is an understatement. Exceptional significance therefore attaches to the meeting of the Assembly of the United Nations, which opens today. Will this gathering of the representatives of more than fifty nations register real progress, or must we read just one more record of disappointed hopes? The omens, it must be admitted, are not auspicious, nor are hopes likely to run high, but before we comment on our immediate problems it is surely wise to examine the implications of this meeting in its true historical perspective.

The United Nations Organization was not the creation of a rosy idealism but of stern reality. The discoveries of science within

World Affairs, 1947 to May 1948

the memory of many now living have served to enrich and some-times to endanger the world, but above all to contract it. We have entered an age when no natural barrier, whether mountain or ocean, can guarantee security against the new weapons which science has placed at the disposal of mankind. Professor Trevelyan in his brilliant book, *English Social History*, wrote: 'Man has changed more in the last hundred years than in the previous thousand.'

Whether we like it or not, we are all now one another's neigh-bours. A century ago, difficulties of communication and transport created shock-absorbers in the world's reaction to events. Now all that is changed. We now all live not only on the same planet but in the same parish and almost on the same street. There is no escape from rubbing shoulders, and so we must seek some form of world order or endure world brawling and world chaos. The Soviet Union, however, seems unwilling either to accept this truth for herself or to allow others to base their collective conduct upon it.

These same scientific discoveries which have outpaced political man have taught us another lesson, that of the interdependence of nations. There is no nation, however powerful and however rich in material resources, that cannot gain more for its people in association with others than by its own individual efforts within its own boundaries. It is the task of the United Nations to give con-structive expression to that interdependence of nations. Here again it is the Soviet Union whose practices have obstructed progress.

Is the present organization of the United Nations capable of fulfilling its task, and is its machinery adequate? That machinery is certainly not perfect. We can probably most of us think of some amendments that we should like to make, and we should probably all start off with the same one—the Veto. But my question is not: Would we like to amend the machinery? My question is: Is it adequate? In other words, can it be made to fulfil our purpose if the United Nations are determined in all sincerity to use it? The answer to this is Yes, emphatically Yes.

The present Charter represented the greatest common measure of agreement attainable when it was drafted. Admittedly that was in the pre-atomic age, but if fairly and honestly used the Charter will work, just as the League of Nations could have been made to work. In my experience of international affairs, it is the human factor, as expressed in the policy of Governments, and not the mechanical shortcomings, that has caused our failures.

The United Nations Charter was drafted on the assumption that all those who were joining the organization would sincerely wish to work it. No other basis was possible. It was certainly never contemplated at the time that the Charter was drafted that the veto would be abused as it has been by the Soviet Union. Not only the records, but the spirit of the discussions at San Francisco show that clearly enough. Indeed, the implication that there should be unanimity between the Great Powers is in itself perfectly good sense for without unanimity, which in its turn implies an example by the Great Powers in the acceptance of a rule of law, the United Nations can never fully serve its purpose. Yet the Soviet Union has so completely distorted the essential purpose of the Charter as to create the inevitable impression that her intention is to make the whole machinery unworkable. The veto in the Security Council has so far been used twenty times—eighteen times by the Soviet Union.

This brings us to the sources of Soviet conduct and to the methods we should employ in the light of that conduct. No advantage is to be gained merely by a policy of appeasement. By this I mean that there is no advantage to be derived for world peace by yielding upon some issue of principle to which we are pledged, merely in the hope that by so doing we shall placate the Soviet Union. Such tactics only weaken our self-respect without gaining the respect of others. On the other hand, while firmness and vigilance are indispensable, neither threats nor bluster are going to get us anywhere. To be unshakable in essentials, to be patient in explanation of what is our point of view, even at the cost of endless repetition, to be cool and to leave the door open for agreement, these should be our present directives.

World Affairs, 1947 to May 1948

It seems unlikely that we shall see any important change in Soviet policies in the immediate future. Their whole trend today seems to be towards excluding foreign contacts and deriding all that is not Communist-inspired. Nor is there any encouragement for us in the new Marxian drive in Russia which includes both art and letters. Even Picasso, it seems, is now proscribed. There is no art but Soviet art. Long live Soviet art, even if nobody wants to look at it. In the Soviet Union, at any rate, nobody will be allowed to look at anything else. This is the most miserable parochialism. In spirit it is poles apart from the spirit of the United Nations.

We should not, however, accept it as inevitable that present Soviet policies will continue for all time. Immediate problems may be vexing and disheartening, but this must not cause us to lose grip of long-term opportunities. However discouraging the present phase may be, we should do well to remember that it may prove to be no more than a phase.

This does not mean that we should be half-hearted in our faith. On the contrary, let us hold to it and understand it. 'Ideals in politics,' wrote Lord Acton, 'are never realized, but the pursuit of them determines history.' How true that is. But we must temper our idealism with an understanding of the problems that confront us. To create confidence and to build peace is a long-term business, and the prize is the greatest that the human race has to win.

The forthcoming Assembly of the United Nations will be crucial. The principal items on the agenda, apart from the Palestine question, are the frontier disputes in Greece and the abolition, or limitation, of the Veto.

Greece displayed unsurpassed gallantry in the late war and suffered severely in consequence. The heroism of her people is beyond question, and, having seen their tense courage in a dark hour, I can never cease to pay it tribute. Unhappily, however, Greece is a country in which political opinions have always tended to extremes. It would, nevertheless, be wrong to pretend that this is the cause of the dangerous situation which has developed on her northern frontiers. This she owes, above all, to her northern neighbours. When, therefore, the United States Government proposed a permanent Balkan Commission of Investigation, which would have allowed the world to know and to judge the truth of events on Greece's northern frontiers, they were suggesting a course which was not only within the rights of the United Nations but their positive duty.

I have little doubt that the mere establishment of such a Commission would in itself have done much to steady the situation. Russia's veto of this proposal was therefore a challenge to the whole purpose of the United Nations, and indefensible on the part of any country which purports to observe the spirit of the Charter.

The Soviet Union, by its veto of the United States proposal, is not only preventing the necessary establishment of facts, but is also preventing any positive action from being taken. Such a state of affairs cannot be allowed to continue indefinitely. No country can prosper under constant threats to the security of her frontiers, still less a country which has suffered at enemy hands as Greece has suffered. It is therefore salutary that the issue should be brought to a head at the Assembly.

Our concern, the concern of all the United Nations, should be for the unity of the world, its freedom and its harmony. These objectives can be achieved only by continual vigilance and by prompt action wherever danger threatens. If, by invariable obstruction on the part of one Great Power, such action is wholly prevented or indefinitely delayed, the right of veto must be restricted or the whole machinery of the United Nations will be brought to a standstill.

These are the stark realities. No thoughtful person can wish to write them down. But they must be faced. This does not mean that it is too late for wiser counsels to prevail. No one who has faith in international organization can be prepared to accept defeat in the struggle at this stage. We must not yet abandon the battle for unity. The stake is too high. The hour is full late, but the Soviet Union can yet show by her conduct at the Assembly that she understands that she, too, has a share in that stake, and will modify her policy to give effect to the true spirit of her own engagements.

D. WESTERN UNION

The representatives of the sixteen nations who had joined together to make a plan for European recovery in answer to Mr. Marshall's offer, met in Paris and agreed on measures for economic co-operation, which were presented to the U.S. Government at the end of September 1947.

The Russian answer to this was a carefully organized strike programme in France and Italy with the object of disrupting the economy of those countries and thus sabotaging the recovery plan or destroying Governments. Co-ordinated Communist action was made easier by the establishment of the Cominform in October 1947. Earlier, Russia had sponsored an economic alliance between Czechoslovakia and Poland and a series of trade pacts with Czechoslovakia, Bulgaria and Hungary.

The London meeting of the Council of Foreign Ministers broke down on December 15th. On December 16th Mr. Eden, at a meeting at Wolverhampton, outlined the situation and called for a closer Western European association without further delay.

On 22nd January 1948, Mr. Bevin reported to the House of Commons on the breakdown of the Foreign Ministers' Council and gave his proposal for a Western Union. Mr. Eden, who had been on a short visit to Iraq, Iran, Saudi Arabia and Greece during the Christmas recess, replied to Mr. Bevin with a full survey of the position and a warm welcome for the Western Union proposals.

The Brussels Pact, by which Western Union between France, Belgium, Holland, Luxembourg and the United Kingdom was formally concluded, was signed on 17th March 1948.

A congress of European Union arranged by a number of United Europe organizations, of which Mr. Churchill's United Europe Movement was one, took place at the Hague in May. The Chairman of the Socialist Party Executive, Mr. Shinwell, had written discouraging Socialist Members of Parliament from attending. This decision met with the approval of the *Daily Herald* and many Socialists. Others made it clear that

Foreign Affairs

they would attend the Congress. M.P.s of all parties gave general support to a motion on the Order Paper for close political union in Western Europe.

On May 5th Mr. Eden opened the second day of the Foreign Affairs Debate with a speech on Western Union in which he referred to this Motion.

As I listened yesterday to a number of speeches in the Debate, one dominant reflection was left in my mind, as I think it must have been in the minds of Members in all parts of the House—how fantastically horrible it is that almost exactly three years from the day of victory we should be making speeches in this House and once again mentioning the word 'war'. It is fantastically horrible, but perhaps it is better than that we should drift into actual conflict in part because we do not understand. It would be wrong in my judgment if this knowledge of the deterioration of our situation were to induce anything in our minds of the nature of fatalism. I do regard the present international situation as very dangerous, but I do not regard it as desperate, and the purpose of my few comments this afternoon, is to try to put before the House some considerations which I hope will be regarded as constructive in character.

I will say a few words about the Motion on the Order Paper and the Amendments.

[*That, in the opinion of this House, steps should now be taken, in consultation with the other members of the British Commonwealth, to create in Western Europe a political union strong enough to save European democracy and the values of Western civilization, and a trading area large enough, with the Colonial Territories, to enable its component parts to achieve economic recovery and stability;*

That for this purpose there should be an emergency policy designed to secure immediate and effective co-operation between the countries of

188

Western Europe, and a long-term policy designed to bring into being a federation of Europe;

That the emergency policy should establish forthwith a Council of Western Europe consisting of representatives of the governments of the sixteen participating countries in the European Recovery Plan, and Western Germany, to lay down the broad lines of common action; that the Council should have power to set up permanent international staffs to co-ordinate the social, economic and defence policies; that the first and most important task of the economic staff would be to frame concrete proposals for the stabilization of the currencies of Western Europe, for the development of trade, for the execution of the European Recovery Plan, for a comprehensive production plan, including agriculture and the heavy industries, and for Colonial development; that the necessary staffs should act under the direction, and by the authority, of the Council of Western Europe, and should be in continuous session;

That the long-term policy should be to create a democratic federation of Europe, with a constitution based on the principles of common citizenship, political freedom, and representative government, including a charter of human rights; that such a federation should have defined powers with respect to such matters as external affairs, defence, currency, customs, and the planning of production, trade, power and transport; and that to achieve this objective, the Governments of the States of Western Europe should take steps to convene, as soon as practicable, a constituent assembly composed of representatives chosen by the Parliaments of the participating States, to frame a constitution for such a federation.]

The conception of European unity is, of course, not new. It has never been quite dead since the days of the Roman Empire when, it is a sobering reflection to recollect, a man might travel and trade between the Scottish Border and North Africa, even perhaps to the Sudan, with security both for his person and his property. Throughout the Middle Ages under the Roman Church, at least until the period of the Reformation, the inhabitants of Europe still thought in terms of a United Christendom, and still regarded themselves in some sense as citizens of Europe.

Foreign Affairs

The Reformation and the bloodthirsty conflicts that followed broke up this unity until M. de Sully, the famous Minister of King Henry IV of France in the early years of the seventeenth century put forward the first concrete proposals for forming a United States of Europe in what he called his 'Grand Design'. Despite dynastic wars and national rivalries, this idea persisted. In more recent times two major attempts by Germany to impose her own form of unity on Europe have been foiled, but each of these in turn left behind it political fears, economic misery and general demoralization to an extent which could scarcely have been imagined by the dwellers of Europe at the beginning of this century. The tragedy of it all is that the more patent the political and economic interdependence of nations, the sharper have become the national rivalries and antagonisms.

As the House knows, I have always been in favour of closer relations between the Western Powers, and, as many members of the present Government know, conversations on this subject had already taken place in general terms before the war ended. There were, however, difficulties in making progress then, one of which was that the exiled Governments quite rightly from their point of view felt some hesitation in committing themselves without fresh contact with their own electorates. Therefore, there is much in the terms of this Motion with which I personally agree. The account which the Foreign Secretary gave us yesterday showed that steady progress is being made with Western Union in many spheres. That is all to the good, and we shall look forward to further accounts from time to time.

The fact that the result of the pursuit of this policy must be to bring us closer to the nations of Western Europe underlines the essential importance of the position of the British Commonwealth and Empire in relation to these discussions. For us in this House as a whole the welfare of the Commonwealth and Empire must always be the first consideration. This is paramount. I hope, therefore, that the Prime Minister will be able this afternoon to give us some information about the conversations which must undoubtedly have taken place on these questions with our great partners overseas. We have seen the speeches of Field-Marshal Smuts and, if I remember rightly, Mr. Mackenzie King warmly supporting the conception of the Western European Union, and I have no doubt the Governments of the Commonwealth are not only being kept informed at every stage of these discussions but, as the right hon. Gentleman said yesterday, being consulted.

It is indeed absolutely essential that in an endeavour on this scale and of this kind, and as the right hon. Gentleman said yesterday, a fresh development of British policy, the Empire should be with us at every stage. That is one reason why I should myself have some reservations about this Motion which is on the Order Paper. I am anxious that the closest possible relationship should be established between ourselves and the other nations of Western Europe, but there is one condition to such progress which must be absolute, and it is that the Empire is with us in the conception and the execution of that plan at every stage.

I would hope that it might be possible in the reasonably near future to have a conference of Empire statesmen on these matters. I know, as the Prime Minister will admit, what are the difficulties in arranging such a meeting; elections, the inevitable concomitant of true democracy, take place at different times and in different parts of the Empire and there are many other obstacles. Still there have been such meetings before at critical times in our history and they have been invaluable—invaluable, may I say, in particular to the Foreign Secretary of the day. In these days of the full exchange of information with the Dominions it is possible to obtain from these discussions with Empire statesmen a point of view that is not only fully informed but fresh, given from a different angle and backed by unrivalled experience. The Prime Minister I know would agree, as would his right hon. Friend sitting beside him, how much help it was in the war to us to have that historic meeting of Empire statesmen. The problems which the House is now considering are equally

Foreign Affairs

as important as any in the war in relation to the future of the world. I very much hope, therefore, that such a meeting may soon be possible.

There is another consideration which must never be absent from our thoughts. It is essential when we are examining, as we are invited to do today, projects for closer relations between whole continents or any parts of them that we should not lose sight for one instant of the fact that there will be no real peace and a true sense of security in any part of the world unless and until there is acceptance by the nations of a rule of law, and unless a world authority is in being which is itself respected and can maintain that rule of law. Unhappily we are far from that state of affairs today. Our world is rapidly contracting in size, and more and more should it be apparent from recent experiences that one single part of the world cannot hope for long to remain at peace or to command prosperity if other sections of it are torn by conflict and shadowed by economic ruin.

Therefore, my first caution in respect both of the right hon. Gentleman's speech and the Motion on the Order Paper is that in considering these various regional agreements we must never forget the world aspect of our problem. When there is an effective world organization, regional organizations can be an invaluable buttress to the world organization. When the world organization is not effective, regional agreements, however good they may be, are only a second best. That I am afraid is the grim reality, but it does not absolve us from the task of seeking to increase a sense of security and with it a volume of trade and material prosperity in those areas where we have a special responsibility. Therefore, I for one would cordially support our efforts to co-ordinate and strengthen the economic, political and military agreements between the nations of the West.

I was glad, but I was not altogether surprised, to note that the Foreign Secretary said nothing at all yesterday to indicate that in his belief the Western Union must have any party political basis whether Socialist or otherwise. Of course, we are all of us

192

World Affairs, 1947 to May 1948

free to hope that there will be majorities in these various Western European lands which correspond to our own political faith wherever we may happen to sit in this House. Surely the essential is that the people of those lands shall be free to make their own choice as between one political party and another. That, we maintain, is what distinguishes the countries west of the Iron Curtain from those behind it.

I say to the Prime Minister, and I hope that he will agree, that it is quite untrue to suppose that in international affairs Socialists in the Government of one country cannot work with, let us say, Christian Democrats or Radicals or Conservatives in the Government of another. Perhaps I may give my personal experience. I never felt any difficulty in working at San Francisco with the Prime Minister himself or with Mr. Spaak, recently Socialist Prime Minister of Belgium, who has contributed a good deal to international goodwill in many spheres; or, in earlier years, with Mr. Blum, of course a Socialist. Equally, I am sure that the present Foreign Secretary does not feel any great difficulty when he is in discussion with the present Prime Minister of France or the present French Foreign Secretary, neither of them being Socialists, or in his conversations with Mr. Marshall. One has to be very careful in these matters. The truth is that there are many variants of Socialists and of Conservatives, and indeed of Liberals too. It is only the Communists who are all of one complexion. That is surely the fundamental difference between the totalitarian philosophy and the free philosophy.

It is so easy to delude oneself, as did so many Socialists at the last General Election, when they thought because they were Socialists they were best fitted to co-operate more and more closely with Soviet Russia. I never could understand that particular line of reasoning. I would remind the House now of some words of M. Herriot, which I quoted as a warning at the time of the General Election. He used them upon his release from German captivity, and I believe his words to be profoundly true. They were:

Foreign Affairs

'In Foreign policy . . . you can do nothing constructive if you subordinate that policy to considerations of home policy.'

I mention all these matters not in connection with the Foreign Secretary's speech yesterday at all, but because of the strange writings which have appeared from time to time in leading articles of the *Daily Herald* lately. For instance, on April 29th last, I read these words:

'We Socialists have a distinctive attitude to questions of European unity.'

(An Hon. Member: 'Hear, hear.') Rather a timid bird. I ask the Prime Minister to tell us when he replies, how is that attitude distinctive? In what way, for instance, does it differ from mine, or from the attitude of non-Socialist Ministers in Western Europe with whom all these negotiations have to take place? On the very next day, the *Daily Herald* went a little further and said:

'Why, then, should any British Socialist blur his party's attitude and confuse public opinion by joining an unrepresentative Congress which includes bitter opponents of Socialism?'

I would like to reply to that. I think that he should join because we seek the same things in Western Union. We seek the same results in foreign policy which the Foreign Secretary is at this time trying to pursue. Incidentally, there will be many distinguished Socialists present from all the countries in Western Europe. It is a misfortune for Europe, and it is confusing to opinion on the Continent, that the Government have adopted this attitude towards the Hague Conference. Surely, if we think we are going to be able to unite Europe it is a little unfortunate if we cannot even unite ourselves on an occasion when we happen all to agree. However that may be, let us hope that out of the considerable effort which is being put into The Hague Congress by many people of all parties and from many lands, including Socialist representatives from the other Western European countries, some constructive and helpful outcome will result which

194

will assist the right hon. Gentleman in his efforts. If so, we shall all be more than content.

There is something a little ungrateful in the attitude to my right hon. Friend the Member for Woodford (Mr. Churchill). I have the record here—it is not secret—of one of Mr. Marshall's interviews at the Press conference when he had just announced what has since been called the European Recovery Programme. It is worth inflicting it upon the House because of some of the answers given by Mr. Marshall. This extract is:

'(Q.) Could we go one step beyond—was the idea of shifting the initiative to Europe entirely an American idea, or did we get some indication from Europe that future over-all planning for reconstruction would be better, rather than by piecemeal?—(A.) No, we did not receive any indications—direct to us, that is. There had been discussion over there. Mr. Churchill had made some announcement about a United Europe. There had been other announcements of that kind. That was the situation as various proposals had developed but none of them had been brought to us direct.—(Q.) Mr. Secretary, Churchill's pronouncement for a United Europe envisaged, did it not, a political purpose for a United Europe?—(A.) Yes.—(Q.) You are not implying that we are following the Churchillian idea of a western political bloc?—(A.) We are following the proposition of their getting together in some way that will make it possible to try to restore the economy of Europe.'

That shows that Mr. Marshall's initiative was not uninfluenced by the initiative of my right hon. Friend. That is all I have to say about The Hague business for the moment. I only hope that the result will gratify the Government in such a way that we can all forget that attitude before the Congress takes place.

There is a further reflection that one ought to make when considering this question of Western Union. I believe that in the present state of the world there can be no more direct contribution to the maintenance of peace than the recovery and the prosperity, and with it the international authority, of the Western European nations. We want to stand on our own feet again, and to do that not only for reasons of self-respect, but also because it is thus that we can make our best contribution to peace. We have also, I regret to say, to accept the fact that in present conditions to build up the strength of the Western democracies must include co-ordinating and reinforcing their joint military effort. There is no escape from this in the world as it is today. In this connection my hon. and gallant Friend the Member for Carshalton (Brigadier Head) made some realistic observations yesterday. Nor do I consider that by ourselves alone—by 'ourselves' I mean the Western European Powers—we can bring our defences to that standard of security which is an indispensable guarantee of peace. For that, we shall need the help of the United States.

That does not mean that we ought not to get together in Europe to contribute the most that we can. Having done that, we should be most encouraged by the words that President Truman used in Congress a few weeks ago. He said this:

'I am sure that the determination of the free countries in Europe to protect themselves will be matched by an equal determination on our part to help them to do so.'

I should like to be assured, if possible by the Prime Minister today, that, so far as the Western European nations are concerned, every effort is being made to integrate our plans and our production effort so that there is the greatest economy as well as efficiency in the joint use of our manpower, of our raw materials, of our industrial power and of our geographical situation.

This brings me to what is the fundamental problem of this Debate, the policy of the Soviet Union, and it relates directly to the Motion which is on the Paper. It has always been part of the Communist ideology that what they call the capitalist world, which appears to be any part of the world that is not Communist, is tottering to its fall. I have asked myself many times in the last year or two, do the men in the Kremlin really believe today that the Western way of life is doomed? It is hard to believe that they really think that, especially when they contemplate the vast efforts, for instance, which the United States is making to rebuild the economy of Europe, a plan in the benefits of which, let us remember, the Soviet Union and her satellites were all invited to share. And if the Soviet Government does not believe this, then it is surely running great risks and hazarding peace in acting as if it did.

No doubt today there are great strains and stresses within the Soviet economy; that must be inevitable after the supreme effort that Soviet Russia made in the last war and after the wide devastation that the German armies caused. Yet is it really necessary, in order to explain those problems to the Soviet people, to pour out this daily barrage of abuse of the Western Powers and their representatives, and to pretend that they are antagonistic to the recovery of the Soviet Union? Maybe it is apprehension of the consequences of contact with the West that is the cause of this clear determination of the Soviet Union to break all these contacts and, in order to break them up, that this barrage of abuse continues day by day. Must the Soviet foreign policy continue to be based on this profound error of judgment? If it is, I fear that, however sincere our efforts, we shall not get far in restoring confidence between nations, because the Western way of life is not about to break up.

In all these projects which we are now considering for strengthening the Western nations, there is no provocation, there is no menace of war; on the contrary, cannot the Soviet Government rid itself of what appears to be this Communist obsession, if we are to judge by their own propaganda, as to the inevitability of war? It is they who always speak of this in their propaganda, and no one of us has the right to say that war is inevitable.

Mr. Scollan (Renfrew, Western): America must not say it.

Mr. Eden: America does not say it.

Mr. Scollan: They are saying it.

Mr. Eden: I say that no one of whatever nationality has the right to say that war is inevitable. The hon. Gentleman ought to distinguish between the daily Government propaganda of the Soviet Union and isolated, unwise voices in the United States of

Foreign Affairs

America. We never hear a single word of it from any responsible statesman in the United States, and we are bound to treat this propaganda as representing the view of the Government which emits it. The argument I have just used seems to me to be the only explanation of the Soviet Government's attitude to the Marshall Plan. The American Government invited the Soviet Government and the Eastern States to come in. M. Molotov refused to have anything to do with it because he claimed that the European Recovery Programme, to use his words, was:

'a violation of the sovereignty of European nations.'

He went further and exerted such pressure on his Eastern European neighbours that they also declined to come in—their mouths might have been watering, but they could not get any of the fruit. I believe that M. Molotov was wrong on two counts: first, because there must always be some merger of sovereignty in any common central organization for any international purpose, whether it is to maintain peace or even to fight a war; secondly, if M. Molotov thought that the surrender of sovereignty was in some way being made to the United States Government, I should have thought that Mr. Marshall's address to the Senate in presenting his programme was a complete answer to that charge.

Let me sum up. There seem to me to be three conclusions to draw from this Debate which I present to the House. The first is this: that there is a well-nigh unanimous desire in all parts of the House for the conclusion at the earliest possible date of the most comprehensive, immediate and practical agreement between the Western European Powers, in association, we trust, in due course with the United States. Secondly, there is a sincere desire for improved relations with the Soviet Union, but an absolute refusal to seek such an improvement by courses of weak appeasement which would fail to recognize the real facts and forces that are at work. In this connection I was glad to hear, and I endorse entirely, the Foreign Secretary's observations on the subject of Berlin. In a situation such as this, there is more danger in standing on a slippery slope than in standing four square on your own rights.

The third conclusion I draw is this: a conviction that successful negotiations can yet be conducted with the Soviet Union, but only from a basis of strength, when the Soviet Government itself learns that neither by sapping nor mining, neither by abuse nor by sabotage, can it force the Western people to change their way of life. I believe that there are men in the Kremlin far-seeing enough to understand this. Having seen something of the devastation in Russia, I find it impossible to believe that there are no men among her leaders who do not feel how desperately urgent is that country's need for peace. We here in this House want her to enjoy such peace, but that can only be on a basis of mutual tolerance, respect and good faith. Then let the Soviet Government face these truths, and let them act upon them, and peace can be preserved, but they must surely understand that to persist in their present methods—such methods, for example, as they have been employing recently in Czechoslovakia and Berlin—is to risk an overwhelming calamity for themselves and, alas, an overwhelming calamity for the world.

Chapter 13

World Affairs, June 1948 to July 1949

INTRODUCTION

GERMANY

During the spring of 1948 the Russian authorities created difficulties for the other members of the Allied Control Council in Berlin. On April 5th a Yak fighter crashed into a British commercial aircraft about to land at Gatow airport. Both aircraft were destroyed and all the occupants were killed. The Russian authorities adopted an intransigeant attitude towards the investigation of the crash.

On June 7th the five Brussels Powers and the U.S.A. signed the London Agreement on policy in Germany, which included the convention of a constituent assembly of the three Western Zones to prepare a federal constitution, the establishment of a Military Security Board and provisions for control by them of the distribution of coal, coke and steel from the Ruhr. The French Government made certain reservations to this last proposal.

The American and British Zones, fused for economic purposes into a bi-zone on 1st January 1947, with control centred at Frankfurt, were facing grave economic difficulties. Constant Russian propaganda, designed to show that only the Russians were in favour of a united Germany, was creating unrest. The economic difficulties were largely due to the prevailing currency in which the Germans had no confidence. Currency reform, though often discussed, had been postponed far too long in the hope of reaching Four Power agreement, but on 20th June 1948 the British, American and French authorities established a new currency (the Deutschemark replacing the Reichsmark) in

200

World Affairs, June 1948 to July 1949

Western Germany including the Western sectors of Berlin. The Russian authorities, who had begun to impose traffic restrictions between the Western Zones and Berlin in the spring, cut off all access to Berlin from the west by road, rail or water on June 24th—first on the pretext of preventing smuggling of the new currency and then on the grounds of 'technical difficulties'. On July 1st the Berlin Kommandatura (the Four Power military authority) was dissolved by its Russian Chairman who declared that the Western Powers had no right to introduce currency reform into their sector of the city, 'which is part of the economic system of the Soviet zone'.

The Western Powers retaliated with the Berlin Air Lift, which, by a remarkable effort of organization, succeeded in sustaining the two and a half million Germans in Western Berlin through the winter and spring. They also gradually imposed a ban on trade between Western and Eastern Germany.

Talks held in Moscow broke down when it became evident that the Russian authorities were issuing to their local representatives in Berlin quite different instructions from those agreed for some relaxation of the local restrictions. It was plain that the Russians were using the blockade for the major purpose of forcing the Western Powers to give up their efforts to unite their zones in Germany.

The Western Powers had consistently refused to negotiate with the Russians until the duress of the blockade had been removed. The Air Lift had been in operation for ten months when, in May 1949, it was announced that as a result of a Russian approach to the U.S. Government a meeting of the Council of Foreign Ministers was to be held in Paris. On May 12th the first lorries and trains started from the West for Berlin, but railway strikes and further disagreements between Russia and the Western Powers caused temporary resumptions of the blockade. In August, traffic was flowing both ways subject to certain restrictions. Meantime, the Air Lift continued, but its intensity was reduced from August 1st. The Russians were losing by the blockade and the peoples in the Eastern Zone of Germany were suffering great hardships. The Russians clearly wished to resume trade.

The meeting of the Council lasted from May 23rd to June 20th. It was soon clear that there was no basis for agreement on a Peace Treaty for Germany, but progress was made on the question of relations between the Eastern and Western Zones.

Foreign Affairs

Western Union in terms of the Brussels Treaty had been welcomed by opinion in U.S.A. and responsible leaders of the British Commonwealth. On 17th March 1948 President Truman had said to Congress:

'I am sure that the determination of the free countries of Europe to protect themselves will be matched by an equal determination on our part to help them to do so.'

Mr. St. Laurent, shortly to be Prime Minister of Canada, had told the Canadian Parliament on April 29th:

'It may be that the free States, or some of them, will soon find it necessary to consult together on how best to establish such a security league. It might form one of the plans for Western Union, now maturing in Europe.'

The Brussels Treaty Powers set up a Military Committee under the chairmanship of Field-Marshal Viscount Montgomery of Alamein, who quickly started work in co-ordinating the military plans and requirements of the five countries. From this developed talks with the U.S.A. and Canada and these led in turn to the Atlantic Pact. In economic affairs sixteen countries of Western Europe participated in the Economic Recovery Programme. The next step was to set up an instrument to guide Western European opinion and discuss plans for securing wider co-operation. The Congress of Europe held at The Hague in May recommended, as a matter of real urgency, the convening of a European Assembly chosen by national Parliaments. This proposal was submitted by France and Belgium to the permanent committee of the Brussels Treaty Powers. In October Mr. Bevin proposed the formation of a European Council appointed by and responsible to the Governments. After discussion it was decided to call a conference of delegations from the five Powers to consider both proposals. The British delegation led by Dr. Dalton, who had earlier opposed European Union except on a Socialist Party basis, contained Government officials and Socialists, whilst other countries sent all-party delegations. This conference failed to reach agreement. In the event the consultative council of the Brussels Treaty Powers, which met in London

World Affairs, June 1948 to July 1949

at the end of January 1949, recommended that there should be a Council of Europe consisting of a ministerial committee meeting in private, and a consultative assembly meeting in public. The British Government accepted these proposals, and the Prime Minister decided to appoint delegates from political parties in proportion to their representation in the House of Commons. The first meeting of the Assembly was held at Strasbourg on August 10th.

NORTH ATLANTIC TREATY

During the latter part of 1948 enquiries were made of the Scandinavian countries and of Italy concerning their attitude to a security alliance with U.S.A. and the countries of the Brussels Treaty. At the turn of the year negotiations on the text of the pact were being carried on in Washington. The North Atlantic Treaty was signed in Washington on April 4th between the U.S.A., Canada, the U.K., France, Belgium, Holland, Luxembourg, Denmark, Iceland, Italy, Norway and Portugal, and came formally into force in August.

EASTERN EUROPE

In June 1948 the Yugoslav Communist Party was expelled from the Cominform. The reason given was that Marshal Tito and the other leaders of the Party had failed to carry out the Cominform line on the basic questions of foreign and domestic policy. Tito immediately took steps to assert that it was Cominform countries, not he, who had deviated from the pure Communist doctrine. Despite manœuvres both inside and outside Yugoslavia to make his position untenable, he survived, and by the end of 1948 was making trade arrangements with the West. The Russians intensified their campaign against him in the late summer of 1949.

During this period the Communist Parties in control of the Eastern European countries consolidated their position. An attack on the leaders of the Churches began late in 1948. Cardinal Mindszenty, the Roman Catholic Primate of Hungary, was arrested in December 1948 and sentenced in the following February to life imprisonment. In that month fifteen leaders of the United Evangelical Church in Bulgaria were arrested and thirteen of them were sentenced to imprisonment. In June 1949 the Czechoslovak police raided Archbishop Beran's palace in

Prague and placed severe restrictions on the freedom of the Catholic clergy.

Meanwhile, signs of resistance to Russian control appeared inside the Communist Parties. Tito had his imitators in other countries. The replacement of a number of party officials in Bulgaria, Rumania and Poland took place at the end of 1948. Nevertheless Yugoslavia was still alone in her challenge to Russia in the summer of 1949. Her defection had important results on the position in Greece and on the Austrian Peace Treaty.

In Greece the rebel leader, 'General' Markos, was dismissed in February 1949, probably for nationalist tendencies, and Yugoslav intervention, which had been on the wane since mid-1948, almost ceased.

Tito's claims for large reparations from Austria and for the territory of Southern Carinthia, which had been one of the two main stumbling-blocks to a treaty with Austria, no longer had the support of Russia at the Council of Foreign Ministers which met in Paris in June 1949.

GREECE

Substantial financial aid from the U.S.A. was now given in the European Recovery Programme. The Greek Army was increased. British troops remained, but on the same terms of non-intervention.

During the summer of 1948 a successful campaign in the north resulted in the capture of Mount Grammos from the rebels, but subsequent efforts to round up other bands and capture other strongholds, which were successful in themselves, led to the loss of Mount Grammos and other important areas. In 1949, under the new Commander-in-Chief, the veteran but well-trusted General Papagos, the Greek Army had a series of successes in which they were helped by the replacement of 'General' Markos. Besides the loss of a good general, the rebels suffered from the direct control which Moscow imposed. By the summer the rebels were reduced in strength to 18,000 compared with a 1948 strength of 28,000; but their activities remained a threat to Greece and the West, an intolerable burden on the Greek economy, and a problem which the Greek Army seemed incapable of solving alone. It was estimated then that in the past three years the rebels had lost 31,000 dead, 45,000 captured and 30,000 wounded. The Greek Army had lost 11,000 dead, 4,000 missing and 24,000 wounded.

World Affairs, June 1948 to July 1949

The elimination of 'General' Markos brought into prominence the claim for a Greater Macedonia, centred round Salonika and including part of Yugoslavia and Bulgaria, now being sponsored by Bulgaria.

THE UNITED NATIONS

The third Regular Session of the General Assembly of the United Nations began at the Palais de Chaillot, Paris, on 21st September 1948. Mr. Vishinsky accused the Western Powers of active preparations for war against Russia, proposed a general reduction by one-third of all present land, air and naval forces, and strongly criticized the existence of the United Nations Commission in Korea and in the Balkans. Mr. Bevin, in reply, attacked the Russians for abuse of the veto in the Security Council, for their 'cold war' tactics in Greece, Turkey and elsewhere, for their interference in the internal affairs of other countries, and for their secrecy over their own armaments which made their disarmament proposals suspect. He reminded the Assembly of the 'Marxist-Leninist conception that there can be no final agreement with non-Communist States, that everything the Soviet Government does is tactics and that they adhere to their given purpose whatever they say in the process'.

The Assembly adjourned its proceedings on December 12th until 1st April 1949, when it met again in New York. Important decisions so far taken included the rejection of M. Vishinsky's disarmament proposals, the continuance of the Atomic Energy Commission and the censure of Albania, Bulgaria and Yugoslavia for assistance to the Greek rebels.

A. THE BLOCKADE OF BERLIN

On 30th June 1948, Mr. Eden initiated a debate on Germany in order to make plain to the world the overwhelming determination of the House of Commons that Britain should remain in Berlin, blockade or no blockade.

Foreign Affairs

The Foreign Secretary in his comments to the House on the German situation last Friday referred to its delicacy. I do not suppose that anybody in the House would dispute that fact, and we shall all, no doubt, wish in this Debate to speak with a full consciousness of our responsibility. At the same time, there are occasions when the House of Commons should make its point of view felt. This seems to me to be such an occasion. It is not an issue upon which this House can keep silent. My own words will be few. I want to refer first, briefly, to the successive actions of the Soviet Government which have brought conditions in Berlin to their present pass, and secondly, to make plain what in our judgment should be the determined policy of His Majesty's Government in these conditions.

The Soviet Government's intentions, as it seems to me, were first made plain in respect of Germany by their deliberate and continuous violation of the Potsdam principle of keeping Germany as an economic whole. That was the agreed basis for work between us as Allies—the basis which had been accepted by the Soviet Government, and the only one which could give practical expression to co-operation between the Allies if a desire for such co-operation really existed. That was the first occasion. The next was when the Soviet Government rejected the Four-Power Pact which proposed, as the Committee will remember, a joint guarantee against German rearmament. This proposal was put forward by the United States with the general agreement of His Majesty's Government and of the French Government.

Let us consider for a moment what an immensely significant gesture it was for the United States to make an offer of that kind, with all the history of that country's previous attitude towards such engagements. Soviet propaganda frequently shows—we keep reading statements to this effect—that the Western Powers are trying to build up Germany against them. If they really feel that,

or if they are really sincere in that belief, how can they reconcile
it with their rejection of the Four-Power Pact against German
rearmament, which pact, I must remind the Committee, copied
word for word the Allied Military Agreement which was reached
in Berlin, and which I remember very well because I was still
Foreign Secretary at the time, in early July 1945, between the
military commanders, including the Russian military commander,
Marshal Zhukov.

Yet, a year later, when this agreement was offered with the
guarantee of the United States, Mr. Molotov tried to add all sorts
of political and economic conditions to the military guarantee. In
fact, he tried to turn a pact which was a guarantee against a fear
of the revival of German military power into a peace treaty
giving effect exclusively to Soviet desires. When that draft was
brought forward twice later, each time it was rejected. I am bound
to say, in view of all that—although I say it with reluctance—that
I do not see how the Committee can escape the fact that ever since
the Moscow Conference of 1947, and its failure, every attempt
that has been made to enable Germany to play some part, as she
must play some part, in the revival of European economy, has
been frustrated by the attitude of the Soviet Government. I cannot see how we can avoid that conclusion from the premises
which I have given to the Committee.

It is not, I ask the Committee and others to believe, that we in
this country have forgotten the recurrent acts of German aggression. Of course we have not. Of course the utmost caution will
have to be used in the supervision of the development of German
industrial power. No one proposes to give Germany opportunities
for rebuilding her military armaments. We understand and
sympathize with our French friends in their feelings on that
subject. At the same time—and this we declared even while we
were waging war, and at the time no exception was taken by our
Allies—we made it plain that it was essential that Germany should
be put in a position economically to play her part in the recovery
of Europe. Otherwise, not only does Germany suffer but we all

Foreign Affairs

suffer, and disintegration sets in which can benefit no one except those who want to see Europe in anarchy and ruin.

This Soviet refusal to co-operate has resulted in many months going by without any constructive step being taken to put into effect an agreed policy towards Germany. Now, at length—and as I think rightly—the position has been reached when the economic reconstruction of the Western Zone, including currency reform, can wait no longer and we must go ahead without the Soviet Union. Equally, the period of stagnation in the political sphere cannot be allowed to continue.

What is the present position? The Soviet Government have chosen to regard this decision as a challenge and have retaliated with a blockade of Berlin, which is an act openly directed against their Allies. It is also a callous threat of untold suffering and hardship to 2,000,000 of the civilian population in Berlin. As my right hon. Friend the Leader of the Opposition said, speaking on Saturday, we are in complete agreement with the Foreign Secretary's statement of May 4th:

'We are in Berlin as of right. It is our intention to stay there.'— [OFFICIAL REPORT, 4th May 1948; Vol. 450, c. 1122.]

I do not ask the right hon. Gentleman today to tell us by what means the Government propose to give effect to the policy contained in that statement. I have no doubt that this has been thought out. The two and a half million citizens of our sectors must be taken care of.

I have read many times, and I have heard it said, that it would be impossible to supply by air our sectors in Berlin, with their large civilian population. Well, that may be so, but I should not personally be completely dogmatic about it: remarkable achievements stand to the record of the R.A.F. and the American Air Forces in the war. There is the brilliant record of the American Air Forces in flying supplies to China over the hump, which my right hon. Friend remembers so well, and which certainly made history in efforts of that kind. There was the 14th Army in Burma which advanced on the wings of the Royal Air Force, and was supplied entirely by the Royal Air Force. Since the war there has been the Allied effort in air trooping, which resulted in so many tens of thousands of men being brought home by air for demobilization.

I only say that it would be rash to assume that air effort cannot meet, to a very considerable extent, the need for supplies in Berlin. Anyhow, if this could be done, whatever effort the Royal Air Force and the joint air forces make, they will be making that effort not in war but in the cause of peace; they will be working to supply a civilian population exposed to cruel suffering; and this time they will be dropping on Berlin not bombs but food.

But however that may be, and whatever the mechanical means by which the Government determine to give effect to their policy, it must be made plain to the Soviet Government that sincere as we are, and sincere as we always have been, in desiring their friendship, we are not prepared to be intimidated by brute force or by blackmail. If there remains in the Soviet mind any possible doubt on this subject, as to our attitude and the attitude of our Allies, then I urge the Foreign Secretary, in the clearest and firmest terms, together as Allies to make a joint communication to the Soviet authorities, not in Berlin where the power is limited, but in Moscow where the ultimate decision lies. I say to the right hon. Gentleman and to the Committee that in the light of what he told us on May 4th—which I have just quoted—it is unthinkable that we should now draw back. Were we to do that the effect on our authority and that of the Western Allies in Europe would be catastrophic.

Germany is today a prostrate and defeated nation; millions of Germans are now looking to the Western States to see whether, in truth, we mean what we say, and we have an obligation to them. We have a greater obligation to the two and a half million in our Allied zones in Berlin, who appear to be showing, in the face of every form of intimidation, a steadiness which we must respect and applaud. But most of all, I suggest, we have an obligation to the smaller but still very important number of Germans who have definitely come forward to try to play their part in building up a free life in Western Germany—a free life in the sense in which we in these islands know it. We cannot, we must not, let these people down. It is essential that our case on this issue should be firmly and clearly presented to the German people, and from what I have been able to learn I am not yet convinced that this is being very effectively done.

Before closing I ask the Committee to picture for a moment what would happen if decisions were taken to withdraw from Berlin the forces of the Western Allies. Within twenty-four hours, perhaps less, thousands of Germans who had been co-operating loyally with the British, American and French military authorities would be torn from their homes and would be placed under arrest. We know then what their fate would be. Newspapers which had been appearing as the organs of information of the Western Powers would disappear overnight. For the rest of the population the whole process of Soviet requisitioning and Soviet confiscation would begin.

But over and above all these things, what would be the effect on our authority and on our position in the remaining free nations of Western Europe and the world? The shock to Austria would be completely devastating; it would seem to amount to an open invitation to the Soviet Forces to repeat in Vienna what had succeeded in Berlin. And what would be the effect throughout the Mediterranean and in the Middle Eastern lands? Particularly, it would be highly discouraging to those forces among the Eastern European satellite States—amongst which we must now perhaps include Marshal Tito—who had sought to show their dislike for Kremlin control.

Finally, if such an event happened how could we, how could this country, really hope to build up a Western Union and to bring Italy within its orbit? Powerful Communist elements in France and Italy would receive a sweeping accession of strength. How could we allay the fears, for instance, of the Scandinavian countries if we ourselves had run away from Berlin? There is another motive which must be present in our minds, and I should hope in the minds of everybody in this Committee, of whatever party, when we decide—as I think we must decide—that this is, above all, an occasion upon which we must stand firm. That consideration, which I want to put to the Committee, is one which ought to be in the minds of the Soviet leaders, too. It is essential that we should stand firm in the interest of ultimate good relations between the Soviet Union and the Western Allies. In spite of its numerous provocative acts, I cannot believe that the Kremlin today intends war. But any vacillation on our part now would only encourage the rulers of the Soviet Union to believe that further pressure will result in further yielding, until at last a stand has to be taken which makes war inevitable.

There is one other warning I would utter. If we are determined to see this business through, as surely we must be, then conciliatory language ought not to deflect us. Only deeds should be taken into account. The gentler words of Marshal Sokolovsky, reported in the Press this morning, are no comfort to me without action to give effect to the words. It sometimes happens in diplomacy that there are alternative approaches to a problem, any one of which may lead to its satisfactory solution; but there are other occasions when only one possible course of action presents itself which can preserve peace. Sir, I believe that we have reached such a point today. If ever there was a time to stand firm, it is now; if ever there was a cause in which to stand firm, it is this.

B. THE THREE UNITIES

The Conservative Party met in conference at Llandudno in the first week of October 1948. Mr. Eden replied to a resolution on foreign policy.

In the course of his speech he referred to Mr. Robert Menzies, the former Prime Minister of Australia and now leader of the Opposition there, who had been visiting Britain.

Foreign Affairs

I would recall to the Conference that since we last met a year ago there has unhappily been a grave and rapid deterioration of the international situation. I myself take a very sombre view of the present international outlook.

We have seen the Soviet Government pursue its policy by two methods: by seeking to undermine the authority of a State from within, and by a direct challenge to accepted international agreement. As an example of the former, that is to say, of undermining from within, we witnessed in the spring of this year the tragic overthrow of the free Republic of Czechoslovakia, and so to our deep sorrow Masaryk and Benes followed in the wake of Maniu, Petkov and Kovacs.

As an example of the direct method, the denial of accepted agreements, we have the blockade of Berlin, and now, after this blockade has been going on for months without the faintest legal sanction, we have a suggestion from the Soviet Government that once again we should return to the method of four-power negotiations in the Council of Foreign Ministers. I consider that our answer to this should be unequivocal. The indispensable condition for any Four Power Conference is that the blockade of Berlin should first be raised.

Looking back over the period since last we met, and indeed much further, we can say that we in this Party have been consistent in the advice that we have given the Government. I will repeat it in another form this morning. Our foreign policy should pursue three immediate objectives, which we can call the three unities. First, unity within the British Commonwealth and Empire. Second, unity with Western Europe. Third, unity across the Atlantic. These three unities I maintain—and I agree with my friend Mr. Amery—these three unities are not antagonistic, but complementary.

Take first the Commonwealth and Empire. There can be no

World Affairs, June 1948 to July 1949

successful foreign policy pursued by this country which is not based on the full approval and co-operation of our great partners in the Commonwealth and Empire overseas. My friend Col. Stanley remarked yesterday that we needed some more specific machinery to deal with economic problems in Europe affecting the Empire. I agree with him, and I also consider that similar machinery is needed to deal with the military problems which affect the Empire.

At any rate, our position as a Party is clear enough. We will work for the closest collaboration that can be realized with our overseas partners in the Commonwealth and Empire, in the political sphere, in the military sphere and in the economic sphere. That is the first unity.

The second is unity with Western Europe, and this is in itself of concern to the Empire. Mr. Menzies has explained that very well—and we have all been very happy to welcome him in this country amongst us. Twice in a generation we have seen conflicts which originated in Europe and which have involved the whole Commonwealth and Empire most gallantly taking their part in the common cause, and so I say to you that Western Union and the Marshall Plan are indispensable elements in the reconstruction of the life of Europe, and never forget that it is in conditions of poverty and fear that Communism thrives.

Many of us in this Party have long advocated Western Union or the wider conception of a United Europe in one form or another. It is indispensable to the recovery of Western Europe and to its defensive millitary strength. Here the Brussels Treaty marked the first step forward. We are glad to welcome as the outcome of that event the creation of a Joint Military Defence Council between the Five Western Powers who have so far adhered to that Agreement. We wish Field-Marshal Montgomery all success in his most responsible appointment. The Marshall Plan is economic first-aid to save Europe from those conditions of chaos in which Communism thrives. Our ability to stand on our own feet when Marshall Aid is over depends upon our success in developing the

213

Foreign Affairs

unity and the resources of the British Commonwealth and Empire, together with those of the free countries of Western Europe.

The third unity of which I have spoken is across the Atlantic. The United States have been wise enough to see and generous enough to act upon their vision. American opinion clearly understands that if the free nations of Western Europe are to be preserved they must be both economically stable and militarily secure. In this connection I would express the warm gratification which I am sure the whole Conference feels that Canadian as well as American staff officers were associated with the Staff talks which led up to the creation of this Western European Defence Council.

In this sense, as you will see—to modernize the words of a great Conservative statesman—the new world is once again called in to redress the balance of the old. We can never be sure of peace or of security upon this earth until the nations accept and maintain certain standards of international conduct and abide by the rule of international law. That is certainly true and that is what we hope for by our support of the United Nations. We must continue to give that support, but unfortunately, however, the United Nations has not yet been able to make its authority widely accepted and respected. Meanwhile, I suggest to you that by means of these three interlocking systems—the British Commonwealth and Empire, Western Europe and the United States—a large part of the world can be organized to this task. We threaten no one, but we say with equal clarity that we will tolerate no further encroachments.

There is another great area in the world where British Commonwealth interests and those of the United States correspond with the interests of the countries within that area. I refer to the Middle East. Unhappily the Palestine problem of recent years has gravely complicated our relations with many of our old friends and allies. Nor can the Government's handling of this issue be regarded by any means as blameless. When we contrast the promises made at the General Election with the performance achieved since, we deplore and condemn the weakness, the hesitation and delays which have led to so much bloodshed and human misery. In any event we must now hope that a settlement of the Palestine problem, on the lines proposed by Count Bernadotte, whose tragic death we all so deeply deplore, may lead to stability, and I trust ultimately to friendship between Jewish and Arab lands. Then the Arab lands, working in harmony with other Eastern States and with the Jewish people in their part of Palestine, with the material support of Britain and the United States, could be built up into another great area of security, security for the nation and economic prosperity for their peoples.

In world conditions as they are today, as was well said by one of the speakers just now, our ability to play our full part in international affairs is dependent upon our economic strength and the state of our defences. As to the latter most of us have felt deeply uneasy ever since the Government's surrender to their own extremists on the issue of National Service more than a year ago. I am not going to argue this morning the merits as between a year and eighteen months, but the Government, having told us after months of elaborate and, to use the modern jargon, high-level planning that eighteen months was absolutely indispensable to efficiency in their view and in the view of their military advisers, forty-eight hours afterwards scrapped the whole plan because of the clamour of some of their own Back Benchers. Well, how can anyone have confidence, in critical times like these, in a Government that conducts policy in such a fashion or in a Minister of Defence who is its feeble and ineffective instrument?

As you and I survey the international scene in these days we cannot escape the constant reflection that man's scientific progress has widely outstripped his political development. Politically, so far as relations between countries are concerned, we have virtually stood still, where we have not gone backwards. Yet discoveries, from wireless to the atom bomb, have revolutionized modern life. The existence of wireless has deprived us of the shock absorbers that used to give time for diplomacy to function.

It is rather grim to have to reflect that in modern conditions improved communications corrupt good manners. The constant succession of new discoveries places increasing power within the reach of mankind and at the same time confronts governments with problems more formidable than they have ever known. If these are to be resolved that can only be done by a government which commands real unity in its Party upon foreign policy. Such unity we can claim that we possess in contrast to the Socialists, an important section of whom pursues a bitter and tireless vendetta against their own Foreign Secretary. Well, if you ask me to choose, as I suppose that Resolution does ask me to choose, I personally much prefer the foreign policy of Mr. Bevin to that of Mr. Shinwell. Mr. Bevin's critics in his own Party are indeed the jackals, barking at the heels of their own Foreign Secretary and fawning upon his enemies. But such dissensions within one Party are not a mark of strength. It is indeed a fatal weakness in these anxious days. I can just imagine how Mr. Bevin felt in Paris when he read Mr. Shinwell's remarks in this country the other day.

I have no doubt that many members of the present Government are sincere anti-Communists, and yet sometimes the position of the Socialist Party in this respect is a little difficult to understand. I hold in my hand a recently published re-edition of Karl Marx's Communist Manifesto. Quite a well-known document! It has been republished by Transport House, by the Labour Party, and we are informed on the jacket that this is to mark the Centenary of its first publication in 1848. Therefore, the Labour Party is issuing this important special edition of the Communist Manifesto. Interesting! A little further down we have an extract on the jacket to guide our thought, from a foreword—you can almost guess by whom—Professor Laski. He describes it in this foreword—printed here and issued by the Labour Party—'It is a philosophy of history, a critical analysis of the social doctrines, and a passionate call to revolutionary action.' I rather agree with Mr. Laski's definition of the Communist Manifesto. But who in the world can be at one and the same time an apologist for Karl Marx and a bulwark against Communism? The Socialist

Party can never lay claim to be in any sense an anti-Communist Party until it has rid itself of its connections with Karl Marx.

Now let me sum up my message to you. Over a large part of Europe hangs an iron curtain. Behind it Communism rules. In some other lands Communism challenges the authority of the free parties. To me, and no doubt to this Conference, the whole Communist creed is utterly abhorrent and odious. It is ruthless, soulless and without mercy. I hate Communism for its materialism and I hate it for its intolerance, because tolerance and not material gain is surely the hallmark of civilization. But it is not enough to say that we hate Communism. We have to recognize that those who hold that creed, hold it with a fervour that is almost religious. If we are to defeat them we must, therefore, believe just as fervently in our faith and in ourselves. It is here, I am convinced, that our Party has a special responsibility and duty towards the world. Only a modern, progressive Conservative Party can serve the nation at this hour. But we must make our faith felt.

If we believe in a property-owning democracy, that conception must be made to live. If we believe in our Industrial Charter, in our Agricultural Charter and in the other policies that are being put before you, we must not only preach but practise them for all to see. We must have the courage of our convictions. In Europe today it is man's right to be free in thought and word and worship that is at stake. We have to defend those freedoms here in Britain. Our success will depend upon the vigour with which we champion our own faith. It is in this spirit that we must send from this Conference a message of confidence to Europe and, indeed, to all the world so that the lamps of liberty may be lit again and man may live in freedom and at peace.

C. GERMANY—A YEAR OF OPPORTUNITY

Throughout these post-war years Mr. Eden closely watched the steps that were being taken to assist German economic

Foreign Affairs

recovery, and to prevent any recurrence of German aggression. Side by side with administrative control and supervision in Germany, he looked to Western Union as a strong guarantee against German aggression. But Western Union could not develop until France was confident that proper steps had been taken inside Germany. The provisions in the Six Power London Agreement of June 1948 for the establishment of a Military Security Board and the International Authority to control distribution of the coal, coke and steel from the Ruhr did not satisfy the French.

On December 28th the six Powers, including France, signed a draft agreement for the International Authority providing supervision over management and distribution of Ruhr coal, coke and steel. In April 1949 a complete programme for Germany was announced by the British, French and U.S. Governments, including the Occupation Statute, and the setting up of a Tripartite High Commission for Western Germany as well as agreement on reparations and internal security.

Inside Germany the German Parliamentary Council was still in session at Bonn and a Western German Constitution had not been settled by the end of 1948.

Mr. Eden wrote the following article which was published in certain newspapers on 13th January 1949.

A Foreign Secretary, when being taxed at an international conference with the rapid changes in the Government of his country, once prefaced his reply by saying, 'Which would you rather have, Mr. President, seven Governments with one policy or one Government with seven different policies?'

It is because the Western democracies are at length approaching the ideal of several Governments pursuing one policy that we can enter the new year in a spirit of hope qualified by experience.

The new Ruhr Authority agreed by the Six Powers is undoubtedly an advance towards the necessary revival of the

World Affairs, June 1948 to July 1949

German economy, but with safeguards against a resumption of military power.

That is not to say it is the final solution. It has been welcomed by the French because its terms now include the measure of supervision over management, as well as over distribution, of the Ruhr products for which they made so strong a case. It has been badly received by the Germans for the same reason.

Gen. Sir Brian Robertson has given the Germans a timely reminder that the Ruhr has indeed escaped lightly, and that the measures now taken to control that area might well have been much more severe. Gen. Robertson's words should be heeded in Western Germany, the more so because, with his American and French colleagues, our Commander-in-Chief has displayed an admirable blend of firmness and understanding in his dealings with the German authorities.

All three Allied Commanders have deserved to win a wide measure of German confidence. To see them at work is to know that this is true. If the German people can be brought to understand and to grasp the opportunities that the Ruhr Agreement opens to them, it will in a large measure be due to these men and to those who serve under them in thankless but indispensable tasks.

The truth is that the Ruhr Agreement is on the whole a statesmanlike piece of work. Its detailed structure has yet to be completed, but so far the Germans have no real cause for complaint about it. They will only arouse resentment and intensify suspicion if they make too loud a clamour. Of course, they will protest, but they should not protest too much.

Macaulay once wrote of Walpole: 'He knew that it would have been very bad policy in him to give the world to understand that more was to be got by thwarting his measures than by supporting them.' This is indeed sound sense and it is the very antithesis of appeasement. For Germany co-operation is the wiser method; it can prove to be the more profitable also.

Reconciliation of French and German interests is fundamental to the whole prospect of West European unity. The outcry in

Foreign Affairs

Germany reflects in significant fashion the nationalist spirit which, in its extreme form, has led to the aggression of two world wars. That nationalism has to be reduced to reasonable proportions, for the benefit of the German people themselves as well as for the benefit of their neighbours.

The powers given to the Ruhr Authority contain no element of discrimination against the healthy participation of German industry in the European economy. The main task of the Authority, in fact, is the allocation of Ruhr products between the home and export markets in relation to Germany's common contribution to O.E.E.C.

Meantime, the decision formulated in the Trusteeship Law, and announced by the Military Government in November, gives into German hands responsibility for the form of future ownership of the Ruhr industries. This law still stands though it raises the issue on which the French have felt their greatest uneasiness.

There is today no spirit of revenge among the Western Allies. This attitude is all the more remarkable and creditable to the countries which were occupied. But even if any of us felt like indulging in vengeance, and I doubt if we do, our own self-interest would restrain us. We have too much need of one another.

Opinion in Britain today, in my belief, underestimates the measure of recovery which France is achieving. We have never clearly understood the extent of the ravages imposed upon France's economy, and still more upon her political and social life, by the German occupation and its aftermath. An enemy occupation leaves behind it an unimaginable heritage of moral and material disorganization.

Despite all this we can see that there is taking place in France a significant economic recovery and some political progress, a landmark in which was M. Ramadier's refusal to accept dictation from the Communists and their consequent exclusion from power in 1947.

It is surely encouraging that there should exist among the Western nations who have suffered the agonies of enemy occupation a willingness to condone the past in a common endeavour to build the future. They want to open a window upon a fresh landscape. All this is in a fair and generous spirit, yet precautions must be taken. The Allies are not obdurate; they would be criminal if they were not cautious.

It would be totally unrealistic to close our eyes to the evidence of German nationalism. The theory to which so many Socialists have clung for so long, that an immediate guarantee of security could be found in the nationalization of the Ruhr industries, is completely artificial.

Such a procedure adopted by a nationalist German Government could have most dangerous consequences. Even if nationalization were carried through by a Government of peaceful intention, a regime like Hitler's would, when it climbed to power, find a nationalized instrument ideally suited to its purpose.

But now the Ruhr Agreement itself makes possible the growth of that confidence in France and in the Benelux countries which was always the first condition for the creation of any true Western Union. Their fears were well founded; they could not just be by-passed or ignored. Now they are in a way to be fairly met, and the true work of reconstruction can begin.

In the light of the history of the last century the Ruhr Agreement cannot be regarded as burdensome. Its faults are rather those of incompleteness, but that does not necessarily mean increased severity.

In three wars the Ruhr has been the arsenal of aggression. The contribution that Germany is now called upon to make to reassure her Western neighbours may, therefore, be regarded by Germany as distasteful, but it cannot be justly denounced as extravagant. It leaves Germany ample opportunity to prove herself a constructive partner in Western Union.

What then is the path to follow if we are to reach a really equitable and lasting solution of the German problem which, as we know, centres on the Ruhr? It is, surely, to see that modern Germany is woven as closely as possible into the pattern of the

Foreign Affairs

free Western democracies. And the framework of Western Union already lies to hand.

Within such a union we could hope to evolve a collaboration between the Ruhr and its complementary industries in France, Belgium and Luxembourg. This would eventually involve the integration of the heavy industry of Western Europe as a whole. Such a scheme, extending from the Ruhr to Lorraine and the Saar, would put international control on so wide a basis, and interweave so many mutual interests, that there would be neither scope nor opportunity for purely nationalistic plans.

The economic as well as the political implications of such proposals need detailed study if the disadvantages, as well as the advantages, are to be seen in their true perspective and a proper assessment made. The Governments of the Western democracies should certainly give, if they have not already done so, full expert consideration to the project. I believe the United States Government has in fact already shown its interest.

So far as the French and Germans are concerned, there are many signs that, despite the immediate repercussions of the Ruhr proposals, they recognize the realities of the new Europe in which they have to go forward not only as neighbours, but as partners.

There was, for example, the French parliamentary motion, during a debate on the Ruhr early in December, which called for the speedy creation of a European political federation strong enough to receive the membership of a revived Germany without being dominated by it.

We may not all favour European Federation or believe it to be realizable, but it is notable that a strong motive for French support of such a movement is a desire to find a solution of the German problem which will result in closer relations between the two countries.

This motion was supported by many parties, M.R.P., Socialist and Gaullist. In Germany, Dr. Arnold, the Christian Democrat Premier of North Rhine-Westphalia, has spoken of the part that a closer association of the Ruhr with neighbouring industry could play in a Western European scheme.

The difficulties are no doubt formidable, and I should be the last to underrate them. But so far no other scheme of things has been set before us which offers a constructive hope for the solution of the vital problem of Franco-German relations. Those who will not accept this conception must at least show us another way.

They must remember, too, that delay and indecision breed their own problem. It has taken a whole year for the Western Allies, without having to wait upon the Soviet Union, to reach the present agreement upon the Ruhr Authority. We must go faster than this or at every stage we shall be overtaken by events.

Another sphere of opportunity opens before Germany in the new year. Western Germany is soon to choose its own Government. That Government will have administrative tasks to discharge, but it will also have political responsibilities.

The doors are, in truth, being opened to Germany and she is being offered a place in a joint partnership with the Western nations. The opportunities in such co-operation are immeasurable. Within a firmly established Western Union a hundred years of history and three wars of aggression could find their final rest, and Communism its decisive answer.

D. THE FORMER ITALIAN COLONIES

The former Italian Colonies of Eritrea, Italian Somaliland, Cyrenaica and Tripolitania had remained under British military administration since they were captured between 1941 and 1943. Mr. Eden had promised in 1942, when he was Foreign Secretary, that 'at the end of the war the Senussi in Cyrenaica will in no circumstances fall under Italian domination'.

After many differing suggestions from the Four Powers for the future of these colonies, the Foreign Ministers agreed in the summer of 1946 that final disposition should be made by them within a year of the coming into force of the Italian Treaty (15th September 1947); if they could not reach agreement, the matter should be referred to the General Assembly of the United Nations. A committee of investigation, after visiting the colonies, completed its report to the Foreign Ministers in July 1948, but there was no unanimity and the Foreign Ministers were unable to agree. The U.S.A. and the U.K. proposed Italian trusteeship for Italian Somaliland, U.K. trusteeship for Cyrenaica, and the postponement for one further year of any decision on Tripolitania. The U.K. proposed that Ethiopia should administer Eritrea with an advisory council of four members of the United Nations. The Russians proposed that Italy should be given trusteeship of all former colonies, a proposal which they had first made just before the Italian elections in April.

In the Foreign Affairs debate in the House of Commons on December 9th Mr. Eden spoke of Italy and made his proposal for the trusteeship of these colonies to be handed to the Western Union powers.

Now a word or two about Italy and her colonies. I hope we all welcome, as the right hon. Gentleman did, the decision of the Italian Parliament to co-operate with Western Union. That decision was reached by the Italian Government with their following of Christian Democrats, Saragat Socialists and others against the Communists, who were supported by our old friends the Nenni Socialists. That is good news, for we certainly all desire to co-operate with the new Italy which is emerging from the war. We also want to restore to the full the old sentiments of friendship and mutual trust which for so long ruled between our two countries.

I think the Italian people are entitled to point with a measure of pride to the record of their achievement since the Armistice. Through their partisans and armed forces they made a valuable contribution in the last months of the fighting in Italy. Since then they have made what I believe to be a sincere and successful effort to restore democracy in Italy—at any rate, the supporters of Fascism have been reduced to a very negligible minority. Italian

World Affairs, June 1948 to July 1949

democracy has survived, without recourse to forceful measures, attempts to paralyse the country's economy by strikes and other subversive action. Finally, in the international sphere they have made it clear, by their co-operation in O.E.E.C. and by public statements by their Prime Minister, and Count Sforza, that Italy has definitely taken her place with the West. That is all to the good.

There is some impression, however, among Government supporters in Italy that in spite of what has happened His Majesty's Government are still holding the Italian Government a little bit at arm's length, in part at least because the Socialist Party here still have a tender feeling towards the Nenni Socialists.

Mr. Bevin indicated dissent.

Mr. Eden: The right hon. Gentleman shakes his head, but may I draw his attention to what has happened? There was an international Socialist conference at Clacton last week, which baulked at the Nenni Socialists being expelled. Yet these are the same Nenni Socialists who have been giving consistent support to the Communists. I do not know whether the *Observer* report of last Sunday was correct; it would be interesting to know if it was, but according to that newspaper the decision not to expel Signor Nenni and his followers was taken after a debate in which Signor Treves, of the Socialists supporting the Government, called for immediate expulsion. At one moment the conference seemed ready to accept his advice, but the British delegate suggested that the decision should be postponed until the next meeting of the conference in April. I do not know whether this report is accurate or not, but if it is it is a little difficult to understand why the explusion of the Nenni Socialists, who are now giving full support to the Communists, should be refused while, at the same time, we are told with so much fervour on so many occasions that Socialist parties are the only possible successful opponents of Communists.

Mr. Sydney Silverman (Nelson and Colne): We will try to explain it to the right hon. Gentleman.

Foreign Affairs

Mr. Eden: Perhaps the hon. Gentleman, in doing that, could also explain why there has been so singularly little praise at any time for the achievements of the Christian Democrats in Italy.

Mr. Platts-Mills (Finsbury): Will the right hon. Gentleman allow me to explain? Has he forgotten that the partisan movement he has just praised was based on the Nenni Socialists and Communists? [HON. MEMBERS: 'Nonsense.'] Has he overlooked that the contribution of the Christian Socialists, under their present Right-Wing Government, has gone a long way towards restoring Fascism in Italy?

Mr. Eden: The hon. Gentleman is completely misinformed on all points. To start with, the guerrilla war, as we all know very well, was virtually nationwide. One of the remarkable things about it—[*Interruption.*] Really, I have as much information about this matter as has the hon. Member for Finsbury (Mr. Platts-Mills). One of the remarkable things about the Italian effort which surprised me was the extent to which it was supported by all sections of public opinion.

Mr. Platts-Mills: Communist public opinion.

Mr. Eden: The mere fact that the Communists say that it all belongs to them does not prove that it does belong to them. As to the recreation of Fascism, as I have said, the Fascists are now a negligible party in Italy. If the voting is to be trusted, the fact certainly came out at the last election that their numbers are negligible. I always feel that these two extremes, Communism and Fascism, encourage each other, so I do not feel any anxiety about it.

Now I come to the Italian Colonies. We have to take into account the history of our undertakings, in particular towards the Senussi. This matter is known to the House and I need not repeat it. Those undertakings must be fulfilled. I do not think, in the light of those undertakings, that this House could agree to handing back the colonies, or any part of them, to full Italian sovereignty. There is a complete deadlock on this issue. The Under-Secretary of State shakes his head. He may not call this position a deadlock, but if you adjourn a thing for five months it is a pretty complete deadlock. I am not blaming the Government. I think they did everything they could to bring the matter to an agreement, but on the face of it it looks as though nothing will be done about it for five months. I call that a deadlock. The hon. Gentleman may call it satisfactory progress.

I have a suggestion to make. My suggestion to the hon. Gentleman is that if we cannot get a satisfactory arrangement at U.N.O., if U.N.O. cannot agree about what it shall do, why cannot the Assembly of the United Nations, in order to facilitate a decision which really must be taken, decide that this is a matter which could well be entrusted to the countries of the Western Union, which Italy has now happily expressed her desire to join? Why could not U.N.O. pass the matter to them? Then the Western Union countries might accept a general responsibility for a trusteeship towards those former Italian Colonies. Under that general trusteeship, it should be possible to arrive at arrangements for the administration of those territories which would honour our pledges and satisfy the other parties concerned. I have no doubt that, so far as Italy is concerned, the most urgent problem of all is that of emigration. Within this arrangement I should have thought it ought to be possible to give some measure of satisfaction to Italy on that issue.

Mr. Rankin (Glasgow, Tradeston): Do I take it that the right hon. Gentleman is suggesting an administratively-created trusteeship for Western Union and that, alternatively, failing that, he would suggest that one particular country in the Union should be given that trusteeship?

Mr. Eden: I was suggesting that the trusteeship for these colonies should be entrusted to the Western Union Powers collectively and that they should agree on the way to administer the respective territories; not that they should administer them all together, which I think is unworkable, but that they should decide who have to administer them. I feel that that way a solution might be found.

Chapter 14

Anglo-American Relations

Mr. Eden has always reacted immediately against any tendency in Britain which might harm good relations and understanding with the people of the U.S.A. He worked long and hard to improve Anglo-American relations from 1931 to 1938 while he was at the Foreign Office. During the war he played a part, second only to Mr. Churchill, in strengthening the unity of the two countries. Since then he has often spoken of the vital importance to the world and to Britain of the closest friendship and understanding between the two Governments and peoples.

Throughout the period covered by the speeches in this book public opinion in both Britain and U.S.A. was unaffected by the occasional differences that arose. There were criticisms in both countries of the other; in Britain, mostly by extreme left opinion. Communists did what they could to divide the two. But Marshall Aid, the North Atlantic Treaty and firm faith in democracy united them even more firmly.

In the summer of 1949, however, criticisms suddenly became more intense, more frequent and more dangerous, on both sides of the Atlantic. In Britain the critics blamed the U.S.A. for the dollar crisis and demanded further help as a matter of right; some said that the failure to give exactly the help that they demanded would be an attempt to dictate the overthrow of the Socialist Government in Britain. In the U.S.A. the critics saw in Britain's new dollar crisis proof of her decay, and accused her of living beyond her means and of not working hard enough. Some of the influential U.S. Press joined in the attack. In Britain the Press, with the exception of certain left-wing publications, remained calm, but some offensive speeches were made by a few Socialist back-bench members of Parliament. In neither country did these critics represent the feelings of the vast majority of the people, but they formed a potential threat for the future which it was wise to note.

Meanwhile important issues faced Congress in Washington. Neither the newly proposed Military aid nor the second year's Marshall Aid had been sanctioned by the third week in August. Two weeks later Mr. Bevin and Sir Stafford Cripps were due to start conversations in Washington with Mr. Snyder and the U.S. Government representatives on vital economic issues.

On August 24th Mr. Eden addressed a meeting of 4,000 people in Anglesey. He turned at once to Anglo-American relations. This speech which was fully reported in all the leading newspapers on the following day, received a warm welcome on both sides of the Atlantic.

N o one now underestimates the critical importance of the discussions which will take place in Washington within the next few weeks. Sir Stafford Cripps and Mr. Bevin are carrying a heavy burden of responsibility. Their concern must be with the future of the whole British people. The outcome of their discussion can influence the future course of Anglo-American relations and therefore of the world history.

I have no doubt whatever that all patriotic political parties in this country, and from this category I exclude only the Communists, wish them well. Certainly we as Conservatives sincerely hope that the conversations in Washington will succeed. The mounting pressure on the shrinking gold reserves of the sterling area, and the consequent widening gap between the sterling and dollar economies, are real dangers. So is the risk of growing misunderstanding between Britain and America.

If these are allowed to continue unchecked, if no solution can be found, if bickering and hard words between friendly nations are to take the place of sympathetic understanding and stern effort, then no one will gain except Moscow. In all the anxieties and controversies of the present time there are two facts we should not allow ourselves to forget. The first is that the relations between the British Commonwealth and the United States are something much bigger than any political party in either country. They are the future of the world.

It is impossible to exaggerate the significance of true friendship between the peoples of our Commonwealth and those of the United States. No issue in present or past history is of greater moment than this. If the United States and the British Commonwealth and Empire stand together and work together, there is no world problem they cannot solve. If they fall apart, there is no world problem that can be solved.

The second is that whatever is achieved in Washington cannot by itself solve our problems. We can only do that ourselves. We can do it most surely by the united efforts of our Commonwealth family. There is, in truth, no other way.

I would now like to make some suggestions as to the temper in which the Government should approach their task. It is true the British people have made notable and praiseworthy efforts in these last few years to restore the ravages of war and to rebuild their export trade. Here is a record of endeavour in which all sections of the British people can take pride. It is for us to argue amongst ourselves how far this effort has been assisted by the action of the Government or retarded by its policies. It is for us to argue how far nationalization has proved itself or how far it has failed. It is for us to argue whether a further dose of Socialism will be a fillip or a poison, but the facts of recovery and the efforts of the British people can and should be stated. At the same time we must not forget that other countries have also made remarkable progress in recovery. Let ardent Socialists avoid the temptation to lecture other countries merely because they conduct their affairs differently or because their ideas are out of line with Socialism. Secondly, the Government should disabuse their minds, and the minds of their supporters, of the idea that any responsible American wishes to try to dictate to the British Government and the British people how we should run our own

Anglo-American Relations

country. Still more extravagantly absurd are any suggestions of sinister plots and conspiracies or unholy alliances against Britain across the Atlantic. The truth is that our American friends have given to us and to Europe as a whole in these post-war years the most generous help without making the least attempt to interfere in any way in our own political controversies. Nobody in their senses can believe that they are likely to change their methods now.

It is desirable once again to put on record what the Canadian and American people have done to assist our national recovery. In the last three and a half years Canada and the United States have advanced just under 7,000,000,000 dollars or £1,750,000,000. These are astronomic figures. Admittedly we have in the past made contributions which unquestionably deserve to be weighed in the scale. In the year when we stood alone we expended a large part of our own overseas investments in America and elsewhere, but that does not belittle the generosity of the help now being given by our friends across the Atlantic. And here I must add a special word of thanks to Canada. Nothing could have surpassed the constant and unwearying succession of acts of thoughtfulness and generosity which Canada has extended towards this country. There is no country in the world whose loyalty and friendship has proved more true in times of stress and strain. It is for this reason all the more deplorable that we should now have to cut our purchases from Canada and thus injure her economy. Here is a problem which we simply must resolve.

I hope that Ministers will not try to make out that their Socialist policies are coming under pressure from abroad. That these policies are coming under relentless and growing pressure is true, but the pressure is the pressure of facts. Whatever Socialist Ministers may say, the fact is that their policies have failed to meet the challenge of the times. The vital gold reserves of the sterling area are declining at an alarming rate. Unless that trend can be checked they will be exhausted within a year. These are the hard facts. They are no doubt unwelcome and may be unfortunate. Socialists will no doubt maintain that their policy ought to be successful. It may

Foreign Affairs

be that it would be nice for them and for many of us if their policies would work. But the fact is that they do not. If they persist in their present economic and financial policies; if they still continue to refuse to listen to the warnings that now shower upon them from every side, they cannot expect to escape the responsibility for the consequences. It is really of no use the Government supporters upbraiding our Liberal friends and ourselves when we point to the stern reality of the dangers that beset us. They would be better occupied in mending their policies and restoring our finances.

It is perfectly true that this dollar problem is a world problem. It is perfectly true that no British Government could by itself alone produce a rapid solution of all its baffling perplexities. It is also true that, as it is in our own interests to keep our head above water, so it is in the interest of the rest of the world to see that we do not drown. The free world cannot survive without Britain; but it would be inexcusable folly on our part to rely on these facts as an excuse for failing to do everything that lies in our power to restore our own economic and financial health, as a nation, as a Commonwealth, and as a sterling area. Our Government's responsibility is to shape their policy, to shape Britain's course, to meet the challenge of the present hour. That is just what they are failing to do. I do not say that Ministers are following the example of some Socialist Backbenchers in blaming all our difficulties on other countries, on the American recession for example. But I do say that if Britain's economy is so grievously affected by the comparatively small change that has taken place in recent months in world trading conditions, then obviously the policies which our Government is pursuing are wrong and cannot stand up to the hard facts of international life.

Meanwhile the precious weeks have been slipping by and the Government refuse to amend their economic and financial policy. That policy is once again bringing us to the edge of disaster as it did in 1947. A heavy responsibility now rests upon our Socialist Ministers. For Britain's sake may they prove equal to it.

Anglo-American Relations

But for ourselves, for the British people as a whole, there is no doubt where our duty lies. Despite all these troubles which it would be folly to ignore, we have no cause to lose faith in ourselves or in our destiny. The character of our people has not changed and we have in our history surmounted problems which may have been different in character but which were just as formidable in their challenge. I have recently many times referred to my own journey through the countries of the British Commonwealth. This experience convinced me more than ever that it is in co-operation with these lands in all our problems of commerce, of population and of defence, that we can find the sure way through which will benefit us all. The worst of all policies at a time like this is one of faint heart or of despair. If we work together as a Commonwealth family there is no reason for the first and no excuse for the second.

Index

Index

Index

237

Index

Index

U

United Nations, 58, 134, 141, 170, 181, 182, 183, 213, 214
Unities, the three, 143, 211 *seq.*
Unity, 118, 169, 186
U.N.R.R.A., 170
U.S.A., 19, 45 *seq.*, 50, 51, 56, 57, 169 *seq.*, 179, 181, 230, 231 (*see also* Marshall Aid and Anglo-U.S. relations)
U.S.A.F., 208
U.S.A. Government, 179, 198, 206–7, 222
U.S.S.R., 131 *seq.*, 177, 180, 181, 183, 184, 196, 197, 198, 199, 201, 206, 207, 208, 209, 210 (*see also* Anglo-Soviet Relations)

V

Veto, Security Council, 182, 183, 184

W

War Cabinet, 169
Warwick, 156
Western Europe, 117, 172, 212–14, 220
Western Union, 142, 143, 180–1, 187 *seq.*, 210, 221, 227

Y

Yalta Declaration, 174

Z

Zhukov, Marshal, 207